Preacher Rehab

Restoring Faith in the Sermon

Ron Cassidy

authorHOUSE®

AuthorHouse™ UK Ltd.
500 Avebury Boulevard
Central Milton Keynes, MK9 2BE
www.authorhouse.co.uk
Phone: 08001974150

First published by AuthorHouse 12/31/2009

ISBN: 978-1-4490-5508-0 (sc)

Cover design by Simon Pantling

This book is printed on acid-free paper.

To
PAULINE
whose light never goes out
and to
REBECCA and JOE
the new lights now shining

Table of Contents

ACKNOWLEDGEMENTS

I am immensely grateful to those whose advice and encouragement launched me onto this project, including the staff of several theological colleges - Dr. David Wilkinson, Principal of St. John's College, Durham; Dr. Christina Baxter, Principal, St. John's College, Nottingham; Chris Green, Tutor in Homiletics, Oak Hill Theological College, London; Rod Symmons, Rector of Redland, Bristol, part-time tutor in Preaching at Trinity College, Bristol; Simon Vibert, Tutor in Homiletics, Wycliffe Hall, Oxford. To Dr. John Applegate, one time Archdeacon of Bolton;

Also to:

Leslie Milton, Tutor in New Testament, Ripon College, Cuddesdon, and Christine McMullen, Vice Principal, Northern Ordination Course, who, though I was not able to meet with them, graciously gave me advice and encouragement by letter.

To the congregations who have been on the receiving end of my preaching, and for their comments - positive and negative yet always constructive - I give my grateful thanks. They are the ones who's opinion really matters to me.

INTRODUCTION

The Vicar was excited. The Bishop was due to come to preach and preside the next day. Alongside the natural pleasure of having the Bishop there was a certain sense of relief that for once he would not need to prepare a sermon. Then came the news he dreaded. The Bishop had flu and would not be coming after all. So the Vicar did what all self-respecting Vicars would do in such circumstances - and told the Curate he would have to preach instead. As the young man stood up in the pulpit he felt his inadequacy at filling the Bishop's shoes. The congregation's sense of disappointment was almost palpable. Nervously and self-deprecatingly he began, "I am sorry I am not the Bishop. I know I am no more than a substitute, just like the cardboard filling in for that broken pane of glass." At the end of the service the churchwardens, seeking to be helpful as all churchwardens do, reassured the curate, "you were no substitute piece of cardboard in the window; you were a real pain !"

Sadly this story reflects the impact that many sermons have on congregations today. While they may not actually be caused pain, they will nevertheless regard many sermons as things to be endured rather than enjoyed.

Preacher Rehab is born out of a strong desire for more people to become involved in the privilege of the ministry of preaching, and for those already involved to aspire to become more effective in that ministry. It has sprung from more than forty years of preaching to Anglican congregations in Lancashire in various situations, from inner-city Liverpool, urban Bolton, semi-rural Mossley and suburban Manchester. This time has had many highs and lows, but through them all has continued the conviction that some of God's most effective works are accomplished by effective Spirit-inspired preaching.

It has to be said, in the words of the Preacher of Ecclesiastes (more or less) that of the making of books on preaching there is apparently no end. Look at any typical bibliography attached to a standard book on preaching and you will find no shortage of excellent treatises on this particular subject. It is a well ploughed field, so much so that any prospective writer such as myself has to begin with an attempt at justifying the exercise itself.

What makes this book different ? Why should the aspiring preacher choose it in preference to other worthy writings ? For one thing, it has a very clear and closely defined setting in life. Look more closely at the above-mentioned bibliographies however and you will discover that not many are written in the context of the English Church scene. Many are written by American authors with assumptions about the social and religious context of preaching that simply do not hold true for English society. Fewer books still are written from within the Church of England setting and which discuss preaching in the Church of England. Why is this important ? It is important because, unlike the non-liturgical or semi-liturgical settings that many of these books assume, within the Church of England liturgy the sermon has to vie with other elements for time and prominence. In many churches, what often passes for worship is perceived as simply a prelude or build-up to the preaching of the Word. The sermon is effectively the central if not the sole substantial element of the service. Within the Anglican set up however such prominence for the sermon cannot be taken for granted, and it's importance is not self-evident. There is the need therefore to set out the proper context for the sermon within the worship of the Church. Many other works on preaching nod in the direction of worship but do not develop the theme in any detail. This perceived deficiency I attempt to make up.

What also is very noticeable is that many of the works on preaching are written by academics, people involved in one institution or another teaching homiletics. I am certainly not saying that such people do not have a valuable preaching ministry. Many do, or at least have had distinguished preaching ministries in the past. I do not wish to detract from their work in any way, and in my book I make many positive and grateful comments on the things they have written. However, it is a passionate concern that preaching is a discipline that cannot be learned in the classroom. It must be learned "on the job", preaching to real people in real-life situations - and getting very real and forceful feedback !

Preacher Rehab therefore is written out of a marriage between academic theology (I have a Ph.D. in New Testament Studies) and practical pastoral practice (forty years as an Anglican parish priest). I believe this is one area where it is possible to have feet in two camps, so that pastoral practice is founded, as it should be, on sound theology. The marriage may go through rocky times on occasions, but hopefully the bond remains strong.

It is also true that preaching is a very individual thing. While every preacher operates in accordance with the same general principles, he or she brings much of his or her unique self to the delivery of a sermon. It could be said that there are as many different styles of preaching as there are preachers. It follows by extension that every book on preaching will be different, and reflect the individual approach of its author. While therefore I gladly acknowledge the contributions of others, "standing on the shoulders of giants", the book is very much *my* book, representing an individual approach to preaching that is not merely a condensation of the work of others.   Certainly, no-one else should be blamed for its deficiencies !

I should offer one word of explanation and apology in advance to my sisters in the ordained ministry.   I decided quite early on that it would soon become tiresome and unwieldy to write "he and she" every time I wished to use the personal pronoun for the preacher.   My use of "he" therefore wholeheartedly includes women priests and preachers.   I am reminded of a speaker at the Keswick Convention once who explained "every time I say 'brethren' I embrace the ladies" ! Incidentally, for that same reason I have included no separate section in the book for "women in the pulpit", believing that the principles espoused apply equally to preachers of both genders.   My short hand therefore in no way implies any lack of respect, and I hope therefore the book will for that reason not be passed over by female preachers.

In short, this book is a personal testimony to the importance and fruitfulness of preaching, and stems out of a real concern for the standard of preaching in the Church of England today. This concern originated when, whilst recuperating from an operation, I had the all-too-rare opportunity of listening on a regular basis to sermons, rather than delivering them. The concern has grown since, having retired from full-time ministry, I have had further opportunities of being on the receiving end of preachers. If I had any hair left, it would frequently have stood on end, or been torn out by now ! Instead of complaining to the Bishop, I have attempted to do something about it. I hope therefore all readers will find something somewhere in the book that will be of value and will enrich them as they engage in the greatest calling anyone can have.

RON CASSIDY, Manchester, 2009

1

THE PREACHER'S PROBLEMS

The preacher is in need of rehabilitation. Fortunately his need is not yet for resuscitation, but rehabilitation definitely. To a certain degree preaching can be said to be in the doldrums, considered old fashioned and ineffective by many. And even among those who still embrace the sermon wholeheartedly, it is often not done well. Forces that militate against the preacher in our contemporary society have simply proved too strong for many aspiring preachers. This is a sad situation, all the more so because I firmly believe that preaching the Word of God regularly to a congregation is the highest calling anyone can aspire to in the service of God. Nothing can compare to the thrill and excitement of seeing lives moulded and shaped, not by the eloquence of the preacher, but by the power of the Word he proclaims.

That there has been a drop in the standard of preaching in recent years seems to be a common statement amongst many authors that have written on the subject. In his preface to John Stott's great standard book on preaching, Michael Green baldly states:

1

The standard of preaching in the modern world is deplorable. There are few great preachers. Many clergy do not seem to believe in it any more as a powerful way in which to proclaim the Gospel and change the life.[1]

The great reformer, John Calvin, is even less kind,

> At the present day there are many who are sickened by the very name of preaching, because there are so many stupid, ignorant men who blurt out their worthless brainwaves from the pulpit

Calvin was writing over 450 years ago of course, but it is to the present writer alarming to be told that the average length of a sermon in the Church of England today is between seven and twelve minutes.[2] Now length is not everything. Some preachers can preach for an hour and the time seem like five minutes. With other preachers the very opposite is the case. Nevertheless seven minutes seems a desperately short time to develop anything worth while, certainly when it comes to exposition of Scripture.

It is of course difficult to move beyond the anecdotal to accurate assessments, because of the difficulty of gathering objective evidence. In the nature of the case, as a preacher you usually get all too few opportunities for listening to other preachers. And I guess that because it is rare, when the opportunity does finally come our expectations are too high. But there does appear to be a consensus that the standard of preaching, expository preaching in particular, has suffered a marked decline in recent years.

Surveying the American scene Old writes

> One could say that America was a nation founded by preaching. Yet I find myself looking round at a country filled with empty churches. There are plenty of pulpits, but few preachers up to filling them. There are many preachers,

but few who seem to be able to hold a congregation. Like so many others of my generation, I find myself asking what has happened to preaching.[3]

Recent years have of course seen great changes, both in the general situation in which the Church finds itself, and within the Church itself. The technological revolution, which continues at ever increasing speed, has had a particular impact on the way people receive information, process it, and subsequently act upon it. We have the great expansion of television services, with satellites that bring to the average living room programmes from all over the world. We have the explosion of IT services, with its infinite variety of means of accessing information, means that very often are a mystery to older people but which come naturally to children. We have the phenomenon known as virtual reality, with people able to live full lives without leaving their home. Killinger comments that these changes have placed us as far from the first half of the twentieth century as the Industrial Revolution was from the Middle Ages.[4] The way we perceive our world and ourselves is being radically altered, and the way we listen to sermons with it.

The Church itself finds the pace of change within its organisation a constant challenge also, as it seeks to keep pace with the changing world. The steady flow of women into the ranks of the ordained clergy within the Church of England, a flow that begins to mirror more accurately the gender composition of those in the pews, continues to mould and shape the ministry of the Church. No longer is the pulpit the preserve of men or the bastion of male attitudes. The female (not feminist !) approach to preaching is something that broadens and enriches the sermon's appeal in the contemporary pulpits. As we move ever further away from one priest in one parish, those same pulpits are becoming populated by a whole variety of preachers, ordained and lay, experienced and inexperienced, trained and untrained, good and - unmentionable. The urgent need to have *somebody* preaching on Sunday means that in many cases quality control goes out of the window.

The continually rising tide of secularism, allied often to unthinking political correctness, threatens to keep pushing the Church to the margins of society and limit the scope of its proclamation. To what extent this is succeeding is a matter of varying analyses. The Church still has wide scope for ministry through schools, both Church schools and non-Church schools for example, as well as through the many who continue to seek its services through the Occasional Offices, Baptisms and Funerals particularly. What secularization does mean however is that preachers can make fewer and fewer assumptions of knowledge of even the basics of the Christian Faith on the part of their listeners. Interestingly enough, this is not always a great disadvantage. People come to listen with a clean slate. If they have no idea at all what Christianity stands for, then they at least come with no wrong ideas ! There is less "rubbish" for the preacher to clear away.[5]

Nevertheless, many of these changes have impacted on the preaching ministry of the Church, and a number of factors have combined to challenge the standard of preaching today, and have succeeded in the eyes of many observers, to lower the general standard of that preaching. As we shall see, it is not simply a matter of the preacher's ability, but a matter of the confidence he may or may not have in the exercise on which he is embarking.

Forces that Challenge the Preacher

A number of currents can be detected in contemporary society that threaten the preaching enterprise and make it difficult for the preacher to keep his vessel afloat.

A Cultural Climate that is less amenable to Preaching

The change in the cultural climate of Britain today, which may be very imprecisely characterized as a shift from a word-based culture to an image-based culture, has undoubtedly provided a great challenge to the preacher. People in modern, or as many would say *post*modern) Britain are far less amenable to the idea of someone standing up and dogmatically telling them what to do than they formerly were. There has been a reaction set in against dogmatic and directive authority, a reaction that has found its way into the pulpit. Congregations are now likely to react sharply against any preacher who is unwise enough to cast himself in the role of autocrat or dictator. Contemporary man, a full product of the Enlightenment, does not want to be told what is true. He wants to discover it for himself, and then decide for himself what to do about it. Instead of being on the receiving end, he wants to be in on the discussion. By its very nature preaching does not allow for such discussion. It belongs to the old, paternalistic pattern of the past, where the pastor feeds his flock.

As one writer puts it,

> If something is worth communicating, don't spoil it by preaching it ! Let it emerge in the give and take of the group. In preaching people are as passive as chickens on a roost - and perhaps just as awake. For whatever reason, the authority of the preacher has become problematic.[6]

Consequently many preachers have become hesitant to be seen to be adopting an authoritarian approach and therefore risk alienating their "enlightened" congregations.

An allied reason for this retreat from pulpit authority has been the rise in the general level of education of the congregations of our churches. Long gone is the time when the Parish Priest was the best or only educated man in the congregation. Many of the people in the pews often have academic qualifications that far outstrip those of the preacher. Some would argue therefore that it would ill become a preacher to set himself up as an expert and to proceed to talk down to the congregation. People respect someone, so the argument goes, who is willing to display his or her weaknesses, doubts and fears, thereby identifying with the people he is addressing.

While there is never any justification ever for "talking down" from the pulpit, the preacher cannot function unless he displays some degree of expertise and authority in the field of Biblical exegesis at least that is not present in the pews. Authority cannot be acknowledged without a degree of expertise is some field or other, theology being the obvious one. As long as the preacher does not stray into areas of knowledge that are not his or her proper preserve, there is no problem. People do want to listen someone who is manifestly human, not a clerical Superman, but who nevertheless knows what he is talking about. I am not persuaded that people want to hear doubts and fears aired from the pulpit. Nor do they want simplistic, pre-packaged answers to the questions that arise from their day to day living. What they do want however is a guide who has knowledge of and confidence in the Word of God and who is sufficiently established in his relationship to Christ to point them in the direction in which the answers to their questions may be found.

The experienced preacher, as well as listening to God, will at the same time be listening to his or her hearers. He or she will be aware of their life-situations, their problems, their joys, their sorrows, and this knowledge will shape the presentation. He or she will heed Jesus' admonition not to cast pearls before swine, whilst at the same time not simplifying his or her message to the point where both their knowledge and their intelligence are insulted. A silent dialogue will in fact be going on all the time.

6

Although there are valid ways of encouraging congregational participation, undeniably the essence of preaching is monologue. Modern educational theory, laying great stress on dialogue and participation, would encourage us to believe that monologue is one of the least effective methods of education. Communication is not simply about getting something said, it is also about getting something heard. We preachers have all had the experience of seeing a glaze coming over the eyes of our hearers in the midst of a sermon, accompanied by the grim realisation we have lost their attention. Acts 20.7-12 tells us of an incident when Paul, so carried away with enthusiasm for his theme, kept on talking until midnight. One young man, sitting by the window as Paul talked "on and on" (v.9) finally succumbed to sleep and fell to his death through the window. Fortunately in my preaching ministry so far I have never actually had anyone die during one of my sermons, though I admit not a few have found the effort of staying awake altogether too challenging. This is the ever-present danger of monologue.

Those involved in the business of communication would therefore argue that many, both preachers and listeners, have a deep-down recognition that the sermon simply is not effective in communicating truth. Any preacher brave enough to do so can test his congregation about how much of the main thrust of the sermon they can recall once the service is over. I suspect many of us are not brave enough to do it because we are afraid of what we would discover. Our communication experts tell us that surveys have shown that the answer to the question about how much they remember would be "not very much". But then they would be only telling us something that all preachers have known for a long time.

One observer wryly observes

> The churches of the land are sprinkled all over with bald-headed old sinners whose hair has been worn off by the

friction of countless sermons that have been aimed at them, but which have glanced off and struck the man in the pew behind.[7]

Now we cannot even be sure it will hit the man behind, always assuming there is someone there in the first place !

Communication experts argue that there is also little evidence of changes of behaviour being brought about by the sermon, although to my mind this is much more difficult to measure, and therefore too much weight should not be put upon it.

Critics of the monologue sermon go further and argue that monologue is a form of relational violence, deliberately creating a sense of powerlessness in the hearers. The preacher is active; the congregation is expected to be passive, at least in the sense that vocal contributions from them are not expected or encouraged.

Bishop David Gitari, of the Diocese of Mount Kenya, tells the delightful story of his father, whose enthusiasm for God made impossible for him to stay quiet while his son was preaching. Frequently he would punctuate his son's sermons with "Praise the Lord" and "Alleuia". Such was the volume of these interruptions that Bishop David found it impossible to continue at times. Taking his father on one side, he solemnly promised that, if he could keep quiet during his next sermon, he would buy his father a new pair of shoes. So, each time his father was prompted to leap up and shout, he would visualize the new shoes and sit down again. Eventually his enthusiasm could not be contained, and he leapt up, exclaiming   "for shoes or no shoes, Praise the Lord!".

The congregation are expected to sit there and - probably - suffer. We are reminded of Trollope's celebrated and much-quoted comment:

> There is perhaps no greater hardship at present inflicted upon mankind in civilized and free countries than the necessity of listening to sermons[8]

One might also think of one of Madonna's early hit records "Papa, don't preach, I'm in trouble deep", a title that reflects the common perception that when trouble comes a one-way conversation from a position of moral superiority is somehow not going to help.

A further perception concerning the authoritative monologue, also known as the sermon, is that it encourages clericalism. The sermon is seen as a means of enforcing authority, and suggests the idea that faith formation is best left to the experts. The congregation are there to be told what to think and believe. Stott caricatured this monological approach as often resembling a message "from a moron to mutes". In an age when people are increasingly encouraged to think for themselves and investigate for themselves, such a patronizing approach is no longer satisfactory.

The Impact of Biblical Criticism on respect for the Bible and the increasing understanding of theology as the preserve of the professional academic

A fundamental *credo* of many scholars engaged in Biblical Criticism is that the Bible should be studied like any other book, with detached neutrality. This has of course sometimes led to many conclusions that are perceived to be negative and destructive of the long- accepted beliefs drawn from the Bible, and maybe destructive of faith itself.

Now some of my scholarly friends would rise up in great indignation at this, asserting that such negativity is not inevitable, and that their aim is not to destroy the authority of the Bible but to enable that authority to be viewed in a new contemporary light. I would certainly not be disposed to argue with them on this point. I am simply making the observation that often the results of scholarly research are *perceived* to be negative and destructive. Where such negative perceptions do filter through to the teaching and training offered to preachers it runs the great risk diminishing reverence for the text in comparison to former days. This will in turn threaten to lessen the impact of preaching, something that is many feel has proved to be the case.

An allied difficulty is that dialogue on these issues has become increasingly difficult for the lay man. Speaking from the vantage point of my own discipline, New Testament Studies, it is quite remarkable how research in that field has become the almost exclusive province of the "professional academic", who invariably is a teacher or lecturer at one institute of learning or another. It does not seem so long ago great churchmen, such as Geoffrey Lampe, Archbishop Michael Ramsey, the Hanson Twins, Wesley Carr and others, men of great faith and pastoral concern, could be numbered amongst those issuing New Testament treatises of some weight. Sadly, very few of these theological giants are around today. It appears very often that it is the University Faculty that produces the vast majority of works on theology in general and the Old and New Testaments in particular. The current Bishop of Durham, N.T. Wright, with his quite prodigious output on New Testament matters, stands out as a glorious exception (though even in his case, much of his formative work was done in Cambridge).

A number of factors have contributed to this state of affairs. Among them is the very natural tendency to want to become more 'professional' in one's profession, in the good sense of 'being the best one can be'. To be professional in this sense means developing a sense of dedication to the single task of interpreting the Biblical text. This process is aided by greater access to the necessary resources of books, linguistic expertise and so on than would be available to scholars outside the

University environment. The extremely high standard of scholarship required by the publishers of scholarly books and journals makes it very difficult for the enthusiastic "part-timer" to compete.

Does this trend matter ? In many ways it does not. It is good to have people who can devote lots of time, energy and resources to study of the Biblical text, the fruits of which study can be passed on. No one would want to argue in favour of half-measures or inferior quality of study. On the other hand, some bridges need to be built between the academic and the pastoral spheres, otherwise frustration will ensue on both sides. Academics for example sometimes complain that the fruits of their studies are not filtering down to the pulpits. Preachers are still propagating understandings of the biblical text that they regard as outmoded.

One scholar writes for example

> It is obviously impossible for thinking Christians to repudiate or even to ignore historical criticism. But that is precisely it seems to me what most of them do. And it is not hard to see why. More often than not the results of historical criticism appear to have no bearing on contemporary issues or upon the faith of the Church. The local congregation scarcely finds edification when the preacher tells them that the Old Testament lesson is the work of J or that the Epistle taken from Ephesians was not written by Paul.[9]

At the same time preachers often complain that they are not being provided by their academic brethren with the tools they need to help them apply Scripture the vast array of practical situations they face. The preacher and the academic often appear to inhabit separate spheres of life that rarely intersect. The academic may be a man or woman of faith, involved in Christian leadership, or he or she may not. The Preacher may be involved in a pastoral schedule that simply leaves him or her no time for serious academic study, even if he or she had the inclination for such. A situation can develop where academics and preachers are asking totally different sets of questions of the text, and therefore coming up with different sets of answers. The academic will approach the text from the world of the Ancient Near East, and see the text in that setting. The preacher and the congregation will often approach the text initially from their world, and the needs that life in that world presses upon them. The academic and the preacher need each other and need to talk to each other. The danger for the academic is that, unless he keeps in touch with the situation on the ground he or she will end up writing things that people are simply not reading, apart from the very few people that share the same elite circle. As far as the preacher is concerned, the danger is that he or she will churn out standard ideas, taken from the three or four commentaries he or she bought many years ago, and that he or she (and the congregation of course) will not find refreshment from the many streams flowing from the world of contemporary Bible Scholarship.

A further complicating factor is that these streams are very diverse and rarely intersect. One observer comments that modern scholarship of the Bible is less united now than ever it has been, and the interpretation of the Bible has diversified to the point where no one person can master it all. It may be that a new synthesis will be found which will draw scholars back together. If so, that synthesis will have to embrace the fruits of critical research, but not in such a way as to deny the legitimate use of the Bible in the devotional life of the Church. The Bible lives as the book of the Church, and it is from the bosom of the believing community that scholars arise to study and expound it. If that link is severed it will not be the Church that dies but academic study of the Bible.

However, the Craddock encouragingly comments:

In spite of all the distance and suspicion generated between those who critically investigate the text and those who preach it, the marriage between sermon and Scripture is in no danger of divorce. In fact, not within this century has the pulpit been so well served by biblical studies, nor biblical studies been so conscious of its relation to the preaching and teaching ministry of the Church.

Craddock points particularly to the development of disciplines such as genre, narrative, rhetorical and reader-response criticism as providing useful tools for the preacher in particular to use in the enhancement of his work. But whether Craddock's optimism here is justified or not, there is still a gap between his assessment and the popular perception in the pew and in some pulpits that academic study of the Bible text is of necessity negative and destructive. We watch to see how things develop.

The Church would be the poorer without such academic study, but not fatally crippled. As has happened in the past, new forms of biblical interpretation would arise to take the place of the ones rejected, and the spiritual life of the Christian community would continue along its historic path.

The continuing expectancy that the Parish Priest will be a Jack of All Trades, good at all the pastoral disciplines, including preaching

Although, with the advent of Non-Stipendiary Ministers, Ordained Local Ministers, Ministers in Secular Employment, Lay Readers and so on the Parish Ministry of the Church of England is infinitely more diverse than it used to be, there is still the expectation that the full-time Stipendiary Minister will be good at everything, including preaching. That this is not the case, and has probably never been the case, is fairly obvious. A man or women may be an excellent pastor, an effective teacher in small groups, a superb leader and administrator, but a terrible preacher. It is simply not possible for one person to combine all the gifts necessary for effective parish ministry, as is demonstrated many times in parish after parish. The whole point that Paul makes about the necessary gifts of ministry in Ephesians 4 is precisely that they are distributed by the Holy Spirit amongst a number of individuals, and not concentrated on one person. And yet this has been the traditional expectation in the Church of England in particular, to which I belong.

Then there is in ever present bugbear of the many administrative tasks that the preacher is called upon to perform. Today's parish is very different from the parish of 50 years ago, when every parish had at least one priest, and sometimes two or three. Now parishes are being increasingly grouped together, and are having to share priests. In these circumstances the parish priest simply has not the time, never mind the talent, to deal with everything. It is no surprise to see that the results of this situation are on the one hand sub-standard offerings from the pulpit from clergy who have simply not the time, resources or energy to devote themselves to proper preparation, and on the other hand burn-out of those self-same clergy.

Not merely the parishioners, but the parish priest himself has to change his mindset, and be liberated from the many mundane tasks he is called upon to carry out, so as to have the time to do what is really the essence of his calling, preaching the Word of God. He is not *the* minister, working on behalf of the congregation, but the one called up to equip *them* to be the ministers.

Interestingly enough, this is not a new problem. As the work of distributing to the widows of the Early Church expanded with the growth of that Church, it began to throw up problems (Acts 6.1-7). The problems were of two kinds. The distribution was not being done efficiently enough, giving rise to complaints, and even of racial bias. The other problem was that the Apostles were finding it taking up an increasing amount of their time, increasingly squeezing the time they had available for preaching the Gospel. Their solution was squash the idea that distribution was something only an Apostle could do, and to recruit extra personnel to do the practical work. As an interesting sideline we note that the new recruits all belonged to the 'Hellenists', the very group that had been complaining about discrimination. The Apostles were thereby freed to devote themselves to the preaching task.

Having said that, it is worth noting that delegation is not always in itself the answer. Delegation can in fact increase the workload, temporarily at least. The parish priest's responsibility is shifted from doing the task himself to administering and co-ordinating those who take the job on. This can itself be time consuming, especially if those to whom the task is delegated prove not to be up to it and in need of support.

Happily in the contemporary church things are changing, whether by insight or necessity, and those responsible for training come to grips with this issue. Not only are laity being encouraged to relieve the parish priest of administration, laity are being involved more and more in the task of the ministry of the Word. Increasingly churches are developing ministry and leadership teams, clergy and lay together, where the necessary pastoral gifts, including preaching, can be effectively distributed. Such distribution lifts the pressure off people, releasing them from tasks they are simply not equipped for, and brings into play gifts and skills that might otherwise be ignored.

A preoccupation with alternative Modes of Communication

Some preachers feel that the traditional sermon is one-dimensional, and as monologue alien to the way communication is carried out in our contemporary world. To

15

a certain extent this is a legitimate response to the increasing diversity of the ways in which men and women receive information. A brief visit to the average Primary School will see the classrooms populated with computers, white boards and a whole range of electronic gadgetry that was undreamed of just a few decades ago. McCluhan's famous division of communication modes into 'hot' (passive and involving only one of the senses) and 'cool' (participational and multi-sense) shows that the array of 'cool' communication modes open to modern people leaves the 'hot' method of the sermon looking a little antiquated.

Then again the buzz word in modern communications is 'interactive'. The sermon by its very nature allows for no such interaction as it is normally conceived. Recent years have therefore seen the 'sermon slot' increasingly filled with the use of audio tapes, CDs, Videos, DVDs and the seemingly ubiquitous 'Power Point' presentation. Only a contemporary Luddite would deny that these modern methods convey great benefits and have a place within the teaching work of the Church. They are, as mentioned above, legitimate responses to irresistible changes in society. And they offer unquestioned benefits for the Church. For example, the projection of the words of hymns onto a screen via powerpoint can greatly enhance the singing of the congregation. Instead of having their heads down in a book, they have them held up, looking at a screen. The increase in volume has to be heard to be believed.

Simply because something is modern however does not mean it is beyond criticism and has no corresponding drawbacks, especially when it is used to aid the preacher. Technology is, like many things, a good servant but a tyrannical master. My observation, sitting fairly regularly on the receiving end of PowerPoint™, is that it carries the risk of oversimplifying the message by the necessity of conveying it in a form which renders it visually presentable. It has always to be remembered that the written word and the spoken word are different media and not always equivalent. In my view it is sometimes better to allow the congregation to visualize something for themselves, rather than draw it or spell it out on a screen. This I believe is especially true when addressing children, whose lively imaginations can be a vital resource for the preacher.

The second risk, in my view, is that it divides the congregation's attention between two visual centres, the preacher and the screen. This may at first glance seem a trivial point, and yet, as we shall reflect later, it is in my view of the very essence of preaching to have a direct relationship between preacher and hearers. This can be a particular problem if the screen is placed any significant distance from the preacher. This can result in the congregation actually looking away from the preacher to the screen without relating visually to him at all. Eye contact is in my view very important. It is through this intimate contact between speaker and listener that the Word of God is conveyed. I would want to argue here that care must be taken when interposing something that threatens to weaken this sense of intimacy. Technology, no matter how sophisticated and effective, will not do the job for the preacher. The person to person element remains the vitally important fulcrum around which the sermon turns.

The Pace of Liturgical Revision in the Church of England in recent years has decentralized preaching in many churches and imposed great restrictions on it

Very few people would deny that the liturgical revision which began in Britain in the early sixties has brought tremendous benefits. There are of course still those who would argue that the advent of the Liturgical Commission was a dark day in the Church of England. This writer is not one of them, and is very ready to acknowledge the benefits of the greater flexibility, clarity of expression and opportunity for use of imagination that the new liturgical forms have brought.

Nevertheless there are one or two negative consequences for preaching that have to be acknowledged. One is that the importance of the Eucharist has been heightened, even within evangelical circles, so that the centrality of the altar rather than the lectern, has become commonplace. It is a discussion for a later chapter of this book, but here we must note that this shift in visual symbolism can bring with it a downplay in the importance of the Word read and expounded. In seeking in the Eucharist to establish a balance between Pulpit and Table, it is inevitable that some churches will tilt the balance in favour of the Table, to the detriment of the sermon.

Then again, the sheer length of the Common Worship Eucharistic Liturgy, if used in its entirety, inevitably imposes severe restrictions of the length of the sermon, making it virtually impossible in most cases to develop a detailed biblical exposition. Proponents of Common Worship would argue that the section entitled Ministry of the Word, with its allowance for three readings for the Bible plus a sermon, gets greater prominence in the liturgy than was the case previously. Nevertheless the time for actual exposition is under great pressure, and any sermon longer than fifteen minutes risks making the whole service unacceptably long. We shall touch on this later as one of the negative consequences of the advent of the Parish Communion Movement.

It would be churlish however, not to acknowledge positive developments in liturgical revision in recent years. The advent of the Revised Common Lectionary and its widespread use in the Church of England are, to this writer, very welcome developments. The appearance also of a number of study aids to the RCL betokens a genuine desire to improve the effectiveness to raise the standard of preaching within the liturgical context, and this is another welcome development.

The basic question is "where is the central focus of worship to be found ?". The fear is that, where once worship would focus on the reading and exposition of the Word, developments in liturgy have in many churches shifted the focus onto other things.

The Charismatic Movement has, in the eyes of some, opened up alternative ways of accessing God's Word other than through the Formal Exposition

This point is in a sense a variation on the previous point, in that within many churches that experience charismatic renewal through the Holy Spirit, the focus of worship has shifted from the exposition of the Word onto music and singing, extempore prayer and the exercise of spiritual gifts. People within this Movement sometimes fall unwittingly into the trap of referring to singing and prayer as 'the worship', as though the Word something added on, an appendix to the act of devotion.

More specifically the exercise of the gift of prophecy has opened up, in some people's eyes, an alternative to the sermon as a means of accessing and listening to the Word of God. Distinctions are made between the prepared exposition and the impromptu utterance within the context of worship. In some cases this has inevitably led to the downgrading of the sermon as somehow being 'lower level inspiration' than the prophetic utterance.

This is not the place to debate the issue in detail, apart from saying that both types of utterance have a place within the Church and that the gift of prophecy, whatever precisely that is, has to be used only in relation to the Canonical Scriptures, to ensure that these charismatic utterances are truly from God. It is sufficient to note the point that in some instances the gift of prophecy can be viewed as a short cut, a means of evading the hard disciplined work of Bible exposition.

Again, I risk losing friends from within the charismatic renewal movement by suggesting that charismatic worship inevitably downplays the sermon in favour of other things. I fully recognize that this would be a parody, and that many models of restoration churches have expository preaching right at the heart of charismatic worship. At its best charismatic preaching drives people back to the Word. I am suggesting that the temptation is a constant one to squeeze the Exposition, with the great demands it makes on both preacher and listener, in favour of things that appear more congenial and less demanding.

New Directions in Preaching

Taking on board many of the criticisms of the traditional sermon discussed above: that it was over-prescriptive and authoritarian, that it encouraged passivity in the congregation, and was in any case ineffective, students of preaching began to look for new approaches, and new models for preaching.

The genesis of this new approach to preaching, styled "**The New Homiletic**" by David Randolph[10], is usually traced to the work of Fred Craddock. Craddock's seminal work, *As One Without Authority*, led to what Richard Eslinger styled "the Copernican Revolution in North American Homiletics."[11]. Craddock's basic and passionate conviction is that congregations should be encouraged to think for themselves, rather than being told what to think by the preacher. This would in turn lead to a much greater assimilation of spiritual truth than traditional ways. It has the further merit of fitting in with new postmodern ideas of how truth is approached.

Craddock coined the phrase the **Inductive Sermon,** in which the preacher, rather than giving the conclusion to the congregation, gives information that will initiate a journey, one in which the preacher journeys with the congregation, with the aim of coming across a conclusion together. The sermon would be thus be open-ended. It would not be entirely so, however, for it would be shaped to a certain degree by the preacher's own reading of the text. The inductive sermon re-creates the process of discovery of meaning in the text.

The essence of the inductive sermon is movement. It moves from the particular to the general, and not the other way round as traditional exposition does. Craddock suggests

> Instead of the sermon beginning where preparation ended, i.e. with the conclusion, why not recreate with the congregation the process of jointly coming to the conclusion?[12]

At the end of the sermon therefore the hearers are not where they started. They have been on a voyage of discovery. The content of the sermon does not come pre-packaged, but is teased out by preacher and congregation together.

The congregation will be encouraged on this journey by a deliberately inserted note of discordance or incongruity. This note will be allowed to continue playing until some later point in the sermon, when the preacher introduces a second note, that of clarification, a "sudden surprise" which dissolves the incongruity. Other exponents of the New Homiletic such as Lowry speak of "crisis-resolution" to make the same point. Unfortunately, many who applied Craddock's ideas lacked his subtlety, as he himself observed with sadness, introducing confusion and obscurity almost for the sake of it. However, the truly inductive sermon would not solve the puzzle completely for the congregation. There would be an element of the Hercule Poirot, with his concluding set-piece consummation. Unlike Poirot, however, the preacher would not tie up all the loose ends. The inductive process draws people in so that, instead of turning to the last page of the detective novel for the resolution, they are able to write that page themselves.

Craddock and those who have taken up his ideas see the inductive sermon as an *event* or experience. It is not the content of the sermon that is of crucial importance, it is participation in the preaching process itself that matters. Preaching is not the conveying of a proposition or concept across the homiletic bridge between the horizons of the text and the hearer; it is an *experience* that is brought across.

These ideas have important implications for the structure of the sermon. If the sermon is seen as a journey of discovery, then the form and structure will be very different from that of the traditional Expository sermon. Indeed, there may well be no set structure. There will be as many structures as there are texts.

Craddock says

> Why should the gospel always be impaled upon the frame of Aristotelian logic, when the preacher's muscles twitch and his nerves tingle to mount the pulpit steps not with three points, but with the gospel as narrative, or parable, or poem, or myth, or song ?[13]

Genre and rhetorical criticism have emphasized the importance of the preacher respecting the literary form and rhetorical situation of the text under review when structuring his sermon. Form and meaning are undoubtedly connected, and it is all to easy to do violence to the meaning of the text by casting it in an inappropriate form. It is a matter of balance. The form of the *original* text must be allowed to influence the form of the sermon, but not be the sole, or even the dominant, factor in shaping that form.

As second major development within the umbrella of the New Homiletic, stemming from the pioneer work of Craddock, was the development of the style of preaching known as **Narrative Preaching.** It has many modern exponents, such as Grady

Davis, R.E.C. Browne, Thomas Troeger, as well as Craddock himself.

But it is with the name of the jazz piano playing preacher Eugene L. Lowry that the narrative sermon is most closely associated in recent times. His book *The Homiletical Plot: The Sermon as Narrative Art Form*, published in 1980, but with a second, expanded edition published twenty one years later, is the definitive statement of the principles that underly narrative preaching.[14]

Helpfully Lowry sets out those principles in his introduction. He urges preachers to put aside, at least temporarily, all cherished norms about sermon structure. One of these norms is the idea that the structure of the sermon is related to and develops from the content of the passage being preached. Typically then the expository preacher chops the text up into equal parts, usually three, and arranges them in logical order.

> We have been taught the science of sermon construction as though we were a strange breed of structural engineers.[15]

Lowry then urges us to develop a new image of the sermon. The sermon is not a doctrinal lecture; it is an event in time, a narrative art form more akin to a play than a book. Hence the preacher is not an engineer, but an artist.

The notion of the sermon as an "event" is a concept that Lowry shares with Craddock. Indeed there is a great similarity between the ideas of Lowry and Craddock, a point that Lowry graciously acknowledges.

> Preaching is more than a faithful witness, more than a topical discussion, more than a moral lesson, more than an exposition of the text. It should be an event in time that

intends a divine-human meeting in the context of corporate worship.[16]

The common denominator in all versions of narrative preaching involves a strategic delay in the arrival of the preacher's meaning. The comedian who repeatedly gives away the punch line too soon will spoil the effect of the jokes and will as a result probably have an extremely short career.

As with Craddock, Lowry emphasises the importance of movement in the sermon. In narrative preaching, the congregation moves from crisis to resolution, or from what Lowry picturesquely describes as being from "oops" to "yeah", or from "scratch" to "itch". This movement involves not merely telling stories (narrative preaching is more than that, argues Lowry) but is brought about by a very carefully constructed "plot". A "story" does not necessarily go in any particular direction - it is just a story. "Plot" moves from itch to scratch, from conflict to resolution.[17]

Variations on the theme of narrative preaching include what may be styled **episodal preaching,** a style associated with Lucy Rose. Here the sermon consists of a whole series of vignettes or episodes, the connection between which is left implicit until the conclusion of the sermon, or at least scarcely named. The episodes are linked together in a way that increases interest with each episode. What is lacking in this style of preaching, if it is to be included under the umbrella of narrative preaching, is the sense of movement from crisis to resolution, ambiguity to closure, that narrative preaching presupposes.

Another variation on the narrative theme is represented by David Buttrick, who explores the language of the sermon and develops the concept of the homiletical "move". The sermon is a "plot" with a series of "moves." The plot terminology means that the sermon has an intention. The preacher is preaching for a particular intention. The sermonic plot is made up of 3-5 minute moves. So the sermon is a Introduction, a number of moves, and a conclusion.

Buttrick speaks of three basic plot forms that are used to construct sermons. The first plot form is "Mode of Immediacy." In this plot form the sermon follows the narrative moves in a text. The second plot form is "reflective mode." In this sermonic approach we use the text as we move from moments of the preacher's reflection. The third plot form is "praxis mode." Here the preacher focuses on a topic and not a text. The plot is a number of steps of theological analysis that will lead one to the Christian understanding of the situation.

Each move has a statement which is a clear indication of the move. Then there is a development of the statement which consists of an explanation. Next the preacher provides an image that helps the congregation to see the point. Finally there is a close statement that summarizes the move.

A growing feeling that arises from reading the work of Craddock, Lowry, Buttrick and other exponents of the New Homiletic is that there is an element of caricature in their portrayal of expository preaching. In most cases it does not devolve into the lecture, the dry recital of propositions. I would not dare to say that nobody preaches in that way, but in my experience the best of expositors have always been sensitive to the genre of the material with which they are working, and have been more than willing to vary the form of their presentation in accordance with it. Effective, good and imaginative expository preachers have always incorporated into their presentation many of the insights reflected in the New Homiletic.

New Wine in Old Wineskins ?

It is at the very least an arguable case to say that Inductive, Narrative and Expository preaching can peacefully coexist in the same pulpit. The good sermon is at times all three. We reflect on the old adage that a half-truth made into the whole truth becomes a complete untruth.

For example, induction cannot represent the sole characteristic of preaching. There are many times when the congregation will, quite rightly be encouraged to use their brains and think for themselves. After all, that is the whole point of the parables of Jesus. They were designed to make the hearers think, something that applies every bit to the congregations of today as it did to Jesus' original hearers. The parables should not be, indeed cannot be, preached in any other way. They are, by their very nature, non-prescriptive.

There are limits, however. To reach sensible conclusions people need to be given information. If the information is incorrect or incomplete, any conclusions they reach are likely to be incorrect. The preacher therefore, no matter how non-directive and non-prescriptive may wish to be in his approach, cannot be indifferent to the conclusions the congregation reaches on the basis of his sermon.

By way of example we can point to Jesus' discussion with Peter about forgiveness in Matthew 18.21-35. In this Jesus places on Christians an absolute command to forgive. Experience tells me that this presents real difficulties for some Christians when considering certain types of people who have committed certain kinds of acts, such as child abuse. If therefore the preacher's listeners decide to tone down or qualify the command of Jesus in the light of their personal experience and understanding, the preacher cannot be indifferent to this, and would feel the need to respond. There have to be certain parameters prescribing the range of destinations to which preacher and congregation arrive on their journey, otherwise we arrive at the situation where "all a man's ways seem right to him".[18] If therefore we allow for a degree of prescription, then the gap between expository and inductive preaching is not as large as we may suppose.

In the case of narrative preaching, we recognise also that the concept of "plot" has something to offer. The notion of movement in the sermon, from itch to scratch is an exciting one. The Ethiopian Eunuch, totally bemused by his reading of Isaiah, receives the key from Philip and goes on his way rejoicing, (Acts 8.26-40). Any sermon that sends our congregations out rejoicing, as the Ethiopian did, gets my vote. His move from "oops" to "yeah" was dramatic. There is no argument against the value of this as *one* approach to preaching. The danger comes, as we have previously stated, when this is represented as the *only* approach. The wide range of literary genres in the pages of the Bible means that multiple approaches will be needed. The concept of plot must not be imposed on material to which it is alien, because the artificiality of such a practice will be very quickly spotted by the congregation. Craddock at least recognises this, and is very careful to point out that the inductive sermon can take many forms rather than a single form.

It has to be said that other weaknesses can be detected in the New Homiletic that would back up the notion that it does not represent the total answer to the malaise of preaching. Craddock himself recognises that it works best in a Christian culture where people are already familiar with their Christian heritage. The reason for this is not hard to see, since Inductive and Narrative preaching focus on form and technique rather than content. People will not learn much about the content of the Christian Faith through such preaching. It is not the answer to the problem of Biblical illiteracy, nor will it do as a recipe for building up and sustaining Christian communities. As a diet for Christian growth it will require supplements.

It's insistence and emphasis on narrative will make it an inappropriate tool for analysing much of the New Testament material. 21 out of the 27 New Testament books are not narrative in form, and therefore not surprisingly are neglected by many exponents of the New Homiletic. The revelatory significance of other genres in the New Testament is seriously underplayed. Above all, the retreat from pulpit authority, no matter how much that authority may have been abused by preachers, does not sit comfortably with the representation of authoritative preaching in the New Testament, which we shall shortly examine, nor the features of preaching in the high points of the Church's history.

It should be said in addition that the New Homiletic has been around now for more than 50 years. It is not exactly brand new. Nor, should it be said, has it ushered in any Golden Age for preaching, nor heralded dramatic growth in the Church. It is not in itself the answer to the malaise of preaching today. Its appearance, however, especially on the reading lists of our theological colleges, is at the very least an encouraging sign that people are open to new ideas and are wanting to improve the quality of preaching and increase its impact. Criticisms of traditional preaching do need to be taken seriously. Nothing is gained by denial, or by the dismissal of such criticisms by a glib retort on the part of those committed to traditional expository preaching. Nor must we blindly plough on, imagining that somehow things will change and come right. We must take on board the many valuable insights that Craddock, Lowry and others have produced. We owe this to those who, in spite of all the alternative modes of communication open to them, still submit themselves week by week to the experience of listening to a sermon.

We would not in fact wish to make a rigid distinction between "old" and "new" preaching. Such a distinction is not very helpful. Certainly there are insights in the newer preaching that need to be taken on board, whilst there are valuable elements of expository preaching that must not be jettisoned. The new wine will *not* burst the old wineskins.   Many of the criticisms of traditional monologue preaching as outlined above could be said to be criticisms of expository preaching done badly. It can devolve into a dry and dusty lecture, a recital of boring propositions. That is down to the quality of the preacher. In the same way narrative preaching can be done badly, introducing the element of "oops" so mysteriously that the poor congregation never get as far as the "yeah". We must not fall into the trap of comparing the worst of one thing with the best of another.

Getting the Best of Both Worlds

Whilst taking on board all the good things that flow from the New Homiletic, we would want to stubbornly argue that preaching as monologue is, when done well, still of great value, and is moreover somehow of the very essence of the Church. The Old Testament community was founded and sustained by the Word of the Prophets, whilst the New Testament Church was built round the proclamation of the Word by Jesus and the apostles. Whilst giving full value to all the newer ideas, we see them as enriching and strengthening traditional preaching rather than replacing it. As we shall observe later, there is a proclamatory element at the heart of God's communication. "Thus says the Lord" is a communication that can be presented only by the anointed preacher or herald. Lowry attempts to make a distinction between "proclamation" and "preaching", arguing that the latter only becomes proclamation when it rings bells, and is "heard" by the receiver. This however does not chime in with the experience of the Old Testament prophets. Prophets were frequently sent to people who deliberately closed their ears and would not listen. This did not make them any less heralds or prophets. The authority of the speaker comes from God as the source of his words, rather than from the ability or willingness of the audience to hear.

It has often been rightly observed that the Church has been most healthy when its pulpit has been robust. Across the centuries we can see that when the Church has been most alive, there was a strong emphasis on preaching and proclamation. Protestantism in particular has never found a substitute for preaching, and it never can.[19]

Above all, the simple fact is that in spite of all the arguments against it, from the educational, sociological and cultural realms, preaching works ! This is not a glib retort to such criticisms, but a fact of experience. Story after story can be told of how people were "hooked" by a particular turn of phrase, or story, or illustration etc in a sermon and came to see themselves and Jesus in a new light. Even more amazingly, these revelatory events have often been brought about by what might be considered "poor" sermons ! Every preacher will be aware of Paul's reminder that we have "treasure in earthenware pots" (2 Cor.5.14) and that God works sometimes in spite of us and not because of us. Yet, in His providence, he uses the sometimes inadequate utterances of preachers to do His work, and we can only thank Him for so doing. We are reminded also of Paul's remark about how God was pleased through "the foolishness of preaching" to save those who believe. [20] The primary reference here is of course to the *content* of the preaching, an incarnate crucified Saviour, something dismissed as a foolish notion by many Greeks, with their spirit/matter dualism. But we can suppose that the modern equivalent of those Greeks would regard the activity of preaching, the standing up and simply shouting it out, is implicit as well. We can see this in the way the open-air preachers at rail stations or outside sports stadia, a phenomenon that has always been part of British culture, are ignored or taunted by modern day passers by. Wright notes that this has contributed to the pejorative understanding of the word "preaching" today.[21]

What we are pleased to refer to as the "authoritative monologue", seems to have been an essential part of the Biblical faith right from the start. In Genesis 1.3 God declares "let there be light". In similar fashion the prophets come along declaring "Thus says the Lord". Their words are autocratic (or more precisely *theo*cratic) statements about how things are and should be. There is no room for debate or discussion. They are definitely not inductive in their approach ! God has spoken - the role of the listener is to hear and obey. It is certainly true that the prophets used a variety of methods to speak to the people, including dialogue, but under girding the prophet's authority was the authority of the Word of God that had "come" to them.

John the Baptist appears in the desert, proclaiming a baptism of repentance. The Greek verb κηρυσσων refers to the work of a herald, and is exactly the same word used a little later to refer to Jesus' coming to declare the Gospel of God.

Peter's sermon in Acts 2 includes the staggering declaration:

> Let all the house of Israel therefore know for certain that God has made Him both Lord and Christ, this Jesus whom you crucified.
>
> *Acts 2.36*

No preacher ever had a more devastating authoritative announcement to make, nor did any preacher get a more immediate and comprehensive response.

For Peter this preaching was what he and his fellow apostles had been called to do.

He (God) commanded us to preach to the people and to testify that He (Jesus) is the One appointed by God to be judge of the living and the dead.

Acts 10.42

The authoritative pronouncement or monologue is a central feature therefore of the work of the Messengers of God, the prophets, John the Baptist, Jesus, Peter, Paul and others.

Preaching as Revelation

Why is this ?   Why is preaching such a central part of the story of God's work as related in the Bible ?   The answer is not too hard to discover.   Christianity is a revealed religion. It is not a story of men seeking God, searching the far corners of the world in search of glimpses of Him, it is the story of how God has come to us and said 'Here I am'.   God lifts the veil that would otherwise obscure our sight and declares Himself to us. He has indeed left His footprints in Nature, but without revelation they would leave us, like the Abominable Snowman, with just a tantalising mystery.

There are many corollaries that follow from this.   For the purpose of this study the one that matters is that men and women cannot know God unless they are told about Him. Paul puts it very concisely when he asks the rhetorical questions:

How are they to believe in Him of whom they have never heard ?

How are they to hear without someone preaching ?[22]

How are they to preach unless they are sent ?

Romans 10.14,15.

People are therefore not going to stumble across the Good News of Jesus in the garden or on the street.   It is not self-evident. Nor will they discover it through debate and discussion. The Bible is very clear that, if people are to come to know Jesus and the significance of His work for them, they need to be told. That requires someone who has already heard and received the message answering the call to pass it on authoritatively and clearly. Of course there is a place for dialogue and discussion. But, as we have argued, discussion cannot discover truth without information. The preacher cannot stand idly by while lack of information allows shared insight to lead the congregation out into a trackless desert. Shared insight is the cart that follows the horse of authoritative preaching.

In Acts the work of the Holy Spirit and preaching are closely linked. The Holy Spirit falls dramatically on the apostles in the Upper Room in Jerusalem. After the initial signs appear, what happens ? They begin to preach. What had happened to the disciples to change their lives ? This can be discovered only through preaching, as Peter does in the way referred to above.

Again and again in Acts, when God is portrayed as doing a great work by His Spirit, the outcome is renewed preaching, so much so that it can be argued without too much difficulty that the primary work of the Holy Spirit in Acts to produce effective preaching.[23]

Preaching as Encounter

The great revivalist preachers had grasped something important about the essence of preaching. Within the act of preaching a great drama is being played out. There are three participants: the preacher, naturally; the listener, (no point in preaching if no one is listening); and the God who inspires the words the preacher is uttering. Within that drama, properly understood, the hearer is being confronted with the Word, and with himself in relation to that Word. Although the sermon

33

will convey information, that is not its primary purpose. The sermon invites a response from the hearer - no, the sermon *demands* a response. The sermon will not necessarily convey new facts, but will invite the hearer sometimes to see old facts in a new light. The purpose of the parable of the Good Samaritan is not to convey facts as much as to confront the hearer with himself and with his attitudes, so that he may "go and do likewise". As the third player in the drama God is present to witness the response and in turn to react to that response.

This notion of the sermon as an encounter with God through His preached Word I find very exciting. The concept is borrowed to a degree from the existential thinkers, especially those who, like Bultmann attempted to apply existential thought to the Christian Faith. It brings a dynamism to preaching which is not always appreciated.

Preaching changes things. Here we find ourselves travelling along very happily with Craddock, Lowry and their colleagues. Their concept of "movement" in the course of the delivery of a sermon is a very valuable one, though we may conceive that movement as going in a number of directions rather that the one they envisage. Something very definitely does happen in the course of preaching, because the word spoken by the preacher is much more than simply a word, and audible sound. It is an eventful word, so full of happening that we may describe it as a "word-event". This is a commonplace of human experience. Any man who has asked a girl to marry him and has heard the word "yes" knows that he is not in the presence of a monosyllable, but of a life changing event. All life is charged with such moments. The words of the Old Testament prophets are *par excellence* word-events, or, to use the parlance we shall take up later "speech-acts". The prophets' words changed the lives of individuals and shaped the destinies of nations.

As Canon Max Warren puts it,

> The astonishing story of the survival of the Jewish people, and the infinite ramifications of their spiritual insights on all the subsequent history of mankind can be understood only if we give full value to the power of words to be themselves creative, to partake of the very nature of the Creator God Himself.[24]

So we see the creative words of the prophets of an earlier day gathering new meanings in the course of history, finding unique expression in the self- disclosure of God in Jesus Christ, and still continuing down history, gathering ever more new meanings. This is the nature of creative words. And the supreme task of the preacher is to take these words and make them speak again, so that once more a word-event may occur. Preaching actualizes the Gospel and brings the hearer face to face with the crucified and risen Christ.

Preaching remains foolishness today just as much as it did in ancient Corinth. The preacher himself must accept that what he does will seem foolishness to many to whom he speaks. He will find within the Church itself who will insist that the day of the preacher is over. At times he will be tempted to agree with them. It is then that he will ask himself two pertinent questions:

> How can they have faith in someone of whom they have never heard ?

and the logical follow up

> How can they hear without someone to tell them ?

The responsibility to "tell" is as urgent today as it was for the Apostle Paul, reflecting on the beauty of the feet of the one who carries the good news to Zion that their God reigns

(Isaiah 52.7). This cry is taken up by the watchmen on the walls, and they, with the preacher, shout for joy.

The preacher is further to be encouraged by the knowledge that the response made by the hearer to the Word of God spoken through him has an eschatological quality about it. This is most easily seen in evangelistic preaching, where the hearer is invited to in some way to say "yes" to Jesus. As the revivalist preachers would put it, with some truth, on the individual's response to that invitation eternal issues may rest. What is true of evangelistic preaching is true, I believe, of every other kind of preaching also. Lots of things determine how people listen to and respond to the preaching of the Word. The sermon, the prophetic word-event, provides the existential "moment" in the continuous flux of peoples' lives. Time and space, and indeed life and death, are changed by it. If we preachers can only grasp this concept more fully, we would be positively running up the pulpit steps !

CHAPTER ONE
ENDNOTES

[1] E.M.B.Green, in Editor's Preface to J.R.W.Stott, *I Believe in Preaching*, (London: Hodder & Stoughton, 1982), 7.

[2] ed. R.Bowen, *A Guide to Preaching* (London: SPCK, 2005),

[3] Hughes Oliphant Old, *The Reading and Preaching of the Scriptures in the Worship of the Church: Volume 1, The Biblical Period* (Grand Rapids: Eerdmans, 1998), 2.

[4] J.Killinger, *Fundamentals of Preaching* (Minneapolis: Fortress Press, 1996), 2.

[5] Nehemiah 4.10 - the people in Judah said, "there is so much rubble we cannot rebuild the wall".

[6] L.E.Keck, *The Bible in the Pulpit: The Renewal of Biblical Preaching* (Nashville: Abingdon Press, 1978), 40.

[7] Ilion Jones, *Principles and Practice of Preaching* (Abingdon: Nashville, 1956), 31.

[8] G.Trollope, *Barchester Towers*, (Penguin Classics) 46.

[9] R.Greer, *Anglican Approaches to Scripture: From the Reformation to the Present*, (New York: Herder & Herder, 2006), 184.

[10] D.J.Randolph, *The Renewal of Preaching* (Philadelphia: Fortress, 1969), 17.

[11] R.Eslinger, *A New Hearing* (Nashville: Abingdon, 1987).

[12] F.Craddock, As One Without Authority, 125.

[13] Craddock, *As One without authority*, 45.

[14] Eugene L. Lowry, *The Homiletical Plot: The Sermon as Narrative Art Form* (Louisville: Westminster John Knox, 1980)

[15] Lowry, *Homiletical Plot*, xx.

[16] Lowry, *Homiletical Plot*, 122.

[17] Lowry, *Homiletical Plot*, 125.

[18] Proverbs 21.2.

[19] An observation of G.Sweazey, *Preaching Good News* (Englewood Cliffs: Prentice Hall, 1967), 6.

[20] 1 Cor.1.24   Greek: του κηρυγμα

[21] S.Wright, *Preaching with Humanity* (London: Church House Publishing, 2009), 3.

[22] Greek: κηρυσσοντες, from the same word 'herald' used in Mark 1.4,14 of John the Baptist and Jesus.

[23] I am grateful to Dr. Martyn Lloyd Jones for this insight. cf. *Preaching and Preachers* (London: Hodder & Stoughton, 1971), 21-24.

[24] M.A.C.Warren, *The Day of the Preacher*, (London: Mowbrays, 1966), 3.

2

THE PREACHER'S ANCESTORS

PREACHING AND PROCLAMATION IN THE BIBLE

Genesis, the very first book of the Bible, starts with something pretty amazing. The third verse of that opening chapter tells us that "God said......". Now that may not seem particularly amazing until you look round and observe the strenuous efforts of men and women, both inside and outside the religious tradition, to probe the mysteries of the universe and to search for something that will make sense of it all. They are investigating what they see as a silent world, one whose secrets may be discovered only by those who stretch every muscle and sinew in diligent search.

But it is not in fact a silent universe. It is one in which its Creator speaks. God's existence and nature is being shouted from hill to valley, from mountain top to ocean depth. In many and various ways (Heb.1.1) God communicates His nature and purpose, and who, through His grace invites human beings to become involved in this process of communication. This is the foundational theological principle on which preaching is based. The preacher speaks and proclaims because God speaks and proclaims. Communication by speech is one of the prime ways in which human beings in general and preachers in particular demonstrate that they are moulded in the image of God.

To continue the Genesis statement begun above, "God said 'let there be light', and there was light". That's also amazing, because we human beings are pretty good at saying things but not quite as good at doing them. For God however, saying and doing are the same thing. It is enough for God to *say* it for it to happen. "No sooner said than done", a phrase we often use in casual conversation is literally true of God.

The writer of Genesis goes on to list the various stages of creation, culminating in the creation of man, and introduces each stage with the same formula - "And God said" (1.3, 6,9,11,14,20,24,26). No intermediate agencies are mentioned. The creative agency is the spoken word of God.

The writer of Hebrews can say

> By faith we understand that the world was created by the Word of God, so that what appears was created out of things that do not appear
>
> *Hebrews 1.3*

The Psalmist makes much the same point

> By the Word of the Lord the heavens were made, and by the breath of His mouth all their host.
>
> *Psalm 33.6*

It would seem that, for the Biblical writers, the expression "word", especially when related to God, is far more than the often casual and imprecise utterances that come from our mouths and just as often mean very little. On the contrary, God's word is very solid and accomplishes things. In what it is sent to accomplish, this Word is irresistible (Isaiah 55.11).

In the Wisdom Literature "wisdom", understood as the sum total of the utterances of God, is presented as an extension of God's personality. This presentation of wisdom borders on personification. So wisdom comes into being before the creation of the world. Wisdom is God's companion and agent in Creation itself. Wisdom rejoices with God in His finished work. All these ideas we can see set out in Proverbs 8.22-31.

In the opening chapter of the Fourth Gospel the Word (λoγoς), understood as the Word of *God*) is presented just like wisdom as the agent of creation, before going on to the stunning description of that same Word becoming flesh (John.1.3,14).

We shall return to this passage for further consideration later, but for now it is important to see the Word of God as the means of God's self-disclosure. For our purpose it is important to note that in all this God uses His *spoken* Word, a process that proceeds through the prophets and culminates in the person of the Incarnate Word, Jesus, to reveal Himself to men and women. The "Word of the Lord" is seen as more than mere verbal utterances; this Word is seen as something emanating from God that carries power, and is an expression of God's omnipotence.

This dynamic concept of God's spoken word is important, because it links together God's speech and action. Kevin Vanhoozer has popularised the notion of "divine speech-act".[1] The Bible is no mere catalogue of inert divine propositions. The Bible is a record also of the mighty Acts of God: in Creation; in the Rescue from Egypt; in Exile and Restoration, and supremely in the Incarnation, Crucifixion and Resurrection of Jesus Christ.

But these acts would not be revelatory without explanatory words. The Rescue from Egypt gains meaning when we understand it as a response by God to His Covenant, as explained in His words to Moses in Exodus 3.

So, says Vanhoozer,

> God is a speech-agent. Much of what He does - warning, commanding, promising, forgiving, informing, comforting - He does by speaking[2]

Vanhoozer's concept of speech-act, which we will see come to the fore when we look at the work of Jesus, is a valuable and helpful way of resolving the old conservative-liberal argument about so-called propositional revelation over against revelation through history. God's word is *both* word *and* act.

God speaks through the Law and the Prophets

The practice of reading and expounding the Word of God within the community of Israel was already well established by the time of the prophets. It has its origins in the events surrounding the giving of the Law and its establishment at the heart of the covenant life of the people. So in Exodus 24 we read that Moses, having come down the mountain from his meeting with God

> told the people all the Lord's words and laws And the
> people responded everything the Lord has said we will do
> *Exodus 24.3*

The word "preached" is not used here, but it seems inconceivable that Moses was here engaging in mere recital without explanation. In v.7 of the same passage the people respond in the same way to Moses' reading of the Book of the Covenant.

We will do everything the Lord has said: we will obey.

This introduces the very strong link between the reading and teaching of the Word of God and covenant renewal. This notion of expounding the word in the Israelite assembly in connection with the renewal of the covenant is widened and deepened in the Deuteronomic tradition. The responsibility for this regular exposition is placed on the **Levitical priests**, to be executed alongside their responsibilities at the altar

> About Levi He (God) said….. he watched over your word and guarded your covenant. He preaches your precepts to Jacob and your law to Israel. He offers incense to you and whole burnt offerings on your altar.
>
> *Deuteronomy 33.8-10*

This aspect of the work of the priest in Israel is perhaps overlooked by many readers. When Jeremiah issues his condemnatory oracles on the priests, he specifically targets their failures in the ministry of the Word.

> The priests did not say, "where is the Lord ?" Those who *handle the Law* did not know me.
>
> *Jeremiah 2.8*

This practice which we have styled "the ministry of the Word" was therefore closely linked to covenantal worship, and had the three dimensions of **remembrance**, recalling God's saving acts; **interpretation**, applying the Law to situations of the day, and **exhortation**, the constant urging of Israel to be obedient to the Law. These are all the dimensions of what we understand to be the hermeneutical task today.

Undoubtedly, however, the emergence of **the Prophets** brought a whole new dynamic to the concept of the ministry of the Word in Old Testament days. A very rough distinction between the Word of the Deuteronomic priests and the prophets would be that the priests' ministry was to a great extent retrospective, looking back at what God had done in the past and soliciting a response, whereas the prophets brought *new* words, new revelation and new calls for obedience from the people.

What the prophets present the aspiring preacher with is an extremely dynamic picture of inspiration and proclamation. The prophets came along as men with something to say, not out of their own minds, but from the God who called and inspired them. In the speaking mode the prophet came before the people proclaiming, "Thus says the Lord."   When the prophet's words are written down the formula changes to "the Word of the Lord came to me, saying…" (Jer.1.4). They saw themselves very clearly as channels for God to speak through. In the case of Jeremiah and others there was a sense of compulsion about it. They had no choice but to speak God's Word.

Jeremiah exclaims

> If I say "I will not mention Him, or speak any more in His name", there is in my heart as it were a burning fire, shut up in my bones; and I weary of holding it in, and I cannot.
>   *Jer.20.29*

There was in some cases a marked sense of reluctance, as in the celebrated instance of Jonah.   This reluctance stemmed from the fact that quite often the message was a message about God's impending judgement, and the need for repentance. There was ultimately no glamour or kudos in being a prophet. To be a prophet involved putting oneself into the firing line and becoming instantly unpopular.

How did the prophets receive their divine message ?   In the previously mentioned formula, "the Word of the Lord came to me", the original Hebrew carries no word for "came". The Word of the Lord mysteriously materialises to the prophet in a way that the text leaves undefined. In Exodus 7.1 we read simply that, "the Lord said to Moses", as naturally as two people conversing in the same room. There is a direct, personal awareness. Even more vividly we read in Jeremiah 1.9 that 'The Lord put out His hand and touched my mouth, and said to me, "Behold, I have put my words in your mouth"'. Not surprisingly a number of passages link this inspiration with the work of the Holy Spirit, but even then the exact mechanics of inspiration are left unexplained.[3] This fits in well with the experience of many preachers. We often descend the pulpit steps having said things we didn't plan or prepare beforehand, and find ourselves asking the question, "where did that come from ?". Prophetic inspiration is at its root an operation that is in its essence mysterious.

At the same time, God's inspiration of the prophetic message does not override the prophet's own personality. The oracles of Amos and Jeremiah are as different from one another as were the personalities of the two prophets. What they did have in common was a closeness to the God who inspired them. A close relationship to God is the *sine qua non* of the prophet. Nobody can speak *for* God unless they are first listening *to* God. A failure to observe this simple principle has led to many a pulpit catastrophe.

The writings of the Prophets are a double witness therefore. They are first of all a record of the words given to the prophet by God through the prophet's close relationship to Him. They are simultaneously the words of specific men in specific historical circumstances.

It is important to add the cautionary note here that the very fact that God uses human authors does not itself imply fallibility and error in the message. It is commonplace for humans to err in the statements they make, but not inevitable. I am not a mathematician (the only member of my family to have to admit that), and yet it is perfectly possible for me to make a series of specific mathematical statements that are all true. Error is not inevitable in *every* statement I might wish to make in the realm of maths. In the same way, it is perfectly possible for God to make a set number of statements through the prophets and for no error to be involved. Certainly the prophets themselves had no sense that what they were saying was anything other than the Word of God itself.

This combination of the divine-human channel in the bringing forth of the Word of God has of course important implications for the preacher. Whilst the full humanity of the preacher is recognised, and careful study required in preparing the sermon, the closeness of the preacher to God will result in nothing other than a message from God.

The Hebrew word for the Old Testament prophet was NABI, usually derived from the Akkadian root NABU meaning "one call, to proclaim". Albright argues successfully that the word should be used passively, to refer to the one who is called, seeing behind the passive the agency of God as the caller.[4] In the course of time it gained the technical meaning of "prophet", and the original meaning was forgotten. NABI occurs in all 309 times in the Old Testament, with 32 occurrences in the Book of Jeremiah alone.

In common parlance, when we speak of "the Prophets" we tend to mean the later so-called "Writing Prophets", whose work we have recorded in the pages of the Old Testament. There were however important examples of prophecy that pre-dated the Writing Prophets.

Various important individuals in Israel were given the title NABI. Abimelech is told that Abraham, in spite of the fact that the latter had deceived him, is a prophet (Gen.20.7). Aaron will be Moses' prophet, speaking the words of God on Moses' behalf (Exodus 7.1). The writer of Deuteronomy sums up Moses, life by exclaiming "there has not arisen a prophet since in Israel like Moses, whom the Lord knew face to face" (Deut.34.10). In Exodus 15.20 Miriam, Aaron's sister, is given the title "prophetess".

A prominent feature of early Israel were the so-called **ecstatic prophets**, groups of itinerants who used to put themselves into trances, using music, babbling out prophecies while entranced. Their work was so infectious that on one occasion King Saul himself got caught up in their activities (1 Sam.10.5). This aspect of prophecy was not confined to Israel however, as the prophets of Baal proved (1Kings 18.19-40).

Major figures like Elijah and Elisha often had prophetic, semi-monastic groups associated with them, often attached to local sanctuaries such as Bethel and Gilgal. Groups of prophets, so-called **cultic prophets** were found attached to the national sanctuary. Their role was to prophesy in response to requests from the King, a role that sometimes caused them divided loyalties, and which consequently brought criticism on them from the Writing Prophets. Hosea exclaims that, in spite of their prophets, "Israel has forgotten his Maker and built palaces" (Hosea 8.14).

Old Testament prophecy reaches its high point, however, with the advent of the **writing prophets**, a phenomenon that came to prominence during the monarchy. With these prophets ecstasy comes to an end, and ties with the cult, the institutions and the monarchy become progressively loose. From now on the word spoken, and then subsequently written, becomes the sole means of communication.

The writing prophets, with such household names as Isaiah, Jeremiah, Ezekiel, Hosea and Amos, were men of widely different temperaments and backgrounds. What they had in common was a closeness to God and a willingness to listen to Him. They are people to whom God is able to speak directly and naturally. They were, in the words of one writer, 'head and shoulders above their contemporaries'.[5]   They were very much men of their own times, but could see beyond them. They were men of the people, but were able, when the occasion demanded, to stand over against them. Proclaiming God's word to the people often brought personal suffering to them, as in the case of Jeremiah, as well as great personal resentment, as in the case of Amos.

Characteristic of the prophet (then and now) was the ability to look beneath the surface of things to see what was really going on in the events around them, along with the ability to see those events from God's point of view. This understanding of the prophet is far more important than the sterile and unprofitable debate about *forth*telling and *fore*telling.   First and foremost the prophet tells the people what God thinks about a certain situation. Only then does he go on to tell them what God proposes to do about it. Analysis of the past and present thus precedes announcements about the future.

The events with which the Prophets were involved were not inconsiderable ones. Isaiah's prophecy (whether from one man or more) spanned the years before, during and after the Exile. Jeremiah and Ezekiel were caught up in the events of that Exile very intimately. Haggai and Zechariah were part of the process of rebuilding the nation and re-establishing its priorities after the return from Babylon.

The message of the Prophets revolved around the twin themes of Judgement and Salvation. They warned when calamity was about to befall the nation, either through earthquake, famine, or ultimately through exile and the loss of their national institutions. They went on to introduce the novel and unpopular idea that these calamities were not just twists of fate, but the consequence of the nation's sin. Nevertheless they would not be abandoned by God - He would rescue them. This salvation was not God taking pity on them in their plight, but stemmed from the nature of God Himself. God is a God who saves, who remains faithful and loving when all around are unfaithful, and who remembers His covenant when all around ignore it. The wonderful phrase "covenant love" (Hebrew: QESED) is the characteristic prophetic description of God. Within the message of salvation and deliverance come all the personal elements that would later coalesce into what we call the figure of the Messiah, the Anointed Deliverer.

At the end of the prophetic era prophecy began to develop into the distinctive literary form known as **apocalyptic**, with its characteristic use of vivid symbolism. Daniel and Zechariah mark the transition from prophecy to apocalyptic, although earlier books contain fragments of the genre (Isaiah 24-27). The rabbis saw apocalyptic as the legitimate successor of prophecy, and with the advent of apocalyptic prophecy itself fades away:

> Up to this point (i.e Alexander the Great) the prophets preached through the Holy Spirit. From then on bow down and hear the words of the wise (the apocalyptic writers).[6]

The Qumran Community treasured the writings of the Prophets to an extraordinary degree, applying many of the prophecies to their own day, which they saw as the End-time.

That the prophets should be seen as genuine preachers, and not simply *ad hoc* proclaimers of the Word need not be doubted. Examination of the books of Amos and Jeremiah and identifies rhetorical structures that are conventionally termed "oracles", but which may just as easily be described as "sermons". The famous oracle of the nations in Amos 1 and 2 is a great example. Amos draws his listeners in by the condemnation of their near neighbours, eliciting their agreement and assent before hitting them with the devastating accusation that their guilt, as ones who possess the Law is as bad if not worse than the others. The oracles of Jeremiah 14 may be understood in the same way.

The prophets were those who spoke first and then had their prophecies written down. It is only natural for us when we think of these men to think of the books we have preserved for us in the Old Testament part of our Bible. But we must always remember that they were speakers and "preachers" first before they were writers. Although the books were written as literary works, with a literary structure of varying degrees of complexity, they are essentially the records of sermons. This ought to give a special dynamic to the things we read.

As preachers, and presenters of the Word, the prophets were extremely versatile. Within the standard, direct speech they would employ a number of literary forms to aid their teaching. Chief amongst these was the MASHAL, or "wise saying". The simplest form of the MASHAL contained a single point of comparison:

> the fathers have eaten sour grapes and the children's teeth are set on edge.
>
> *Ezekiel 18.2*

Used in a disparaging way this comparison becomes a taunt:

> you will take up this taunt against the King of Babylon, "how the oppressor has ceased, the insolent fury ceased".
>
> *Isaiah 14.4*

Like the oriental, the wise man of Old Testament times loved a dark saying or riddle to unravel. In this way the MASHAL merges into HIDAH, "riddle", something not easily interpreted. So the writer of Proverbs asks for divine guidance

> to understand a proverb and a saying, the words of the wise and their riddles
>
> *Proverbs 1.6*

50

A variation on the wise saying was the allegory, used by Isaiah for example in his description of Israel as God's Vineyard (Is.5.1-7). A far more spectacular example of the use of this medium was Nathan's entrapment of David, in his story of the rich man who stole the poor man's lamb to feed his guest, with its damning conclusion *"you* are the man !" (2 Sam.12.1-7). David's penitent response shows the effectiveness of this particular literary device.

The most characteristic prophetic preaching vehicle, and potentially the most powerful, was the "acted oracle", or, more accurately, "the embodiment of prophetic teaching in the life of the prophet". Ezekiel, for example, acts out a number of bizarre sketches as his means of getting teaching across (e.g. Ezek. 4.1f).

At other times the prophet is so closely involved with God and His Word that his own life becomes the embodiment of that teaching. Most famously Hosea moves into an unwise marriage in order to teach Israel the consequences of unfaithfulness (Hosea 1.4-9). Jeremiah has to abstain from marriage and keep away from celebrations to help the people realise that the impending judgement is a time for mourning and not rejoicing (Jer.16.2-9).

For them preaching the Word of God was a costly business, and involved the giving up of normal life in order to pursue the work of the prophet. Being a prophet was not something they slotted into a part of their lives - it involved the whole of that life.

The processes by which the prophecies came to be written down varied with the prophet concerned. In Jeremiah 29 we see a letter composed by Jeremiah himself to the Babylonian exiles. A few chapters later we read of the same Jeremiah employing Baruch as a secretary, to write down "all the words of the Lord that he had spoken to him"(Jer.36.4). By far the most likely means by which the words of the prophets came to be recorded was through groups of disciples associated with them. So Isaiah orders "bind up the testimony and seal the teaching among my disciples" (Is. 8.16). The imperatives suggest a definite act, a precise (almost legal) securing of Isaiah's message against any accusation that he did not say this or that, and against subsequent tampering or adding to it.

In the last few decades Old Testament scholarship has produced a number of literary hypotheses, in some cases quite complex ones, that have resulted in the fragmentation of Old Testament books, including the prophetic books, according to various traditions of literary composition. Besides the books of the Pentateuch, the Book of Isaiah is an obvious example, with its theory of 'multiple Isaiahs'. There is not space here to debate the issues involved in detail. We would however agree with Motyer that the fragmentation hypothesis of Isaiah is not simply to be assumed to be true just because it is accepted by a majority of scholars.[7] It is not impertinent to comment also that many of the fragmentation hypotheses involve a severe limitation of the dimensions of the prophetic vision, taking the forthtelling/foretelling dichotomy to its ultimate conclusion.

We should say also that such hypotheses, except where they can be said to be limiting or denigrating the prophetic vision, do not detract from the picture we have been painting of the prophet as the vehicle for the spoken Word of God. The prophet, responding to the call of God, and standing in close relation to God, speaks the Word of God to the people, sometimes being almost crushed by the gravity of the message he was delivering, and always at personal cost to himself. Aspiring or even established preachers need to study them well, as inspiring examples and as heights to be attained.

It is well known that after the exile prophecy as such died out, giving way to apocalyptic and other forms of address.

However, in accordance with promises of the eschatological revival of prophecy (Deut.18.15; Malachi 3.1; cf.John 1.14) it was spectacularly restored in the person of John the Baptist and then, supremely, in the work of Jesus Christ.

John the Baptist walks the intermediate land between old and new. In the words of Jesus Himself. "the Law and the Prophets were until John; since then the Good News of the Kingdom of God is preached" (Luke 16.16). In a very real sense then John is the end-point of the line of prophetic inspiration.

It is not difficult to see John among the prophets. He "appears" (no word in the Greek) in the desert, as the place where Elijah and others received their prophetic inspiration and which sets him symbolically over against the people. His dress sense and eating habits are enigmatic, and go to further emphasise his distinctiveness.

His message embraces the twin prophetic emphases of judgement (hence the need for repentance), and salvation (through the Jesus who will baptize in the Holy Spirit). It is interesting that, though he presents John's ministry as primarily a preaching of repentance, Luke concludes his description of that ministry by saying that

> With many exhortations John continued to preach *good news* to the people
>
> *Luke 3.18*

In his brief and rather stark opening to his Gospel, Mark presents the ministry of John the Baptist as "the beginning of the Gospel of Jesus Christ, the Son of God" (Mark 1.1-4). John is very much part of the Gospel message. Mark underlines the point in the same passage by using the Isaianic quote to set John's ministry in its proper eschatological context. John the Baptist is a crucial part of the salvific act of God in Jesus that brings in the New Age. Though the message of repentance may be a harsh one, it is a necessary preliminary to receiving the good news of salvation. John's message is therefore definitely good news. It was Martin Luther who once said that the Gospel must be received as *bad* news before it can be seen as *good* news. If further proof were needed, it is seen in the great crowds from town and country that flock to John at the riverside. John's message meets their needs and strikes a chord in their hearts.

His preaching style is characteristically prophetic, both in its directness and in its use of vivid verbal imagery. The Jewish leaders in the crowd are condemned as a "brood of vipers", crawling out of the kindled fire. The people are warned that "the axe is already laid to the root of the trees", and that "the winnowing fork" is already at work.

John's sophistication in his use of imagery is seen in a clever play on words, recorded in Matt.3.9/Luke 3.8. John warns his Jewish listeners not to place too much reliance on their Abrahamic descent, because "from these very stones (Aramaic: EBENIM) God is able to raise up sons (Aramaic: BANIM) for Abraham". It is a mischievous use of words entirely lost in translation from the original language, but is very much a preacher's stock in trade.

Then again, John's message is not simply a bland message of the need for repentance, but of the need to "bear the *fruits* of repentance". It was an extremely practical, concrete message, with a great note of urgency. It is not enough for a person to *say*, "I repent" - evidence must be provided to show the truth of the statement. In case hearers should be confused about what this means, John helps them out. In the extended description of John's ministry provided in Luke 3.10-14, various groups within the crowd come to him asking "what shall we do ?". Unhesitatingly, John gives them solid advice. The crowds are to be unselfish and share; the tax collectors are to collect no more than they are authorised to do, and the soldiers are not to abuse their power in order to extort money by threats or false accusation. Here we have a good example for preachers. Part of the aim of preaching is to motivate people to action, as we shall see later. Too often our attempt at motivation is too vague, and our hearers are not given enough practical guidance as to how our exhortations are to be worked out in practice. Listeners of course vary enormously, and something like repentance (for example) will have different practical implications for each of them. As we noted in our earlier discussion of inductive preaching, we must not fall into the trap of being too prescriptive, directing people's lives or living their lives for them. Nevertheless it is no use offering people the vision of a journey without giving them *some* travel directions. John may be said to have been sent from heaven, but is very much a man of this world, with his feet set firmly on the ground.

We argued earlier, on the basis of Luke 16.16, that John the Baptist marks the end of an era, the last of a long line of prophetic messengers sent to God's people, Israel. But John of course bestrides two eras. He not only points back, he points forward. His overall significance is as the Forerunner of Jesus, "the One who comes after me, whose sandals I am not worthy to untie" (Mark 1.7 *and parallels*). The point is amplified in the Fourth Gospel, where the preaching of repentance disappears and the emphasis falls entirely on John as the witness to Jesus. The common explanation given by scholars for this is that numbers of John's followers, after his death, were getting confused and coming to see John as Messiah, or at least on an equal par with Jesus. To them the writer of John says clearly, "he was not that light, but came to bear witness to the light" (John 1.8). To underline the point, the Fourth Evangelist describes him simply as "John", dropping the characteristic Synoptic designation as "the Baptist". In John 3.30 John himself affirms that "He (Jesus) must increase, I must decrease".

What is interesting from our point of view is the Johannine portrait of John's preaching as "witness" to Jesus. It reminds every preacher that he or she is simply a vehicle for God. The preacher's task is to point away from himself or herself to Jesus, the One who reveals God. John in the Fourth Gospel is therefore a wonderful reminder of the need for all preaching to be Christ-centred.

In this connection Jesus' description of John as a "burning and shining light" is a particularly vivid image for the preacher. Light was given by burning flames, active and energetic bursts of energy, dynamic and alive, being consumed in the process of giving out the light. A better inspiration for the preacher would be hard to find.

God speaks through Jesus Christ

> In many and various ways God spoke to our fathers by the prophets, but in these last days He has spoken to us by His Son.
>
> *Hebrews 1.1*

These are the striking and spectacular attention-grabbing opening words of the anonymous letter to the Hebrews. The twin adverbs πολυμερως and πολυτροπως emphasise the rich variety of the methods used by God to communicate with mankind, and take us back to the individuality of the prophets that we previously noted. Like the supporting acts, the dancers, singers, comedians and so on, of the now old-fashioned Variety or Vaudeville shows, the prophets serve to warm the audience up and prepare them for the appearance of the main act, the big star, who appears as the climax of the evening's entertainment. Jesus appears as the culmination of a long process of *verbal* communication from God. Although non-verbal communication is always possible, the mention of the prophets here tells us that what the writer is talking about is communication specifically in spoken words.

We are immediately reminded of the description of Jesus in the Prologue to the Fourth Gospel as "the Word" (ο λογος) in a passage that shows affinities with the Wisdom Literature, the Word is portrayed as standing alongside God, whilst at the same time being identical with Him (John 1.1, cf. Proverbs 8.22).

λογος, a term found also in the writings of Philo of Alexandria, may be seen as the sum-total of the verbal communications of God, His complete communication. Of course, the whole person of Jesus is seen as revelation and communication. In Jesus we see the person and character of God revealed. This revelation is on a higher, qualitative level from that provided by the words of the prophets. Nevertheless, the choice by the writer of λογος as his description of Jesus has to be seen as focussing primarily on the revelation brought through the words Jesus spoke.

Just as we saw in the Old Testament, the words of Jesus are seen as powerful, dynamic utterances that cause things to happen. For example, the healings of Jesus rarely involve any elaborate rituals or spells, as was often the case with contemporary magicians. The word of Jesus is enough. To the leper Jesus simply says, "be clean" (Mark 1.41). To the woman with the haemorrhage He says in similar fashion, "Be healed of your disease" (Mark 5.34). In common with the contemporary practice of exorcism Jesus drives out evil spirits and demons by His Word ("come out and be silent", Mark 1.25 ; "come out, you unclean spirit" Mark 5.8). The Syrophoenician Woman is told to "go home", for the demon has left her daughter (Mark 7.29) even though Jesus has been nowhere near her home. His word is enough. That word is a word of command "follow me", that the disciples obey instantly (Mark 1.17). When told to launch out into the deep, they at first protest that in their opinion it will prove fruitless, but then say "at your word we will let down the net" (Luke 5.1f).

Most dramatically, the Word of Jesus extends its power over the world of nature. A dramatic storm, so fierce that seasoned sailors in the boat are despairing of their lives, is calmed by the words "peace, be still" (Mark 4.39). No wonder those same disciples are prompted to see Jesus, whose word calms the raging elements, as someone who can scarcely be contained within human categories.

The word of Jesus covers the realm of sin and forgiveness. The watching and listening scribes at Capernaum are enraged when Jesus tells the paralysed man "your sins are forgiven" (Mark 2.5). They correctly understand that Jesus is going way beyond the priestly pronouncement of absolution to exercise the prerogative of God Himself. Far from backing down, Jesus tells them that in this case the ability to heal the man and to forgive his sins are well within the scope of the utterance of His word.

The key element of the Gospel presentation therefore is that of the power of Jesus' spoken words. Jesus had a very obvious authority in the way He spoke and in what His words achieved. Having listened to His preaching the crowds recognised that Jesus' words had an authority not possessed by the scribes, their usual teachers (Matt 7.28,29). The guards sent to arrest come back, their mission unaccomplished, with the exclamation "no man ever spoke like this man" (John 7.46).

It is not the case that everything Jesus taught was new and original to Him. Many Jewish and Christian scholars have sought to place Jesus in His Jewish setting have come to that conclusion. But that is not the point. It is the *authority* that Jesus claimed and possessed in presenting this teaching, and authority about which He was later challenged that His listeners needed to respond to (Matt.21.23-27).

Further staggering claims about this authority are seen in His presentation of the "new law" (Matt.5.19-48) and in His assertion that though heaven and earth may pass away, "my words will never pass away" (Matt.13.31).

What is interesting in examining Matthew's use of Mark is that in Matthew's redaction of the miracles the miraculous element is often reduced in favour of emphasising the relevant verbal exchanges. Certainly in comparison with the work of contemporary Jewish and Hellenistic healers the miraculous element is very sparse. It would be going too far to suggest that Jesus' healing miracles were simply visual aids for His teaching. On the contrary, they are genuine works of compassion, prompted by Jesus' reaction to what He saw about Him and in the people who approached Him for help. Nevertheless it is not the miracle itself that is revelatory. Indeed John tells us that miracles prompted both faith *and* unbelief[8] . It is the combination of miracle and word that offers a glimpse of God. Here we are back to Vanhoozer's concept of divine speech-act, in which the act is inseparable from the word. The word acts; the act speaks. It is worth noting that the word "miracle" does not occur in the Gospels to describe what Jesus does. In the Gospels they are described as "works" (εργα), wonders" (τερατα) "signs" (σεμεια). In all cases it is the *combination* of speech and act that make these incidents significant.

Like John the Baptist before Him, Jesus comes on to the scene as a preacher and herald.

> After John was arrested, Jesus came into Galilee, proclaiming the Gospel of God and saying, 'the time is fulfilled and the Kingdom of God is at hand. Repent and believe in the Gospel
>
> *Mark 1.14,15.*

Mark thus sets Jesus' whole ministry in the context of preacher. Jesus is essentially a preacher, proclaiming a message.

The "Kingdom of God" (η βαριλεια του θεου) was a concept not unfamiliar to the Jews. The idea was a development of the basic notion of Yahweh as King and, whenever this Kingship was demonstrated, the Kingdom could be seen. Rather than the flat, material concept of a realm or territory, the Kingdom was a dynamic, spiritual concept. The Kingdom transcended national and geographic boundaries. Since Yahweh was King of the whole earth, so His Kingdom was demonstrated on a universal scale.

In traditional Jewish thought the full manifestation lay in the future, beyond this present Age, with the General Resurrection (Daniel 12.1,2) and Judgement forming preludes to the golden Final Age.

In adopting these categories Jesus was a Jew of His day. What was arresting and startlingly new in Jesus' presentation was His pronouncement that this Kingdom had "drawn near" (Mark 1.15). There was now a new opportunity to enter the Kingdom, and opportunity that was not to be missed, (Matt.25.1-11). In His story of the Great Feast Jesus stresses that the invitation to enter the Kingdom is no longer confined to the Jews but is universal; anyone may enter who is willing to respond (Matt.22.1-14). This invitation to all is intimately linked to His own person. His ministry amongst them, and His death in particular, is opening a door for all who will respond. Jesus stresses that His death is something that has to happen - "the Son of Man must (μει) suffer" (Mark 8.31) - not because of anything He Himself has done, but for the benefit of others.

In interpreting His ministry and death Jesus weaves together Old Testament strands concerning the Messiah (occurring as a title only in Daniel), the Isaianic Servant and "the one like a son of man" (Dan.7.13). Space does not permit a discussion of the mechanics of this process (a much debated subject) so that we must confine ourselves to the summary statement that the imagery surrounding these figures was used by Jesus to present His death as clearing the way for people to enter the Kingdom. The key now to entering the Kingdom will be the response a person makes to Jesus. By their stubbornness and rejection the Jewish Leaders have missed the opportunity to enter the Kingdom, whereas the tax collectors and sinners, by their enthusiasm to listen to Jesus, have grasped the opportunity with both hands.

Jesus firmly rejects materialistic notions of the Kingdom in favour of its spiritual dynamics. The Kingdom is not about national identity or physical descent; nor is it about wealth or power. In the Fourth Gospel the phrase η βασιλεια του θεου virtually disappears, being used in just one passage (cf. John 3.3,5). In His dialogue with Pilate Jesus crucially tells Pilate "my Kingdom is not of this world" (John 18.35), that is, it is not a kingdom based on military power, but one based on truth. In the Fourth Gospel the phrase "eternal life" (ζωη αιωνιος) appears to take on the eschatological dimensions of the synoptic "kingdom". Receiving eternal life is the Johannine equivalent of entering the Kingdom, and as such is something that is possible in the present through receiving the word of Jesus

> Whoever hears my word and believes in Him who sent me has eternal life. He does not come into judgement, but has passed from death to life.
>
> *John 5.24*

Although the emphasis in Jesus' teaching, especially in the Fourth Gospel, is on what is happening in the present, there is an assurance that this is not all there is, and that a future consummation awaits. All the traditional emphases on Judgement, Resurrection, Heaven and Final Glory are present in the Gospels on the lips of Jesus. The work of scholars like

C.H.Dodd (Synoptics) and R.Bultmann (John) who argued that the future dimension had been squeezed out by Jesus, has been shown to oversimplify the position.

What Jesus is saying is that, whilst the future blessings of the Kingdom remain real, those who receive Him can begin to enjoy those blessings here and now. The dramatic Raising of Lazarus becomes a vivid demonstration of this principle. These blessings, available now, reach their full flowering in Heaven.

It works the other way as well. Any casual observer will notice that by no means everyone accepts the rule of God. Many continue to rebel. The door to the Kingdom is open, but many refuse to go through. Final victory over this rebellion is assured, through the Cross, but many battles remain to be fought. A helpful illustration is that of D-Day and VE-Day. The success of the Normandy landings could be said to have been the vital moment when victory was assured; yet the war continued for another year or so.

Believers in Jesus will therefore find this world uncomfortable. They are destined for another world, where the Reign of God is perfectly expressed and universally accepted, and yet perforce must live in a rebellious world. So, whilst the blessings of the Kingdom are truly present now, they are not present in their complete form. There is a "now, but not yet" tension that pervades all the Teaching of Jesus and indeed the whole of the New Testament. The importance of this "eschatological tension" for our understanding of Jesus' message cannot be over-stressed, and is the key for interpreting many of the parables.

Jesus' Preaching Method

Jesus is seen in the Gospels as a model of flexibility when it comes to the methods used to get His message across. We may take Mark's statement in 1.14, quoted above, as a summary statement, at least in relation to Jesus' early ministry in Galilee. Jesus came 'proclaiming' (κηρυσσων). Jesus is first and foremost a **preacher**, a herald. He doesn't come to make suggestions or initiate discussion - He comes to proclaim. It is not unreasonable therefore to see all Jesus' spoken ministry as different aspects of proclamation.

Like the prophets before Him, Jesus took opportunities to **preach to crowds**. He didn't have to seek out such opportunities, since in the Galilean Ministry we are told that crowds followed Him everywhere, to the extent of intruding on His privacy. Crowds create their own dynamics and shape the way the message is presented. The most famous passage of public teaching from Jesus is the section in Matthew 5-7 almost universally referred to as the "sermon" on the Mount. We are told that the listening crowds were struck by the authority showed by the way Jesus taught (Matt.7.28,29).

On occasions the audience was made up of His own disciples. Some of His most valuable teaching is committed to them. Sometimes it is by way of extended discourse, as in the celebrated "Farewell Discourse" of John 14-16, and in the "Eschatological Discourse" of Mark 13/Matthew 24/Luke 21.

Not all the crowds that listened to Jesus' discourses were friendly and receptive of course. In the Synagogue at Nazareth Jesus delivers a set-piece **Exposition of the Scriptures,** taking what was for Him the key text of Isaiah 61, (cf. Luke 4.16-30). His exposition is well received, and people are impressed by the Preacher. They are even receptive to the amazing claim "today this scripture is fulfilled in your hearing", until somebody in the audience points out that this is the son of Joseph, whose workshop is just around the corner. Jesus anticipates the consequent hostile reaction by quoting "physician heal yourself; what you did in Capernaum do in your father's home town also" (v.25). Exposition thus turns into hostile debate, and Jesus is well able to handle both.

The Fourth Gospel records a series of **discourses** given to crowds on various occasions, e.g. the discourse on Bread of Life that follows the Johannine account of the miracle of the loaves (Jn.6.1-14). The response to this speech-act is mixed. The crowds speculate "Is this the Prophet that is to come into the World ?" (v.14), whereas the Jewish leaders find occasion to dispute with Jesus. Yet again a number of His erstwhile followers draw back and no longer walked with Him (6.60). Similar hostile responses are seen in the discourses of Chapters 8-10.

The variety of responses to His teaching caused these "sermons" to flow into **debate.** Jesus uses leading questions for example to make His audience receptive to what He wanted to say. When asked by a lawyer "what shall I do to inherit eternal life ?", Jesus replies with another question "what is written in the Law; how do you read it ?" (Luke 10.25,26). In response to the Lawyer's further question, "who is my neighbour ?" Jesus tells the story of the Good Samaritan (vs. 30-37).

Another example of the use of key questions to confound His antagonists comes in the debate about authority (Matt.22.23-27). Jesus is interrupted whilst teaching in the Temple Courts by the Chief Priests and Elders. Jesus skilfully turns the leading question "by what authority are you doing these things ?" back onto the questioner by asking their opinion of John the Baptist, a question that traps them on the horns of a dilemma. Beware asking questions without anticipating all possible answers ! In similar fashion the question "whose inscription is this ?" on the coin presented to Him paves the way for an answer that turns the tables on those who would try to encourage Him to make politic statements about loyalty to Caesar (Matt.22.15-22). Other examples of "hostile" dialogues can be seen in the debate about resurrection (Matt.22.23-32), the Great Commandment (Matt.22.34-40), the sonship of the Messiah (Matt.22.41-46).

Jesus the Preacher is therefore extremely skilful in turning monologue into dialogue and dialogue into monologue. He delivers pre-planned, set-piece sermons, but He is able to respond to hostile and potentially-hostile interrogations with authoritative statements. He is not engaging in debate *per se* but using the questions as a jumping off point for further proclamations. Anyone who has encountered Jehovah's Witnesses will know how much time can be spent in fruitless debate and discussion without much that is worthwhile and proclamatory being communicated.

The Parables of Jesus

The most distinctive element of Jesus' proclamation method was His use of the parabolic form. Parables and parable-like sayings were not of course unique to Jesus, but they were characteristic of Him.

In our above discussion of the prophets we have already noted the use of the MASHAL, the enigmatic saying that dresses the truth up in a way that causes people to think. The parable, as developed in Classical Literature and in the New Testament, refines the MASHAL and develops it as a vehicle for teaching truth. The parable was used widely by such figures as Aristotle and Homer.

Aristotle writes:

> The parable is a comparison of the known with the unknown, where the reader is left to grasp the point of reality so as to set in motion the thought processes by which the point of analogy is reached.
>
> *Rhet.2.20*

In Classical Greek literature the parable form is clearly distinguished from the allegory, a form not used until relatively late Hellenistic times, and the *riddle* (αινιγμα) – a puzzling, indistinct image whose meaning is deliberately hidden.

The parables of the Gospels, occurring only on the lips of Jesus, fall into three main groups. There is the **simile**, a saying that has a single point of comparison, e.g. "the Kingdom of God is like…..", just as we might describe Snow White's hair as "black as night". Strictly speaking the simile is not a parable at all, and a lot of expositor's time would be saved if the distinction were maintained.

Then there is the **parable** proper, the typical example of the genre. Here the simile is developed into metaphor, and the whole form elaborated. The parable proper is a story, true to life, that is drawn from a situation that the hearers are familiar with and readily understand. A good example is the story of the man who had two sons, one of whom failed to keep his promise to go into the field and work, and the other who repented his initial refusal and went out to work. The story is told in a fresh, vivid way that engages the hearer. The story of the persistent widow is another. The accessibility of the situation to the hearer is an absolutely crucial element of the parable. Having said that, it is crucial to recognise that the parable is not necessarily representing a situation that is *typical*. Commentators sometimes get hung up on elements in parabolic stories that are abnormal. "The story can't be true, they say, because things didn't *normally* happen that way." To the teller of the story that does not matter. For the purpose of the story it is sufficient that the situation depicted happen this way once only. One scholar described the parables as the Bible's "once upon a time stories".[9] This helpful comment reminds us what the parables essentially are - stories. We don't know for example if there actually was a man who had two such sons, or whether Jesus knew of an actual case of a widow driving a judge to distraction. It doesn't matter; it doesn't affect the story as a story.

The oft-repeated statement that parables have only one point of comparison needs a degree of modification[10]. In some cases this statement betrays confusion with the above-mentioned simile. To be fair, this narrow view of parable interpretation arose as a reaction to the elaborate allegorical interpretations popularised by Origen and other Early Church Fathers. But it risks overlooking much of value in the text. What may be said is that the parables as stories have one *principal* point of comparison (just as a good sermon will have one major theme). This doesn't rule out the exploration of minor themes, however, such as how two brothers can have such widely different temperaments and react in such opposite ways to their Father's request. In the case of the other parable about sons in Luke 15 many interpreters (including the present writer) find it well nigh impossible to identify a single major theme. Hence the varying titles given to the story - "the Prodigal Son", "The Waiting Father" and so on.

Dodd, who did much pioneer work on parabolic interpretation comments, with not a little irony

> By all means draw from the parables any lesson they may suggest, provided it is not incongruous with what we may learn about their original intention. We shall not easily exhaust their meaning. [11]

A third literary category normally associated with the parabolic form is that of the **exemplary story.** This form presents a single event, real or imaginary, that draws a moral lesson. The best-known example is that of the Good Samaritan, where the hearers are exhorted to copy the Samaritan's behaviour (Luke 10.25-37, esp. v.37). Another example is that of the Rich Fool, where the hearers are warned not to be like him, ignoring the eternal dimension of life, and imagining that material possessions were everything (Luke 12.13-21). The Story of the Rich Man and Lazarus falls into the same category, but is a much more complicated, multi-layered story (Luke 16.19-31). The lesson presumably is that earthly status is no guide to heavenly destiny, though many other minor themes can be identified as well.

The Purpose of the Parables

The question as to why Jesus chose the parable as His main vehicle of teaching is a complex and intriguing one, and an important one for preachers.

The easiest answer is that Jesus was familiar with the understanding that every preacher has that illustrative stories will **engage the interest of the hearers** and make them more attentive to the teaching he wishes to put across. The parables did just that. As we have already noted, the parables of Jesus were stories taken from life, from situations with which His hearers were well familiar and could readily understand. Galilee being farming country, for example, Jesus naturally told stories about farmers planting seeds, growing crops, separating sheep from goats, etc.

The celebrated "I am" sayings of the Fourth Gospel, whilst not strictly speaking parables, were similes or illustrative statements drawn from life that illuminated important aspects of Jesus' self-attributions. Contrary to what is sometimes claimed by scholars, they are inclusive statements, pointing to the universal needs people have. Far from being esoteric code language, they were statements designed to arrest attention and to show that the revelation brought by Jesus was for everybody and not merely an exclusive few.

Having said that, not all the "I am" statements were addressed to the general public, "I am the resurrection and the life" being reserved for Martha alone (John 11.24-27).

The parables went beyond the simple clarification of spiritual truth to carry elements of shock and surprise, **to challenge the hearers preconceptions and prejudices**. The outstanding example of this is the story of the Pharisee and the Tax Collector (Luke 18.9-14). Conventional understanding of the Pharisees as devout religious people (reputation in the main justly earned) predisposes the audience to see the Pharisee of the story as the one in good standing with God. Sharp intakes of breath follow the pronouncement of Jesus that it was the man who had no self-worth but simply threw himself on the mercy of God that was justified before God (v.14). Two thousand years of seeing the Pharisees as the "bad guys" has lessened the impact of this particular story. The story of the Good Samaritan is another clear example of the shock value of many of Jesus' stories (Luke 10.25-37). Jesus' plays on local political and national prejudices to ram home the point of his story - loving others has no boundaries; need is the only criterion. The story is so universally relevant that it "works", even when extracted from its original context, something that is true of many of the parables.

People were not simply entertained by the parables then, but **were challenged to think**. Notwithstanding the fact, noted above, that parables were drawn from circumstances and situations with which the hearers were familiar, their meaning was not immediately obvious. The meaning was dressed up in a way that made it accessible only to those who were prepared to work at it an unravel the puzzle. To those who were unwilling or unable to think this through then the stories would remain as stories, opaque ones at that. Even the disciples are thrown into confusion by the Parable of the Sower, and need to come to Jesus privately for an explanation (Mark 4.10). What is true of the parables could be said to be true in a sense of all Jesus' ministry. At the key points concerning His ministry and identity Jesus resorts to allusion. As we have noted, parables were extremely flexible teaching vehicles, and came in several different forms. Instead of saying 'speaking in parables', we should rather speak of "a parabolic way of speaking", an allusive, indirect way of presenting spiritual truth, especially the truth about Himself. When the disciples of John the Baptist come to ask on John's behalf for Jesus to affirm his messianic claim Jesus, rather than giving a simple, direct answer, directs John to observe that the things happening in Jesus' ministry are a fulfilment of the things prophesied for the Messiah in Isaiah 61, the passage used by Jesus as the framework for his ministry (Matt.11.2-6). People have to think things through and make the appropriate connections before the teaching of Jesus becomes clear. The parable of the Tenants (Matt.21.33-44) invites people to consider who the vineyard owner's son may be referring to. It is not spelled out for the hearers. Even the aforementioned "I am" sayings, including the absolute use in John 8.58, have to be set in the appropriate context before they are seen as the staggering self-claims they actually are.

It is the allusive element of the parables that encourages people to think. A truth gained as the result of careful search is a truth more likely to be valued and retained in the mind than a truth simply handed to listeners on a plate, something we preachers are needlessly afraid of. We are often obsessed with "spelling it out" to our congregations, lest we leave them in confusion and dismay. The urge to play safe and not take risks is often too strong for us to resist. It comes as no surprise when our failure to engage our hearers' minds, hearts and imaginations results in slowness in appropriating and practising the teaching we are seeking to present. This was not the way of Jesus.

"That they may indeed see but not understand"

This leads naturally on to a discussion of a key saying of Jesus about the purpose of parables that has caused much misunderstanding and, it has to be said, no little heartache.

In Mark 4.11,12 Jesus says:

> To you has been given the secret (μυστηριον) of the Kingdom
> of God, but for those outside (τοις εξω)everything is in
> parables, so that (ινα) they may indeed see and not perceive,
> and hear but not understand, lest (μηποτε) they should turn
> and be forgiven.

This is based on a quotation from Isaiah 6.9-13, where the
Isaiah who responds to the vision of God in the Temple is
given the most difficult of tasks. As Motyer remarks:

> Isaiah's message, and his task, at first sight seems the oddest
> commission ever given to a prophet: to tell people not to
> understand and to effect hardness of heart and spiritual
> blindness ! There is, however, no way to evade the plain
> meaning of the verses.[12]

Motyer goes on to point out helpfully that Isaiah's teaching
was marked by simplicity and clarity, to the point that the
sophisticates of his day scorned him as scarcely fit to teach
in kindergarten (Isaiah 28.9,10). Isaiah saw it as no part
of his task to deliberately complicate the message in order
to make it difficult to understand. Yet inevitably even this
plain, straightforward approach would be too much for his
hearers, and would expose them to the danger of hardening
their hearts to the point of no return. The choice was not to
preach at all, or to preach knowing the processes of rejection
that such preaching would set in train.

The problem with Jesus' use of the Isaianic passage is not
interpreting it. On the contrary, its meaning is all too clear.
The problem is to fit it into the declared purpose of Jesus'
mission to open the Kingdom of God to all who would come
in. Matthew seems to sense the problem by changing Mark's
ινα to οτι in the parallel passage (13.13), suggesting that
blindness is the inevitable, but not intended, *consequence* of
the parabolic teaching. The suggestion might be then that in

God's eyes purpose and consequence merge into each other. It would certainly make some kind of sense to suggest that Jesus resorted to apparently simpler preaching vehicles because of the slowness of people to latch on to what He was saying.

Several things prevent us adopting this convenient way out of the dilemma. In the first place, we have noted several times that parables are far from simple vehicles for the presentation of truth. In many cases they are highly sophisticated forms of teaching. Then again, μηποτε "lest" (retained by Matthew) does seem to suggest that parables have a preventative purpose.

It is just possible that μηποτε can carry the hopeful sense of "perhaps", i.e. "perhaps they will turn and be forgiven". It carries this sense in 2 Tim.2.25-"God may perhaps grant them repentance". But this is definitely not the sense of the Isaiah passage.

The disciples are told clearly by Jesus that it is to them specifically that the μυστηριον (secret) of the Kingdom of God is given and not the crowds. Almost any occurrence of μυστηριον in the New Testament rings bells with those scholars who wish to emphasize the links between the Mystery Cults and the New Testament. However, the subsequent commission of Jesus to the disciples to take out the message of the Kingdom suggests that Jesus is not treating them as initiates who are meant to retain a hidden truth. The word here bears the same sense that it bears elsewhere in the New Testament (cf. Eph.3.16) of a "truth once unknown, now revealed". The secret of the Kingdom of God is the secret of the person of Jesus. God's plan and purpose could not be revealed until Jesus came. Now the secret is out; it is there for anyone who will receive it.

Certainly it is of great significance that Jesus chose the Twelve and took them to one side in order to interpret His teaching to them in a more intimate way than He did to the crowds. But the purpose of this was not to create an elite, but to use them to reach the masses. In the process of this He discovered that slowness of understanding was not confined to "those outside", as this inner group constantly struggled to grasp what He was saying !

There is, in short, no easy answer to the problem of Mark 4.10-12. The text has to be accepted and interpreted in the broadest possible context of God's dealings with men and women, seen in two dimensions. The first is the dimension of the sovereignty of God in election. The disciples are chosen, not because they are bursting with obvious natural gifts, by in accordance with God's will. They are part of that long process traceable through the Scriptures, of God choosing unlikely-looking individuals, such as Jacob and David, and using them for His sovereign purposes. In Jesus God is working in a particular way, and it is not the place of the clay to dispute with the Potter.

The second dimension concerns the level on which God's truth is understood. Cranfield applies the thought of Isaiah 55 by commenting,

> The idea that God's thoughts and ways are not men, but that they are His secret, not obvious to human wisdom but which He may reveal to those He chooses, was familiar to any who listened attentively in the synagogue[13]

So, the mystery of the Kingdom is the revelation of God in the person and work of Jesus. But this revelation is accessible only by faith. It is veiled revelation, but it *is* revelation nevertheless.

The ministry of Jesus is a fascination mixture of openness and veiledness. He doesn't run an exclusive school for pupils - He teaches crowds openly. His entry into Jerusalem, as well as His trial and crucifixion were public events. At the same time, as we have noted above, His teaching was allusive and indirect.

This openness and veiledness exist in tension in the Gospels, even in the Gospel of John. But though veiled revelation, it *is* revelation nevertheless. The truth is there, but there is just enough room left for doubt and unbelief. This allusive revelation, which the parables represent *par excellence*, places men in a crisis. A separation between faith and unbelief is brought about, and the blindness and sinfulness of men are shown for what they are. It is part of the dynamic of preaching that such a separation is brought about whenever preaching takes place. That's what makes it such an exciting and, one might say, dangerous enterprise.

Thus the parables are not "nice stories", such as a parent might tell to a child. Their truth is not theoretical, but extremely concrete, concerning what Jesus is doing in His ministry before their eyes. Set against the background of Isaiah 6, the parables remind us that God's purpose in Jesus is not simply to bring about salvation, but judgement also. It is extremely daunting and humbling for every preacher of the Gospel to realise that he or she is part of this process also.

God speaks through the Apostles

One of the least-contested ideas of New Testament Studies is the common authorship of the Gospel of Luke and the Acts of the Apostles. Another widely accepted corollary of this is that Luke and Acts represent two parts of the same work. As Luke himself says, His Gospel is the story of what Jesus *began* to do and teach (Acts 1.1). The Acts of the Apostles may be taken therefore as representing the story of the continuation of that same work. Indeed Luke hints at this when he says that the earthly work of Jesus concluded by His giving commands to the disciples through the Holy Spirit (1.2). This thought is further strengthened by the prophecy that the coming of the Holy Spirit on the disciples will give them power to be witnesses to Him (1.8). Although Jesus is physically absent, the Holy Spirit, working through the disciples, continues His work.

It is not surprising therefore to discover preaching as the centre of the work of the Early Church. The thread that links together the work of Peter, Philip, Paul, Barnabas and the other leaders of the Early Church is the witness to Jesus and the Resurrection through the spoken word. Sometimes this word takes the form of a "set piece" sermon, as on the Day of Pentecost, or as in the case of Paul before the Areopagos, or spontaneous responses to events and experiences that befall the Apostles. A number of sermons are delivered under severe pressure. Then again, there are the various *apologia* that Paul has to make before various Jewish and Roman authorities. For the purposes of our discussion of preaching we will discount the Pauline *apologia,* in favour of what we might more commonly understand as sermons.

That preaching was central to the life of the Early Church in Acts scarcely requires demonstration. The outpouring of the Spirit at Pentecost results in a multi-lingual outburst of praise, but then leads to a definitive sermon from Peter to the assembled pilgrims. When Peter and John are called before the High Priest in connection with the healing of the man outside the Temple (Acts 3.1-11) it is not the healing work they are called into account for, but their preaching in the name of Jesus (v.17,18). When the High Priest uses his authority to try and silence them they reply:

> Whether it is better in the sight of God to listen to you rather than to God you must judge, for we cannot but speak of what we have seen and heard.
>
> *Acts 4.19,20.*

At the conclusion of the "prayer and praise meeting" following this healing we are told that the assembled group were all filled with the Holy Spirit. What was the result of this filling ? The outcome was that they "continued to speak the word of God with boldness" (4.31). In this passage of Acts we have the clearest of links between the Holy Spirit and the Apostolic Preaching.

The priority of that preaching for the early followers of Jesus becomes even clearer in the incident recorded in Acts 6, an incident that could be said to represent the first organisational crisis for the infant Church. The process of sharing and dividing goods, headed up by the Apostles (4.35) was breaking down under the weight of its own success. Such a major task was it becoming that complaints of unfairness and neglect were being received from a section of the recipients (6.1) and that the time needed to supervise the distribution was hindering the Apostles in what they saw as their primary task of preaching the Word of God (6.2). It wasn't of course that distributing to widows was beneath the dignity of the Apostles (a modern preacher or pastor knows he has to be prepared and willing to do *anything*, but that they couldn't do that as well as preach. They appointed the seven deacons therefore so as to free themselves and give themselves the time necessary for the work of preaching. They saw the preaching the Word as the primary task of the Church. Other things were certainly important; but they would not achieve the purpose of God if they caused preaching to be neglected. In point of fact the work of these deacons, as we shall see in the case of Stephen and Philip, was wider than the welfare element and included preaching also. This only serves to underline the priority given to preaching. The greatest impulse in the nascent Church was the impulse to preach the Gospel of Jesus wherever and whenever they could.

Much time has been spent by eminent scholars in analysis of the preaching of the Apostles and deacons in Acts. C.H.Dodd did wonderful pioneer work in isolating a common core in all the preaching, what he styled the kerygma.[14] On Dodd's view, developed later by others, there were certain basic elements common to most, if not all, sermons delivered in Acts. These elements included:

- *A number of statements concerning the historical life and ministry of Jesus.* The number and scope of such statements is admittedly limited, but they are sufficient to assure the listener that the preacher is speaking about a real, historical person. The alleged facts are verifiable.

- *The life and ministry of Jesus is the fulfilment of Old Testament Prophecy.* Jesus came as the continuation and climax of the work of God begun long ago.

- *The crucifixion of Jesus was part of that divine purpose, and the subsequent resurrection declares Jesus to be the promised Messiah.* This was no mere theoretical statement: it was a statement that carried a great barb for the Jewish listeners in particular. "let all the house of Israel know for certain, that God has made Him both Lord and Christ, this Jesus whom *you* crucified" (2.36). Amazingly the accusation does not provoke a riot but gets a positive response from the listeners (2.37-41).

- *This Jesus will one day return in glory.* Salvation History (German: *Heilsgeschichte*) has a goal and culmination in the exaltation of Jesus.

- *The preaching of the crucified and risen Jesus requires a response.* The coming of Jesus makes two outcomes possible, salvation and judgement. The response made by the hearer will determine which of these two outcomes the hearer will inherit.

Not all these elements appear in all the sermons in Acts, nor do they appear in the same order. What we are arguing is that there is enough evidence in all the sermons, taken as a whole, to suggest that this was the fundamental basis of the Acts preaching about Jesus. Like all good sermons, they were based on solid fact, had a practical purpose, and called on the listener to respond.

Before going any further, we must briefly try to summarise and assess the critical study of the speeches of Acts, stemming originally from the work of Martin Dibelius, which sees the speeches as very largely the work of Luke the writer, rather than words of actual speakers on actual occasions.[15] Dibelius argued that the general unity of style and language was unusual for sermons allegedly given on separate occasions by different speakers, and that they fitted the context of the book of Acts better than they fitted their individual contexts. He further argued that the uniform linguistic style of the sermons was suggestive of Luke, rather than the individual speakers. He concludes that Luke is following the style of contemporary Hellenistic historians such as Thucydides, who allegedly freely composed his reports where sources were not available to him.

It must be said straightaway that what we have in the Acts of the Apostles is in all probability not verbatim accounts but summaries only of sermons. In fact Luke specifically tells us that Peter said more to the Jerusalem pilgrims on the Day of Pentecost than that which we have recorded in Acts, "and with many other words he bore witness and continued to exhort them" (2.40). Having made that important concession however, we are compelled to argue that such scepticism as shown by Dibelius and others with regard to the accuracy of Luke's reports is scarcely justified.

We have seen already that the speeches, or sermons, are held together by a common thread, the κηρυγμα, the basic message of Jesus.   It is scarcely surprising therefore that the sermons should show similarity in content. And as we shall go on to see, in our survey below, the sermons are in fact remarkably well suited to their individual settings. The Areopagos speech of Paul for example shows great flexibility and adaptability on the part of Paul. The individuality of the speeches which we shall go on to demonstrate makes Dibelius contention that they fit the literary context of Acts better than the circumstances of the occasion one to treat with great caution. *Of course* Luke has integrated them into his literary work, as any good author would, but it does not follow that in doing so Luke has isolated them from their original setting . The same could be said of the language of Acts. The very fact that they are part of a literary unity will inevitably mean that the language has a Lukan 'cast' over it, as a reminder that the document is second-hand reporting.   It is worth noting however, as a number of scholars have observed, that the language in the direct speech of the sermons is distinctly more semitic than in the narrative parts of the work.[16] In addition there are apparent inconsistencies that would be surprising in an artificially constructed work. The brief message of the angel to Cornelius for example occurs in slightly different forms in 10.4-6 and 10.31-33. The point is further underlined by the different use of Psalm 16.10 "For you will not abandon me to Sheol, or let your Holy One see corruption" in Acts 2.27, where the parallelism is preserved, and Acts 13.35, where only the second half of the quotation "You will not let your Holy One see corruption is preserved." The idea of both being Lukan compositions assumes Luke has the ability to imitate two kinds of rabbinic exegesis, a big assumption if Luke is a Gentile Christian.

The comparison of Luke and Hellenistic historians is very misleading.   While Thucydides did admit to occasional artificial composition, he did so only where he had no original sources. He admits that he could not recall all the speeches he heard word for word, and would therefore fill the gaps in his memory by making the speakers speak in a way demanded by the occasion, whilst concluding,

> of course adhering as closely as possible to the general sense of what was actually said.
>> *History of the Peloponnesian War, I.22.1*

Far from justifying fabrication, Thucydides is arguing for the substantial historicity of his work. Some of his contemporaries specifically condemned those "historians" who countenanced deliberate fabrication.[17]

At the end of the day there is no reason for scepticism with regard to Luke's reporting of the Acts' sermons. To suggest otherwise is to suppose that Luke had the ability to create sermons as different as those of Acts 2 in Jerusalem and Acts 17 in Athens; to imitate the style of the Greek Old Testament in the early part of his narrative and semi-classical Greek style in the latter; to vary his theology from speaker to speaker. As improbability piles on improbability it seems preferable to assume that sources underlie Luke's writing.

It must be remembered that these sermons were all delivered on public occasions. There were plenty of people around who knew what had been said and who therefore knew the truth of the matter. Luke had no need to invent, and, had he done so, there were plenty who could have discredited him by bringing such invention to light.

Peter the Preacher

Conveniently, the sermons of Acts fall into two categories, those of Peter and those of Paul. In the first part of the book Peter is the main preacher (though a major sermon by Stephen is included), whilst in the second part Paul takes centre stage.

Arguably the most important of the Acts sermons is that of **Peter in Jerusalem on the Day of Pentecost**, recorded in Acts 2.14-39. It is important because the events of that day are commonly understood to represent the beginning, if not of the Church itself, then of the Church's missionary enterprise at the very least. In that respect it is important to recognise two aspects of the context of the sermon. The first is that it follows the coming of the Holy Spirit on the disciples (2.1-11). This coming is accompanied by multi-lingual praise that grabs the attention of local residents and pilgrims. The very next thing that Luke records is the preaching of the Gospel of Jesus. This links the Holy Spirit and the preaching of the Word in the intimate way that runs through Acts. It can be said to be the first fulfilment of the promise of Acts 1.8, "you shall be witnesses when the Holy Spirit comes upon you".

The other important element in the context concerns the audience. In the words that every Whit Sunday lesson reader dreads, we are told that these come from over all the Jewish world. It seems highly probable therefore that among the 3,000 or so that responded to Peter's message were a number of pilgrims, who would take the Gospel back home with them once the Festival was over. Peter's message therefore was of great strategic value, giving great momentum to the Church's missionary beginnings. It reminds us also that sermons often reach areas far beyond the preacher's expectations.

Peter begins with a brief explanation of the Pentecost phenomena. After the quite reasonable suggestion that drunkenness is unusual at the third hour of the day, he explains that the strange behaviour of the Apostles is the result of the fulfilment of the prophecy of Joel 2.28-32.

He follows that with his reference to the historical Jesus, and particularly His crucifixion and resurrection, which he again sets in the context of Old Testament prophecy, applying the words of Psalm 16.8-11 to the resurrection. Peter does not simply quote the psalm, but bases an argument upon it. The passage is an early piece of exegesis.

The argument runs:

- it is prophesied that God's Holy One will not see corruption in Sheol;

- the phrase 'Holy One' cannot refer to David, by common consent the author of the psalm, since David died in the normal way;

- it must therefore refer to the Messiah and,

- since Jesus was raised and preserved from the corruption of Sheol, Jesus must be the Messiah, *q.e.d.* !

With reference to our earlier discussion, the very lack of sophistication in the argument argues in favour of its originality.

As Messiah, enthroned at God's right hand, a statement based on yet another Old Testament quote, (Psalm 110.1), Jesus has brought about the things they have seen and heard.

Having set out his argument, Peter moves to the devastating punch-line:

> let all the house of Israel know for certain, that God has made Him both Lord and Christ, this Jesus whom *you* crucified
> *Acts 2.36*

Such directness could well invite anger and maybe physical harm for the preacher. In this case it does neither, and Peter's reward for his Spirit-inspired courage is the open question:

Brothers, what shall we do ?

Acts 2.37

How many preachers would give their right arm for that kind of sincere, open response to their sermons ? Peter does not make his audience grovel, but in a very concise way sets out the appropriate method of response to the appeal of the Gospel:

- Repent

- Be baptised in the name of Jesus Christ for the forgiveness of your sins

- You will receive the Gift of the Holy Spirit

Building on the work of John the Baptist, Peter tells them that repentance (μετανοια), literally, a "change of mind", is the necessary first step. They must first recognise their need for forgiveness and then, as a second step, be baptised into Jesus, as the One who brings them that forgiveness. Notice that forgiveness in Jesus is being offered by Peter even to those who crucified the Messiah.   The third step is one over which they have no control, the gift of the Holy Spirit to those who complete the first two steps.

How can we summarize Peter's sermon in terms of structure and 'technique'?

- It was well grounded in the Scriptures, and contained reasonable argument based on those Scriptures.

- It was offered as an explanation of what had been going on in the sight and hearing of the listeners. Contrary to Dibelius, it was rooted in the historical circumstances of the Day of Pentecost.

- It was centred on Jesus, and contained a clear statement of the implications of Jesus' life and ministry.

- It was direct and pulled no punches.

- It offered clear directions for an immediate response to the message. The hearers were offered clear, concise directions as to what their response should be.

Peter's further work that day is described as witness and exhortation. Peter does not put the Jews on the spot for the sake of it, to condemn them, but to win them, another salutary reminder for preachers.

In the next chapter Luke records a sermon by Peter **in Solomon's Porch** (3.17-26). Although briefer, this bears some similarities to the Pentecost sermon. A number of the same elements are present, though not in the same order. It is offered for example as an explanation of phenomena, as the Pentecost address was. Peter observes the people's reaction to the healing of the man at the Temple's Beautiful Gate (3.1-10) and offers them an interpretation. It is an interesting example of how miracles in Acts are often followed by preaching. The pattern again is reminiscent of Vanhoozer's concept of speech-act that we noted above.

Here Peter declares that the action of healing was a consistent with the process of God's glorification of Jesus (12,13). Specifically it was the God of Abraham, Isaac and Jacob at work in Jesus, the God who declared His plan for the restoration of all things through "all the prophets since Samuel" (21-24, esp.24). Just as he did on the Day of Pentecost, Peter confronts his hearers bluntly with their culpability in the death of the "Author of Life" (το αρχηγον της ζωης), (13-15), something Peter and his fellow Apostles are there to bear witness to. The point is rammed home further by Peter's assertion that it is through the agency of this same Jesus, "killed" by them, that the man standing before them now has been healed.

Once again, the sermon is not designed merely for condemnation, but for salvation.   So there is an appeal. There was an element of ignorance in their actions, a note Paul picks up later in his address to Athens, but it is nevertheless sin from which they need to repent so that their sins may be blotted out (17-19).

This time the sermon gets a mixed reception. From the listeners it gets a very positive response, as "many who heard the word believed" (4.4). However it leads to the arrest of the preachers by the authorities, a mixture of priests, the Captain of the Temple Guard, and the Sadducees, "greatly annoyed" that they were teaching in the first place (presumably because they were not rabbis) and that they were proclaiming the resurrection, anathema to the Sadducees.

It is a reminder to preachers that directness will always have positive and negative consequences. People will be moved to respond by preachers who "tell it as it is". Yet there will always be those who react with annoyance. They may not have at their disposal "captains of the guard", but will be able to express their annoyance in plenty of other ways! The preacher's responsibility is to ensure that fear of the angry response does not lead to cowardly evasion of the implications of the message.

The consequence of **the arrest of Peter and John** is that they are hauled up in front of the highest Jewish authorities, Annas and Caiaphas no less, along with all the high priestly family and a collection of rulers and scribes (4.5,6). What a congregation ! It is the sort of congregation any preacher worth his or her salt could only dream about having. We can almost see Peter's eyes lighting up and hear the adrenalin coursing through his veins at the opportunity and challenge this presented. Then, on top of that, we are told that Peter was "filled with the Holy Spirit" (4.8).   Powerful people though they were, there was a great need for Peter's audience to brace themselves for what was to come.

The record of the sermon here is the barest summary. Yet in a few words Peter manages to pack in many of the elements of the κηρυγμα that we have previously seen:

- *Explanation* -it is through Jesus of Nazareth that this man has been healed;

- *Accusation* - this Jesus is the One *you* crucified;

- *The Fulfilment of Old Testament prophecy* "the stone rejected (by you) has become the cornerstone", Psalm 118.22;

- *Salvation available through, and only through, this Jesus.* - no other name by which we must be saved.

The reaction here is not repentance, but astonishment. This astonishment stemmed from the fact that Peter and John were αγραμματοι, "lacking in education". Bruce argues that some of the earlier translations that pressed the term to mean "illiterate" go too far, and that the phrase is more likely to mean something like "unversed in the learning of the Jewish schools".[18]   It is the disciples' ability to carry on a learned theological debate with leading Jewish authorities that causes eyebrows to be lifted.

An interesting further note tells us that the authorities recognised that Peter and John had been "with Jesus" (4.13). We have to guess, because we are not told precisely, what the point of resemblance was. As likely a theory as any is the idea that they remembered Jesus' ability to dispute theologically, though apparently He had never studied (cf. John 7.15), and the authority with which He spoke (Matt.7.29).   We might

86

also point out that the otherwise inexplicable ability of Peter to engage in the sort of Old Testament exegesis we see in his sermons may also emanate from the masterly example he had in Jesus.

In these verses and the verses that follow we get several further intriguing glimpses of the priority placed on the activity of preaching by the Apostles. The outcome of Peter and John's appearance before the Jewish Leaders is that these leaders seek to curb the activity of preaching. They are not worried about the other things the Apostles are doing - it is their preaching, particularly the preaching of the risen Jesus, that they observe to be the threat.   Their decision therefore is to warn them off from preaching (4.15-18). This warning meets with a polite but firm rebuff:

> Whether it is right in the sight of God to listen to you rather than to God you must judge, for we cannot but speak of what we have seen and heard.
>
> *Acts 4.19,20.*

They had no choice in the matter: the events they had witnessed and their significance were so incredible they simply could not keep quiet. To talk about Jesus was for them as natural as eating and sleeping.

Later the same day the Apostles and their companions gather to discuss the new situation brought about by the hostility of the Jerusalem authorities, and to pray. Very significantly the main thrust of the prayer is that God would grant to His servants to continue to speak the Word with all boldness (4.29). That was what they wanted most of all.

Not even a brief experience of imprisonment (5.17-26) could deter them. As soon as they are mysteriously freed, they go back to the Temple to preach (5.21).   By the time they are brought before the Council a second time the stakes are considerably higher. The leaders add to the charge of defiance the sinister "now you intend to bring this man's blood on us" (5.28)

Far from backing down, Peter picks up the high priest's allegation as the start point for his presentation. After reaffirming that they must obey God rather than men (5.29), Peter goes on to make the by now familiar presentation of all the elements of the kerygma,

- *The God of our Fathers* - the Old Testament reference,

- *Raised Jesus*

- *Whom you killed by hanging him on a tree*

- *He is at God's right hand as Leader and Saviour, to give repentance to Israel and forgiveness of sins*

- *We are witnesses to these things, as is the Holy Spirit*

The accusatory element has greater point here, since Peter is speaking to the very ones responsibility for arranging and carrying out Jesus' death. But repentance and forgiveness are mentioned in a general way as being offered to Israel. There is no direct appeal or offer to Peter's hearers in this particular case. Not surprisingly there is a strong reaction, and only the timely intervention of Gamaliel prevents something nasty happening to the speakers.

There is thus abundant evidence from these early chapters of Acts of the high priority given to preaching the Gospel of Jesus by the Apostles. Threats of violence and imprisonment, far from deterring them, served only to spur them on.

And, if any further proof were needed, we get a summary statement at the end of Chapter 5,

Every day in the Temple and house to house, they did not cease preaching and teaching Jesus as the Christ.

Acts 5.42

Stephen the Preacher

As a bridge between the preaching activity of Peter and Paul, we have the intriguing interlude of Stephen the Deacon (Acts 6 & 7). Against the background of the success of the Gospel, especially amongst the priests (6.7), Stephen emerges "full of grace and power". The implication may be that Stephen is one of the leading figures in this missionary progress. A consortium of those opposed to this progress bring charges against him, having previously failed dismally in face to face argument and disputation, and bring him before the Council (6.9-14). The charge is officially that Stephen is attacking the Temple, based on the allegation that Stephen has said that "Jesus of Nazareth will destroy this place and change the customs that Moses delivered to us" (6.13,14). On first hearing it all sounds a bit fishy and contrived, and a long way from anything Jesus is actually recorded as saying in the Gospels. It is a reminder of the strange positions people will often put themselves into in their attempts to evade the challenge of the Gospel message. Far from being unsettled and resentful about the unfairness of the allegations, Stephen displays a serenity that makes a great impression on those around him (6.15). Like Peter and John before him, Stephen turns a situation of great personal pressure into an opportunity to preach the Gospel. Stephen fully subscribes to the view that the best form of defence is attack.

The first part of Stephen's address is a long recital of Israel's history, beginning with Abraham, then ranging through Jacob, Joseph and Moses, through to David. It is history however with a definite "spin". As he goes through Stephen highlights the theme of rejection. Joseph was persecuted by his brothers, who sold him into Egypt. Moses started life by being hidden from the persecution of Pharaoh, to be brought up in Egypt as a prince. When he intervened on behalf of his people, to save a slave from death, he was spurned. Yet, in the providence of God this Moses, whom they rejected saying, "who made you a ruler and judge over us ?" God sent as both ruler and redeemer (7.35). But even after Moses had successfully led the people out of Egypt still they refused to follow him, urging Aaron to make Egyptian-style gods for them (7.39,40). This rejection of God caused God in turn to reject them (7.41).

Stephen's point is that the rulers' rejection of Jesus is the latest stage in a long process by which Israel has rejected messengers and leaders sent to them by God. It is not a one-off. Stephen challenges them to identify any stage in the peoples' history where examples of this rejection cannot be found. In effect the leaders of the nation are resisting the Holy Spirit continually (7.51).

As far as the Temple is concerned, Stephen argues that it creates an unhelpful sense of permanence. Even Abraham, though he was directed to the land in which they live (7.4) was given no security there, not even a foot's length (7.5). He was a pilgrim, and the first 400 years of the nation's life would be as pilgrims, living in a land that belonged to others. The presence of God was symbolised by the tent of meeting, that moved along with them. Although Solomon, David's son, built the Temple, even he recognised that it was totally inadequate to represent the presence of the Living God (7.48-50).[19]

It is in fact the static, unmoving heathen gods that live in temples. Devotion to the Jerusalem Temple has sent them down a blind alley and caused them to limit God in His acts.

Not surprisingly these accusations cause great anger and teeth-grinding. It would have gone no further had not Stephen gone on to relate his vision of the Son of Man at God's right hand (7.56). The use of "Son of Man" outside the Gospels is unusual. It appears only on the lips of Jesus, and the debate amongst contemporary scholars on its precise significance shows no sign of abating. But understanding the meaning of the phrase is perhaps not important here. The important point is that Stephen relates the son of man figure as *standing,* not sitting, i.e. pleading Stephen's cause before God. This proves too much for the listeners. Order breaks down completely, and Stephen is dragged outside and stoned to death (7.54-60). We note that officially the Jews were not allowed by the Romans to have the power of judicial capital punishment. This was mob violence rather than execution. However, it is unlikely the Romans would have sufficient interest to intervene in any way in occasional happenings like this.

Stephen's sermon, spoken like those of his fellow Christian leaders, was delivered with great courage, empowered by the Holy Spirit, and resulted in great personal cost. It does, however, have unexpected consequences. One of the audience, a young man named Saul, witnesses the riot and its aftermath. It is difficult to think of any other reason for Luke's mention of Saul's presence here other than to suggest that Stephen's words made a great impression on him and influenced his own subsequent preaching. The idea has merit, since Paul's Jewish history is often located on those fringes of Judaism that were likely to have some sympathy with Stephen's analysis of Old Testament history. It is a reminder to all preachers that we can't second guess God, who often uses our words in ways we don't anticipate. At the end of the day it is *His* word, not ours, we seek to preach.

Paul the Preacher

The latter part of Acts, from chapter 13 onwards, is concerned with tracing the preaching ministry of Paul. Many would argue that Paul's lasting contribution to the Early Church comes in his letters, preserved in the New Testament. But his preaching, recorded in Acts, and commented upon in his letters, is in many ways just as significant. Again a number of people, reading between the lines, argue that preaching was not Paul's strong point, and that he wasn't a very convincing orator. They refer to Paul's own statement

> When I came to you, brothers, I did not come proclaiming the testimony of God with lofty speech or wisdom. For I decided to know nothing among you except Jesus Christ and Him crucified. And I was with you in weakness and in fear and much trembling. And my speech was not in plausible words of wisdom, but in the demonstration of the Spirit and of power; that your faith might not rest in the wisdom of men, but in the power of God.
>
> *1 Cor.2.1-5*

One or two things need to be pointed out about what Paul says. The contrast he is making is with the particular styles of oratory familiar to Corinth. Like many Greek cities of the time, Corinth was a centre for philosophy and the rhetorical styles associated with it. What Paul is saying is that he is not trying to emulate contemporary rhetorical and oratorical styles, but making a "plain" presentation of the Gospel of Jesus in a way that allowed the power of God to be demonstrated. Deliberately attempting to adopt a way of speaking not suited to him would have hindered that demonstration.

Then again, the "fear and trembling" to which he refers in v.3 is not the fear of *men*, but the fear of *God*. "Therefore, knowing the fear of the Lord, we persuade men" (2 Cor. 5.11) reminds us that Paul's greatest fear is that of being found unfaithful in discharging his task of preaching. He disciplines himself constantly, so that he may in the end not be disqualified (αδοκιμος γενωμαι),(1 Cor. 9.27). God's opinion of him mattered far more than the reactions of those in his audiences. Paul in fact shows great courage on a number of occasions. He addresses the Areopagos Council on his own, without the backup of his companions, who had not yet caught up with him. At Ephesus he has to be restrained from entering the Great Theatre, where a 25,000 crowd is rioting because of him

(Acts 19.30,31). This is courage bordering on foolhardiness ! Paul is a salutary reminder for all preachers that the One to fear is the One who has charged us to preach, rather than those to whom He has sent us. At the end of the day it is what He thinks that counts.

Paul is nothing if not honest. He knows what people say about him,

> His letters are weighty and strong, but his bodily presence is weak, and his speech is of no account
>
> *2 Cor. 10.10*

Paul doesn't specify who "they" are, but he does refer to some kind of contrast that was being drawn between the way Paul wrote, addressing serious matters, and the way he spoke and acted in person. Paul refutes this contrast (v.11), but he does make the point that, if his letters do appear to be serious and heavy, they do not mean that they should be afraid of meeting him in person. People are capable of being both serious, when the occasion demands, but also quite human and personable. Avoiding the opposites of severity and frivolity is another important lesson for preachers !

Paul was of course an itinerant preacher, covering many, many miles in his work of spreading the Gospel and founding Christian communities. As well as crossing geographical frontiers, he also crossed cultural boundaries as well, becoming popularly known as the "Apostle to the Gentiles". Like all popular titles it is an oversimplification. It was certainly Paul's aim to preach to Jews as well as Gentiles, though Jewish resistance and opposition hindered the pursuit of that aim. Then again, 1 Peter 1.1 suggests that at some point in his ministry he had also worked amongst the Gentiles of Asia Minor.

As we have seen, Paul was very much a "driven" preacher, under divine compulsion to preach. This compulsion was linked to his sense of debt. He was the "worst of all sinners" 1 Tim.1.15, because he had been a persecutor of the Church (Acts 9.1). The wonder that God could forgive even him gave Paul a sense of the breadth of God's love, a breadth that could include everyone, even emperors (1 Tim. 2.7). The debt he owed could never be repaid, and yet Paul felt compelled to do as much as he could. And underlying it all was the dramatic Damascus Road experience, where Paul the persecutor had his life changed round forever, to become Paul the preacher. Quite what happened in that experience we don't know, but we certainly can see its effects. Paul's own accounts suggests that what he saw was the Risen Christ in his heavenly glory.[20] As far as we know Paul had not encountered or seen the earthly, pre-resurrection Jesus, although he was aware of this phase of Jesus' life. What Paul saw, and based his message on, was the Christ of Glory. This vision was what gave the dynamism to Paul's preaching.

As we said earlier, we exclude the *apologia* from our survey as not being representative of Paul's preaching. It is encouraging to discover that no less a person than Donald Coggan agrees with this judgement[21].

Instead we will content ourselves with a discussion of three sermons, conveniently divisible into a sermon for Jews (Acts 13.16-41), a sermon for Gentiles (Acts 17.16-31) and a sermon for Christians (Acts 20.17-38).

After parting company with John, Paul and his companions arrive at the city of **Antioch**, the most prominent city of **Pisidia**, in south west Asia Minor. In the synagogue on the Sabbath day they find themselves courteously invited as guests to offer any word of exhortation that they might have (13.15). After using the normal liturgical gesture of motioning with his hand, Paul, not one to miss such an opportunity, begins to speak. It is interesting to note that he addresses his audience as; "Men of Israel and those who fear God" (13.16b). The latter group are Gentiles who have not yet become proselytes but who have attached themselves to the synagogue. Paul would see them as naturally receptive to his message. He addresses them directly again in v.26.

The structure and content of Paul's sermon shows similarities with both Peter in Acts 2 and Stephen in Acts 7. It includes those basic elements of the κηρυγμα with which we have become familiar.

- The coming of Jesus is the culmination of Israel's history (16b-25). Here he retraces much of the ground of Stephen's speech (which must have been burned on his memory). At the end of this long process Jesus comes as Saviour (23).

- Sadly this culmination in Jesus was not recognised by those living in Jerusalem and the leaders, even though they had the law and the prophets pointing to Him. They had Him executed and laid in a tomb (27-29). Paradoxically, though they didn't realise it at the time, they were fulfilling the words of those same prophets (27b).

- But God's purpose could not be defeated in this way. God raised Him up in accordance with the Scriptures, an action that has many witnesses (30-37).

- Because of all this, forgiveness of sins is available to all (38-41).

In similar fashion to Peter's Pentecost sermon, Paul's sermon shows signs of Jewish hermeneutical traditions, in the way Paul uses Psalm 2.7 and Psalm 16.10 as part of his explanation of the resurrection, as well as a quotation from Habakkuk 1.5. Paul is weaving the Scriptures together in a midrashic way to create a solid framework for his message of Jesus. His decision to turn to the Gentiles he justifies by a quotation from the Servant prophecy of Isaiah 49.6. We see the early preaching of the Church not merely as a recital of facts, but as a scripturally-based interpretation of those facts in order to help their listeners understand.

The sermon gets a positive response, and they are invited back to say more on the following Sabbath. Some, including "devout Jews and converts to Judaism," can't wait a week to hear more and follow Paul and Barnabas outside. How many preachers have had that happen to them ?

A mass audience greets them on the following Sabbath, but events are disrupted by "the Jews" (13.45), to whom Luke ascribes the most basic motivation of all, that of jealousy. The fact that Luke describes the opponents as Jews implies that it is the Gentiles who are giving the ready response to Paul's message. This jealousy could have been prompted by several things. It could be simply that they resented what they considered Jewish blessings being shared with Gentiles. Or it could be more simply still that they resented the fact that Paul's mission to the Gentiles of Antioch was more successful than their own.

However that may be, Paul announces his decision to go to the Gentiles, recognising where his receptive audience lay, a decision that prompts great Gentile rejoicing (13.46-18). Paul had recognised what every preacher sooner or later recognises, that is, that some audiences are more receptive than others. He or she has therefore to decide whether to hammer on locked doors, hoping to wear the listener down, or to move on to more potentially fruitful pastures. This is well in accord with Jesus' teaching about "do not cast pearls before swine" (Matt.7.6) and "shake the dust off your feet" (Matt.10.14). It will involve making sensitive judgements, and yet these are judgements that the experienced preacher is able to make.

In fact Paul does not abandon the Jews. The statement of 13.46 should not be taken negatively as a rejection of the Jews, but positively, as a decision to embrace his new, receptive audience. His letter to the Romans reveals how Paul could never reject his own people, and that he recognises the divine priority of the Gospel as being to the Jew first (Romans 1.16). In most major cities he subsequently visits Paul seeks out the synagogue first.[22] But in Antioch of Pisidia a pattern is set. Paul goes to the synagogue first, because he recognises that he has some kinship there in a city where he was unknown, and that in the synagogue he could gain a foothold in the place. Yet rejection follows (usually from outside the particular synagogue), so that he has to make alternative arrangements for preaching. As a true preacher, Paul is infinitely resourceful in this respect.

The **City of Athens** presents Paul with quite different challenges. Athens, the archetypal Greek city, presented Paul with ostensibly no foothold at all. Every conceivable type of Hellenistic philosophy flourished there. She was the greatest university town in the world, to which men of learning came from all over the world.

However, it is not the pluralism of the city that strikes Paul as he wanders round the streets alone, awaiting his companions arrival. Recalling my own personal experience of arriving in Sydney alone, and finding it an alien place, Paul begins to reflect. It is the preponderance of idols that strikes him. It was said that there were more statues of the gods in Athens than in all the cities of Greece put together, and that in Athens it was easier to meet a god than a man. When Paul later says, "Men of Athens, I perceive that in many ways you are very religious" (17.22) he means it positively. His sadness is that their religion is misdirected. Athens this is where Paul's missionary strategy comes from.

Not waiting for his companions, Paul courageously wades in, engaging the Athenians both in the synagogue and in the market place. In the latter locations he finds no shortage of people to engage with him. Representatives of two leading local philosophies, the materialistic Epicureans and the deterministic Stoics, both well verse in face to face dispute, come to him. In spite of their rude description of Paul as a "babbler" (ο σπερμολογος) they take him seriously enough to haul him before the Athenian Council, the Areopagos. Here, in a setting where we are told people were constantly open to new ideas, Paul is given *carte blanche* to present his message.

The structure of the sermon is quite different to others in Acts, though it does show similarities in some respects.

- Paul states his aim: "what you worship as unknown, this I proclaim to you". He acknowledges their religious spirit, and starts from where they are.

- God is not something "made" - He is the Maker (24-26). He cannot be glorified by anything made with hands, or contained in any building made by man.

- This God guided history and determined the rise and fall of nations in past ages.

- Man has a natural closeness to God. All that God has done is meant to encourage men and women to reach for Him. And it is not a long reach, for "in Him we live and move and have our being", and "we are his offspring" to quote the Greeks' own poets.[23]

- But the days when God was content to allow men to grope tentatively towards Him are past. This is the sting in the tail of the sermon. Now there is an obligation to repent, because in Jesus God has announced Himself and determined the ground on which judgement is to be based. This ground will be the acceptance or rejection of Jesus.

- The proof of this is the resurrection of Jesus.

The mention of resurrection brings the listeners' patience to an end, and they resort to mockery, a common resort of those faced with unpalatable truths. It is important to note, however, that what the Greeks are rejecting is not the resurrection of Jesus specifically, but resurrection as a general principle. The Greeks took the diametrically opposite view of the immortality of the soul. Once death occurred, the body was of no further concern.

At first sight the sermon may appear to have been a failure. But this is not necessarily the case. The phrase "we will hear you again about this" may well stand in contrast to the dismissive mockery, and therefore represent genuine interest. At least one member of the Council, Dionysius believed, along with some unspecified men, a woman named Damaris, and "others" (17.24).

Considerable discussion has taken place as to the extent to which the sermon at Athens marked a change of approach for Paul. Put simply, the argument runs like this. Paul uses natural theology at Athens and attempts to reason with his listeners; this approach was a failure, and resulted in mockery; when Paul therefore goes on to Corinth he abandons this approach and settles for a simple Gospel presentation. In the opening chapters of 1 Corinthians there is much said about weakness and "the foolishness of what we preach" (1 Cor.1.21). Paul seems to deliberately reject the use of 'eloquent words of wisdom' (1 Cor. 1.17).

This argument misunderstands what Paul is doing at Athens. Paul is not engaging in an exercise in natural theology as such, but is dealing with the specific question of idolatry.

That is the point at issue. Paul begins where his hearers are, as any good preacher does. Having thus engaged them and "hooked' them, he brings in the presentation of Jesus, according to the κηρυγμα. The Gospel content here is admittedly minimal, but we can suppose that Paul would have gone much further had the mockers not intervened. Paul is here simply acknowledging the fact that his audience is a philosophically-minded Gentile audience, quite different from the one to which Peter spoke in Jerusalem or even that the one Paul preached to at Antioch of Pisidia. Although Corinth and Ephesus were also Greek cities, the cultures of which were thoroughly Hellenistic, the issues were different, and required a different approach.

As for the Corinthian correspondence, Blaiklock wisely reminds us not to overlook the heavy irony that marks the early chapters of 1 Corinthians. He says

> The remark to the Corinthians must be seen in the context of the restrained irony which characterises the first four chapters of the epistle. With the shallow intellectualism of the Corinthians, Paul was disposed to waste no time. He was not prepared to give them a Christianity diluted with their pseudo-philosophical ideas, or necessarily expressed in their attenuated terminology. Nor had he been prepared to do that in Athens, as the final confrontation of his address amply demonstrates.[24]

Paul is here being the classic evangelistic preacher, starting from where his hearers are, then leading them on to Christ.

His sermon to a Christian audience is delivered to the **Ephesian Elders at Miletus** (Acts 20.17-38). The setting and occasion of the sermon are much disputed. Why speak to the *Ephesian* elders at Miletus rather than at Ephesus itself ? The ostensible reason given by Luke is that Paul wants to be in Jerusalem in time for Pentecost (20.16) and realises that any stay in Ephesus would be unlikely to be a short one, and would therefore unduly delay him. Less charitable scholars argue that Paul is steering clear of Ephesus deliberately, remembering how he "fought with lions there" (1 Cor.15.32). Both answers have an element of truth in them, although our discussion of Paul in Athens shows that he was not lacking in courage by any means. In any event Miletus was only a relatively short journey from Ephesus by road (and even quicker by sea), so that the journey was well worthwhile in order to be able to listen to Paul in peace.

Because this is a sermon (the only sermon in Acts) addressed exclusively to Christians, its structure and content are quite different from the other sermons in Acts. It is an intensely personal address. Paul is speaking first about himself, and then about the Elders themselves. It runs

- A review of his ministry in Ephesus (20.18-24, 26-27).

- A note of pathos, as Paul expects the Elders to see him no more (20.15).

- A look forward to what the Elders may expect in Ephesus and how they are to react (20.28-35).

Paul begins by looking back at his ministry in Ephesus, insisting he had been open and honest, holding nothing back. This self-justification seems strange in Paul, and may have been prompted by some strong criticism of his work circulating in Ephesus. As part of this defence Paul disclaims responsibility for any man's blood (20.26), a possible reference to some trauma that had followed his departure. It could however be metaphorical, using images drawn from such passages as Ezekiel 18.13; 33.1-6. Having heard his message, the hearers are responsible for their own responses. He himself has been open and honest in his presentation of the Gospel of repentance and faith, both to Jews and Gentiles in Ephesus. He cannot be held responsible for the troubles he experienced in the city, for his task was simply to proclaim "the whole counsel of God" (πασαν την βουλην του θεου). He then turns to the future and warns the Elders what to expect (20.28-31). The flock are to be ravaged by fierce wolves (λυκοι βαρεις) who will attack the flock from outside, reference being in all probability to a Jewish counter-attack. This attack would differ from past attacks from Jews in that it will come from a strand of Judaism that shows affinities with local Anatolian philosophies and seeks to draw Christians away, rather than from direct physical or rhetorical assaults.[25] The situation will be compounded by the coming forward of people from within their own ranks of leadership who will distort the truth and confused members of the Church (20.30). The situation confronting Timothy, as described in the Pastoral Epistles, seems to bear out Paul's words. The elders are to be alert (20.31) and fulfil their duty as 'overseers' (επισκοποι). επισκοπος is a word common in secular Greek denoting anyone in a position of supervision and oversight. Applied to the Christian Church, and set in the context of Christian love, it comes to carry the sense of "caring shepherd". The leaders have the responsibility of care over those who will be going through the traumas anticipated by Paul.

Linking past and future together is the extremely personal note of 20.25 that predicts that the Ephesians will see Paul's face no more. Again, sceptical scholars, such as Haenchen, see this as a reference to the fact that Paul was already dead by the time acts was written, and that these words have been inserted by Luke.[26] Reading between the lines of such letters as 2 Corinthians and 2 Timothy it can fairly be concluded that Paul in the back of his mind saw death, whether at the hands of Jews or Romans, drawing steadily nearer. It is perfectly feasible therefore to conclude that Paul would have a strong sense that this would be the last time he and the Ephesian Elders would meet in this way, especially as Paul appeared to have plans to travel westward as far even as Spain (Rom.15.24,28).

We do not need to make the assumption of Paul's actual death to make sense of this prediction.

In this sermon therefore we encounter a quite different Paul - not the bold evangelist, who uses the Scriptures to frame the challenge of repentance to his hearers, but the caring pastor. The Miletus sermon is an intensely personal sermon, baring his own soul, and bringing himself and his hearers to tears (20.36-38). It is a reminder to all preachers that what we are engaged in is not the delivery of a dry academic address, from which our own thoughts and feelings are kept at a safe distance. When we impart the Word of God, our whole being is involved in the exercise, just as our aim is to touch the whole being of our hearers. We cannot do one without the other.

Paul on Paul

Paul saw preaching as central to his ministry. In his debate with the Corinthians Paul states that he did not want to become embroiled in arguments within the Church about baptism, because, as he says : "Christ did not send me to baptize, but to preach" (1 Cor.1.17). For him preaching was not an option he had taken up but a compulsion:

> Yet when I preach the Gospel, I cannot boast, because I am compelled to preach. Woe to me if I do not preach the Gospel !
>
> *1 Cor.9.16*

Paul uses both κηρυσσω and ευαγγελιζω to describe his work. In Romans 16.25 the word groups overlap: "now to Him who is able to establish you by my Gospel (το ευαγγελιον) and the proclamation (το κηρυγμα) of Jesus Christ."

Paul states very clearly that the content of his message is Christ crucified (1 Cor. 1.23) and risen from the dead (1 Cor.15.12). He variously describes this core message as "the Word of God"

(Rom.10.8), "Jesus Christ as Lord" (2 Cor.4.5), "the Gospel" (Rom.1.16; 16.25; Gal.2.2; Col.1.23), "the testimony of God" (1 Cor.2.1) and "the unsearchable riches of Christ" (Eph.3.8).

Paul sees himself as having been "entrusted" with the Gospel (Titus 1.3) and therefore responsible to preach openly and honestly in order to discharge that trust. In the ancient world a herald was regarded as a person of integrity, who had the responsibility of discharging his message accurately. To change the message would be regarded as tantamount to treason. In another passage Paul changes the metaphor slightly to make the same point, describing himself and his fellow workers as "ambassadors" (πρεσβευομεν, 2 Cor.5.20). To this he adds a wonderful statement about the immediacy of preaching, "as though God were making His appeal through us". This represents a great encouragement for any preacher to reflect on the dignity of his calling, as well as a great challenge also.

Paul lived and ministered in a world where sophisticated oratory was prized. Reading between the lines, many scholars have come to the conclusion that Paul was not a gifted orator *in the classical style of Greek oratory*. This is actually far from saying that he was not a good or effective preacher. It is simply that, measured against the superstars of the Hellenistic oratorical world, Paul probably didn't rate very highly.

But then, Paul tells us that it was in fact no part of his ministry to attempt to compete with his contemporaries on the podium. He knew that clever oratory was not in fact the key to effective preaching.

> When I came to you I did not come with eloquence or superior wisdom as I proclaimed the testimony of God. For I resolved to know nothing while I was with you except Jesus Christ and Him crucified. I came to you in weakness and fear and with much trembling. My message and my preaching were not with wise and persuasive words, but

with the demonstration of the Spirit's power, so that your faith might not rest on men's wisdom, but on God's power.

1 Cor.2.1-5

There are many cautionary words here for every preacher. We do of course strive for appropriate speech in the pulpit, and to speak in ways that will command a hearing. There is no justification for slovenliness in a preacher's speech. But eloquence and rhetoric are no substitutes for spiritual power, the origins of which lie not in the preacher's education or knowledge, but in the Word he proclaims and in his relationship with God who seeks to speak through him.

Nevertheless, in spite of his oratorical shortcomings, recognised by friend and foe alike, and not least by himself, Paul's preaching was extremely effective, resulting in the opening of doors and the foundation and growth of Christian communities all through the Mediterranean World. He remains a great encouragement to all who might be tempted to think that they do not possess the natural attributes of a preacher. What matters ultimately is the call of God, and the willingness of individuals to readily respond to that call.

Paul's Letters as Sermons

Were we to regard the material in Acts as the only source for Paul's preaching, then that would be to ignore a tremendously valuable source of information contained in his letters. Whilst undoubtedly literary compositions, they bear a closer relationship to Paul's oral ministry than is commonly supposed.

We should say immediately that the written word and the spoken word represent distinct disciplines. People who are extremely eloquent in speech sometimes struggle to express themselves on paper, and vice versa. I recall what was a relatively new experience for me, that is, reading a paper on

Ephesians to a conference of scholars in San Diego. The paper had of course been composed at home in my study, and, all modesty apart, seemed all right to me. When I stood up and began reading my script word for word, as the nature of the exercise required, it felt extremely strange and restrictive. It was not a natural thing for me to do. I was very glad to be able to lift my head from the script from time to time and speak directly to my listeners, just as I would from the pulpit. That felt much more comfortable. That rather traumatic experience serves as a permanent reminder to me that not only are literary and oral styles distinct, there are subtle distinctions within the range of oratorical themselves.

Nevertheless, there are strong arguments for saying that Paul's letters contain more than a strong echo of his oral preaching style, so much so that they may be taken as representative of Paul's sermons. Paul himself tells us that they were not put onto paper directly by him, but were dictated to an ammanuensis, or secretary. The words of the letters began life as spoken words, subsequently written down. Barclay comments

> They were not carefully written out by someone at a desk; they were poured out by someone striding up and down the room as he dictated, seeing all the time in his mind's eye the people to whom they were to be sent. Their torrential style, their cataract of thought, their involved sentences, all bear the mark of the spoken rather than of the written word.[27]

This notion is backed up by Paul's instruction that his letters were to be read out loud in the recipient churches (cf. 1 Thess.5.27; 2 Thess.3.14), and shared with other churches (Col.4.16). Not only were they to be read out, they were to be explained by the couriers. They were to be seen as making up for Paul's physical absence in the Church:

> We are in our letters when we are absent, we will be in our actions when we are present.
>
> *2 Cor.10.11*

The letters are filled with oratorical flourishes such as "I say", or "I want you to know", things that would normally more at home in oral rather than literary compositions. The letters convey the full range of human emotions, from the relatively eirenic Ephesians, the obvious warmth of Philippians, the reflective atmosphere of 2 Corinthians, to the palpable anger of Galatians and 1 Corinthians. The passion and feeling of a speaker lie scarcely disguised beneath the surface.

The rhetorical approaches of the orator can be detected in the different styles of Pauline writing. So Paul's letters are written to convey encouragement and consolation (παρακλησις), directed at sustaining and developing communities; argument and debate, with full use of traditional rhetorical styles such as diatribe (dialogue with an imaginary oppponent); ethical instruction (paranesis); theological reflection (cf. Phil.2.6-11; Col.1.15-20) and repetition (the reminder of things that he has already said to them).

Bearing in mind then our initial cautionary note that the written media and spoken media are not exactly the same, then we may take Paul's letters as indirect examples at least, of Paul's preaching style.

In his excellent book, *Preaching Like Paul,* James Thompson gives us a number of examples of what he considers to be Pauline sermons:

1 Thessalonians 4.3-8: Sanctified or sanctimonious ?
1 Thessalonians 5.1-11: Children of the Day
1 Corinthians 13.1-13: The Better Way
2 Corinthians 1.15-23: Promises to Keep
2 Corinthians 4.1-6: Jesus Christ as Lord
2 Corinthians 5.11-20: A New World
Romans 6.1-11: God's Unfinished Business
Romans 9-11: When Nothing Makes Sense. [28]

The reader will make his or her mind up about Thompson's titles and his analysis of these passages, but all would agree that he has performed a useful service in identifying what stands as the basis at least for sermonic material.

If we were to pick out just one for closer scrutiny, then the classic passage on love from 1 Corinthians 13, which Thompson titles (appropriately) "the better way", would be a good one to choose. I would take a wild guess and suggest that most preachers who take this as their text break it down thus:

- 1-3 The importance of love - nothing is of any value at all without it;

- 4-7 The characteristics of love - never selfish, not insisting on its own way;

- 8-13 The endurance of love - love is important because it outlasts everything else.

If you have approached it differently, I apologise. But the thought remains that if this arrangement suggests itself so directly and so naturally from the verses, then almost certainly that is because that is the way Paul spoke/wrote it and intended it to be understood. In other words, it may well be a sermon.

The caution we must observe before rushing to that conclusion about this passage, indeed about all the passages listed above, is that it has to be seen in its literary context, that is, the long discourse on spiritual gifts that is made up of 1 Corinthians 12-14. Nevertheless it is arguable that, within that wider setting, chapter 13 does stand out as a distinct unit, an oratorical "aside" that bridges the teaching on proper attitudes within the Body of Christ (Chapter 12) and the guidelines concerning the exercise of spiritual gifts, especially tongues, in Chapter 14.

Although we acknowledge that the ancient world did distinguish between the letter and the address, we can persuasively argue that Paul's "letters" came to being in the territory in between literary and oral phenomena, and contain some of the characteristics of both. We might style them as representing what Paul would have said had he been present in the Church to which he is writing.[29] Certainly our survey of New Testament examples of preaching would be significantly incomplete without them. I suspect that we cannot establish the link between the oral and the literary in Paul's letters to justify Thompson's further claim to see Paul as the model for preachers, but, as we shall see in a later chapter, there is certainly no shortage of things we can learn from Paul to enrich our preaching ministries.

CHAPTER TWO
ENDNOTES

[1] Vanhoozer, K., *Is There a Meaning in the Text ?* (Leicester: IVP, 1998)
[2] Vanhoozer, 171.
[3] cf. Numbers 24.2; 1 Sam.10.6,10; 19.20,23; 1 Kings 22.24; Joel 2.28,29; Hosea 9.7; Zech.7.12; Micah 3.8, etc.
[4] W.F.Albright, *From the Stone Age to Christianity* (New York: Doubleday, 1957), 303f.
[5] J.Muilenburg, 'Old Testament Prophecy' in eds.M.Black & H.H.Rowley, *Peake's Commentary on the Bible*, (London: Nelson, 1962), 475.
[6] Seder 'Olam Rabbah 30
[7] J.A.Motyer, *The Prophecy of Isaiah* (Leicester: IVP, 1993), 25.
[8] Classically in the incident of the man born blind in John 9.1f.
[9] M.Boucher, *The Parables* (Wilmington: M.Glazer, 1980).
[10] A view originating from A.Julicher.
[11] C.H.Dodd, *The Parables of the Kingdom* (1935), vi.

[12] J.A.Motyer, *Isaiah*, 78.

[13]   C.E.B.Cranfield,   *St.Mark,*   Cambridge   Greek   Testament Commentary, (Cambridge: CUP, 1963), 153.

[14] Set out in his classic work, *The Apostolic Preaching and its Developments* (London: Hodder & Stoughton, 1944)

[15] M.Dibelius, *Studies in the Acts of the Apostles* (ET London, 1956)

[16] See especially   F.F.Bruce, *The Speeches in the Acts of the Apostles* (London, 1944); M.Wilcox, *The Semitisms of Acts* (Oxford: Clarendon, 1965); D.F.Payne, 'Semitisms in the Book of Acts', in *Apostolic History and the Gospel: Biblical and Historical Essays presented to F.F.Bruce* (Exeter: Paternoster, 1970), 134-150.

[17] e.g. Polybius, *xii.25.I.8 cf.* F.W.Wallbank, *A Historical Commentary on Polybius* (Oxford, 1967),397-399.   Lucien of Samosata, 'history cannot admit of a single falsehood' in Lucian vi, in K.Kilburn, *Lucian* (London, 1959), 1-14.

[18] F.F.Bruce, *The Acts of the Apostles: The Greek Text with Introduction and Commentary* (London: Tyndale Press, 1951), 122.

[19]   cf. Psalm 11.4; 1 Kings 8.27.

[20] Acts 9.3; 22.6; 22.11; 26.13.   See also M.E. Thrall, 'The Origin of Paul's Christology' in ed. W.W.Gasque & R.P.Martin, *Apostolic History and the Gospel,* (Exeter: Paternoster, 1970), 304-316.

[21] D.Coggan, 'Paul the Preacher' in ed. G.Hunter, G.Thomas and S.Wright, *A Preacher's Companion,* Oxford: BRF, 1990), 24.

[22] See Acts 14.1; 16.13; 17.1,10,17; 18.4, 19; 28.17.

[23] The source of the first of the two quotes is difficult to trace. The nearest suggested source locates it in Crete, either from Minos (to his father Zeus) from Epimenides (cf.Titus 1.12). But Paul's wording is neither poetic nor in the expected Greek dialect. It may be that Paul is making a reference to something well known but which he cannot recall exactly. The second quote is from Aratus of Soli's *Phaenomena,* appearing in a slightly different form in Cleanthe's *Hymn to Zeus.*

[24] E.M.Blaiklock, *The Areopagus Address*   , Third Rendle Short Memorial Lecture (Bristol, 1964), 16,17.

[25] See discussion by Lampe, who argues that this attack comes from a strain of Judaism that had both 'gnostic' and Essene elements, rather like the system confronted by Paul at Colossae. G.H.W.Lampe, 'Grievous wolves' in ed. S.Smalley & B.Lindars, *Christ and Spirit in the New Testament,* (Cambridge: CUP, 1963), 253.

[26] E.Haenchen, *The Acts of the Apostles: A Commentary.* Translated by

Bernard Noble and Gerald Shinn. (Philadelphia: Westminster Press, 1971).

[27] W.Barclay, "A Comparison of Paul's Preaching" in W.Ward Gasque and R.P.Martin (eds) *Apostolic History and the Gospel: Essays presented to F.F.Bruce* (Exeter: Paternoster, 1970), 170.

[28] J.W.Thompson, *Preaching Like Paul: Homiletical Wisdom for Today* (Louisville: WJK, 2001), 149-165.

[29] Thompson, *Preaching*, 32.

3

THE PREACHER'S PREDECESSORS

PREACHING IN THE CHURCH OF ENGLAND SINCE THE REFORMATION

The history of preaching in the Church of England is of course indissolubly linked with the history of the Church of England itself. The quality and style of this preaching has ebbed and flowed with the various movements and changes seen in the five centuries of its existence.

The Reformation and the Bible

The Church of England was born in the heat of the controversies that formed what we call the English Reformation. Superficially it came about because of the King's wish for a divorce; those who look beneath the surface will however see it as the outcome of a movement that had begun some time earlier, a movement that focussed on the Bible as the Word of God. Put very simply, the theological issue that inspired the Reformation was the degree to which the common people, as opposed to the theological elite, should have direct access to the contents of the Bible.

Leading Biblical scholars of the Reformation such as John Wycliff and William Tyndale were unequivocal in their answer to that question. The Word should be made accessible to everyone, thus allowing the individual believer to sustain and develop his or her relationship with God without the intervention of third parties.

Foxe describes an argument with a "learned" but "blasphemous" clergyman, who had asserted to Tyndale that,

"We had better be without God's laws than the Pope's."

In a swelling of emotion, Tyndale is reported as making his prophetic response:

"I defy the Pope, and all his laws; and if God spares my life, I will cause the boy that drives the plow in England to know more of the Scriptures than the Pope"

By way of making good his vow, Tyndale proceeded to translate the New Testament into the modern English of his day. Although a number of partial and complete Old English translations had been made from the 7th century onward, and Middle English translations particularly in the 14th century, Tyndale's was the first English translation to work directly from Hebrew and Greek texts. All these other translations had been based very largely on the latin Vulgate, produced by Jerome a millennium earlier. The process pioneered by Tyndale (at the cost of his life, of course) resulted eventually in the 1611 King James Version of the Bible, the standard Bible in English for many years.

It is important to recall that Tyndale and his fellow translators (e.g. Wycliff, Coverdale) did not begin their work *ex nihilo*. They were following through a process begun in the earlier Renaissance movement, when the desire for new learning led to an accompanying desire (outside Italy at least) to get back to the earliest texts. It was no longer sufficient, in any areas of learning, to accept simply what had been passed on. It was important to get back to roots, to the earliest expressions of knowledge, and find the source of the ideas adopted by society.

One of the earliest fruits of this movement as far as the Bible was concerned was the emergence of the so-called *textus receptus*, a work begun in 1516 by the Dutch Scholar and humanist Desiderius Erasmus , on the basis of some six manuscripts, containing between them not quite the whole of the New Testament. Although inadequately based by modern standards of textual criticism, it is hard to overestimate the importance of Erasmus' achievement.

The Bible was now an open book, not only for readers, but particularly for preachers. Medieval preaching had been characterised by the endless cycling of a relatively small amount of Biblical material, and by the widespread use of *exempla*, or "stories". Many preachers simply did not themselves have the education or spiritual resources to venture any further afield. Now preacher and listener alike had a deep, new fund of material with which to work, greatly enriching the preaching experience of both preacher and listener.

It seems surprising to us, centuries later, that there could have been such fierce opposition to Tyndale, Wycliff and others who were engaging on such an obviously worthy enterprise. What we have to understand is that the enterprise not only challenged the power base of Bishops and their clergy, but inspired genuine fear of a breakdown in order. This stemmed from the indissoluble welding together of Church and State in the concept of "Christendom". If every man were to be free therefore to come to his own opinion about all matters Christian, then the inevitable result would be theological and (eventually) civil anarchy. The idea of a freely-arrived at consensus was impossible to comprehend by those in authority in Church and State in that era. But in the work of Tyndale and his contemporaries the stable door had been well and truly opened, and would consequently prove impossible to shut.

Preachers of the Reformation

The history of the Reformation developed around great individual figures, such as Tyndale and Wycliff, the translators; Thomas Cromwell, the statesman; Thomas Cranmer, the statesman and liturgist; and Ridley, the lawyer. All were important figures in different ways. However, the one who stands out in the early history of the Reformation for his *preaching* in particular was **Hugh Latimer.** Born into a family of Leicestershire farmers, Latimer grew up as an exceptional scholar, entering Cambridge at the age of fourteen.

All Latimer's contemporaries spoke well of him. He was extremely eloquent in speech, and could with justice be described as the most notable preacher of his day. Although essentially medieval in style, his sermons belonged firmly to the days of reform. They were racy, full of anecdotes, reminiscences and humour, rich in homely English phrases like "belly cheer", so that Latimer's sermons could be taken as prime examples of the vigour, courage and outspokenness which belonged to the new era. This bluntness, vigour and general lack of sophistication however, whilst appealing to the common man, were to incur the condemnation of later writers.

Thomas Birch, for example, the biographer of John Tillotson, writes

Latimer's sermons are defective in dignity and elegance, his frank remonstrances to persons of the highest rank being delivered in expressions of peculiar levity, intermixed with frequent stories unsuitable to the solemnity of the place or the occasion.[1]

Latimer was of course a child of his time, and one cannot imagine him being particularly   concerned about Birch's strictures, even supposing he had been aware of them.

It has to be said that his sermons contained little of doctrine, but instead spurred his hearers on to godliness through upright living and devout prayer.   They were essentially practical.   The influence of Latimer's preaching became every year greater.   In December, 1529, he gave occasion to new controversy in the University by his two "Sermons on the Card", delivered in St. Edward's Church, on the Sunday before Christmas, 1529.   Card-playing was in those days an amusement widely favoured at Christmas time.   In his sermons Latimer does not actually express disapproval of the pastime, though the Reformers generally were opposed to it. The early statutes of St. John's College, Cambridge, forbade playing with dice or cards by members of the college at any time except Christmas, but excluded undergraduates from the Christmas privilege.   What Latimer in fact did was to use this seasonal card playing to illustrate spiritual truths in a way his hearers would understand.   In drawing spiritual lessons from what were essentially secular practices Latimer was to a great extent ahead of his time.

But as well as being down to earth, vigorous and practical, Latimer's sermons were thoroughly biblical.   In expounding the Scriptures Latimer was no unsophisticated literalist. He had for example a real understanding of rudimentary hermeneutical principles.   So in answer to a contemporary who had attempted to draw out the literal implications of Latimer's approach in order to demonstrate their absurdity he says:

Do we not know that in all languages and all speeches, it is not on the image that we must fix our eyes, but on the thing which the language represents ? For instance, if we see a fox painted preaching in a friar's hood, nobody imagines that a fox is meant, but that craft and hypocrisy are described, which are so often found disguised in that garb.[2]

Always the outspoken and courageous preacher, Latimer's directness duly incurred the wrath of leading figures in the Church such as Wolsey and Gardiner. He did however enjoy the favour of King Henry VIII, largely because of his support for the quest for annulment of the King's marriage to Catherine, as well as for his denunciation of the Pope, something guaranteed to make him popular with the King. However, Latimer was willing to risk even this if necessary in order to stay loyal to Christ. Thus, in an introduction to a sermon before the King Latimer began exclaiming,

Latimer, Latimer, thou art going to speak before the high and mighty King, who is able, if he think fit, to take thy life away. Be careful what thou sayest. But Latimer, Latimer, remember thou art also about to speak before the King of Kings and Lord of Lords. Take heed thou dost not displease Him.

Latimer's influence reached its height when he was made Bishop of Worcester in 1535. As well as giving him a prominent platform for his own preaching, his bishopric gave him the opportunity of sponsoring other preachers, just as his contemporary, Thomas Cranmer was doing. Many of the men sponsored by Latimer were local men, though none of their names have survived[3]. He used his position to give further prominence to preaching by ordering that other ceremonies in the regular Sunday service should be foreshortened, so as to not intrude on the time given to the sermon.

Amongst all the key figures that make up the English Reformation, Latimer undoubtedly stands out as the greatest preacher of the time. His preacher's flair for rhetoric did not desert him even as he approached the martyr's pyre, alongside Nicolas Ridley. He is famously quoted as saying to Ridley:

> Be of good comfort, Master Ridley, and play the man; we shall this day light such a candle, by God's grace, in England, as I trust shall never be put out.

Thanks to courageous and lively preachers like Latimer that light still shines.

The Elizabethan Settlement

Whilst the new learning radically affected the Church in England as a whole, it had not penetrated all parts of that Church. Elements of both old and new thinking were represented amongst the ranks of clergy and laity. If the two elements were to coexist, a *modus vivendi* needed to be found. This was attempted in the 1558 Elizabethan Settlement, regarded by many Anglican historians as defining the classical Anglican position. The settlement, embodied by the Thirty Nine Articles of Religion, was deliberately designed to provide a middle way, in which strands of both Catholic and Protestant belief could exist side by side in a national Church.

The desire for peace was reflected in the style of preachers. Tiring of seemingly endless controversy, Elizabeth herself issued instructions for preachers to be uncontroversial, and limit the scope of their utterances to the Gospels and Epistles, the Ten Commandments and the Lord's Prayer:

So,

> The Queen's Majesty understanding that there be certain persons having in times past the office of ministry in the Church, which now do purpose to use their former office

in preaching and ministry, and partly have attempted the same, assembling specially in the city of London, in sundry places, great number of people, whereupon riseth among the common sort not only unfruitful dispute in matters of religion, but also contention and occasion to break common quiet, hath therefore, according to the authority committed to her highness , thought it necessary to charge and command, , that they do forbear to preach, or teach, or to give audience to any manner of doctrine or preaching other than to the Gospels and Epistles, commonly called the Gospel and Epistle of the day, and to the Ten Commandments in the vulgar tongue, without exposition or addition of any manner, sense, or meaning to be applied and added; or to use any other manner of public prayer, rite, or ceremony in the Church.[3]

No doubt it was not easy for preachers to operate under such limitations, especially when their imposition comes from the monarch !

Further attempts to control the output of the Elizabethan pulpits can be seen in Articles issued by Archbishop Whitgift, instituted in 1583. They appear to be directed against 'rogue' or freelance preachers working amongst the common people.

So

1. Preaching must not take place in private places amongst people who are not of the same family. This is unlawful and a "manifest sign of schism."

2. No one should be allowed to preach unless at least four times a year he conducts worship according to the Book of Common Prayer.

3. Preachers should at all times wear the authorized ecclesiastical garments.

4. No one should be allowed to preach unless he is a priest, or deacon at least, "admitted thereunto according to the laws of this realm". [4]

Requirements for ordination itself were tightened up when in 1575 it was decreed that prospective deacons must be at least 23 years of age and serve a period of at least a year as a deacon before proceeding to the priesthood. The effect of this was to increase the attractiveness of education before ordination, and increasingly the pulpits of the land became populated with preachers who were graduates of the universities. Ironically this was not a universally welcomed development on the part of the Church's leaders, for it meant it's clergy were being trained in an environment outside their control. A good grasp of theology would not necessarily figure highly amongst the qualifications of these new graduates, nor would they be characterised by a readiness to slip compliantly into the structures of the Church. Whitgift and his fellow leaders had often to resort to disciplinary measures and the law to keep them in line. It was not until the time of William Laud that the Church succeeded in establishing a measure of control over the training of its preachers.

The independent spirit of many of these university trained preachers did not easily contribute to an eirenic spirit over the land, and controversy continued to rear its head. This controversial ethos was intensified by the rise of the Puritans, displeased with the terms of the 1558 Settlement. Compromise was not possible for them, a problem that would eventually lead to their moving out of the Church of England altogether.

Among the many points at issue between the leaders of the Church and the Puritans was the central importance of preaching. Although Whitgift, for example, recognised the importance of preaching, he did not see that the priest was therefore committed to the production of a freshly-crafted exposition of Scripture each week. For him, the traditional homilies would often suffice. For the Puritans, however, this was a wholly inadequate strategy. The need for exposition of Scripture was paramount. Thus they sponsored "lectureships", independent preachers set in market towns and other places where there was a significant population. Not surprisingly their independent spirit brought them into conflict with the Church leaders, especially the Laudian bishops. Common sense prevailed, thankfully, and these lectureships were often linked with the parish churches, ensuring that the benefits of their preaching could be appreciated without disturbing the status quo.

Echoes of the ethos of controversy of the time can be seen in a further set of "Directions for Preachers", issued in 1622, dictated apparently by James I himself. According to these directions preachers were to ensure their sermons conformed to the Thirty-Nine Articles, the Catechism, the Creed and the Ten Commandments. Funeral sermons were apparently excepted. Unless they were above the rank of Djean they were to avoid "the deep points of predestination, election, reprobation or the irresistibility of God's grace". Exasperated by constant criticism of his foreign policies, which many thought were over-generous to Catholics, he forbade preachers preaching about princes and meddling in affairs of state. And, most of all, they are to avoid

> Causelessly and without invitation from the text, fall into bitter invectives and indecent railings against the persons of either papists or puritans...especially when the auditory is suspected to be tainted with one or the other infection.[5]

It was not easy therefore to be a preacher in this particular period, with such proscriptions of occasion, tone and content on the sermon.

Perhaps the best known Church of England figure in this time was **Lancelot Andrewes** (1555-1626), who held high positions in the Church of England during the reigns of Queen Elizabeth I and King James I. During the latter's reign, Andrewes served as Bishop of Chichester and oversaw the translation of the King James Version of the Bible. Andrewes was one of the foremost contemporary scholars, but is chiefly remembered for his style of preaching. As a churchman he was typically Anglican, equally removed from the Puritan and the Roman positions. He emphasized a positive and constructive statement of the Anglican position.

Andrewes preached regularly before King James and his court on the anniversaries of the Goweries Conspiracy and the Gunpowder Plot. These sermons contributed greatly to the development of the doctrine of the Divine Right of Kings. In these sermons, and at times in his behaviour towards the King, Andrewes may appear to modern readers to err on the side of sycophancy. For example, when preaching on Jesus' command "do not touch me" to Mary Magdalene in John 20.17

> The matters likewise, prince's affairs, secrets of the State, David calleth 'great and high above you' (Ps.131.1), and so points too high, too wonderful for us to deal with. To these also belongeth this 'touch not'.

Andrewes was considered, next to Ussher, to be the most learned churchman of his day, and enjoyed a great reputation as an eloquent and impassioned preacher, but the stiffness and artificiality of his style render his sermons unsuited to modern taste.

By many later analysts his style was considered pedantic and verbal. But as T.S.Eliot wrote:

To persons whose minds are are habituated to feed on the vague jargon of our time, when we have a vocabulary about everything and exact ideas about nothing - Andrewes may seem pedantic and verbal. It is only when we have saturated ourselves in his prose, followed the movement of his thought, that we find his exmination of his words terminating in the ecstasy of assent. [6]

Yet Andrewes, least of all great preachers, can be judged by excerpts. His sermons were too close-knit to be an easy target for the critic. His phrase has been described as jerky and abrupt; and yet every phrase is moving towards a predetermined end, and is itself determined by that end. He was a particular master of the use of the short sentence, something that might interrupt the flow of the prose, and which was, nevertheless, integral to the delivery of the sermon. Ninety-six of his sermons were published in 1631 by command of King Charles I.

Anglican Preachers of the Puritan Era

Andrewes was, like Latimer, in the mould of the medieval preacher. But his work marked the end of that particular phase in the development of Anglican preaching.

Thomas Birch, whose biographical work has been referred to above in connection with Hugh Latimer, is notable for the severity of his judgements on preaching prior to the dawn of the 17th Century. Latimer, Dodd and Andrewes have all their faults laid out. For Birch the pulpit had become infected with coarseness and a lack of sophistication[7]. Again, we might consider Birch's opinions overstated; nevertheless undoubtedly a new tone came into preaching with the dawn of the new century. Several important names are associated with preaching in the era of the Stuarts.

The first name to note in this period is that of **Jeremy Taylor**. Taylor was another whose career shadowed very closely the political upheavals of his day. His closeness to both

Laud and the King made him politically suspect when the Parliamentarians triumphed in the Civil War and executed both Laud and the King. Taylor was imprisoned several times, before being released to preach in Wales, where he became Chaplain to the Earl of Carberry. The Restoration of the Monarchy brought Taylor back to prominence, but instead of receiving a prominent post in England, he was appointed as Bishop of Down and Connor in Ireland, as well as vice-chancellor of the University of Dublin.

Taylor's preaching is remembered chiefly for its poetic style. As one writer says,

> With Taylor the *exemplum* (illustration) flowers into a thing of haunting and magical beauty [8]

Taylor's imagination was so fertile that on occasions his illustrations became so elaborate and sophisticated that they would confuse the hearer and defeat the object for which they were given. This sometimes laid him open to attack from contemporaries such as Robert South. Nevertheless in general these illustrations were meant to contribute essentially to his line of argument in the passages with which they are connected. The greater number were in fact integral to the development of his themes. It is a fair judgement on Taylor that in his preaching we see poetic imagery in full bloom.[9]

John Tillotson, the son of a Puritan clothier in Sowerby, Yorkshire, became Dean of St. Paul's in 1689 and was persuaded two years later to accept the Archbishopric of Canterbury. He inherited decided puritan views from his parents, but quickly became disillusioned with the more radical puritan preachers, and moved in a more moderate presbyterian direction. With the passing of the Act of Uniformity in 1662, Tillotson conformed to the Church of England, and severed his formal links with the Presbyterians. The result of his study of the patristic writers, together with the influence of John

Wilkins, master of Trinity College, Cambridge, was seen in the general tone of his preaching, which was practical rather than theological, concerned with issues of personal morality instead of theoretical doctrine. This plain style of preaching is reflective of the late 17th century, when the integration of reason into Protestant theology came to be seen as one of the most important elements of its stand against Roman Catholicism.

Tillotson is considered by many writers to be one of the most notable figures in the development of preaching in the Church of England. He is credited with freeing the Anglican pulpit not only from the metaphysical flights of the medieval preachers, but also to an extent from the influence of the Puritan tradition, contributing in the process to the development for the first time of a distinctively "Anglican" style of preaching. In an age weary of religious controversy and beginning to feel the cold wind of secularism, he believed that good preaching and holy living would be powerful influences for good. Whilst he was in his manner less dramatic and emotional than many of the Puritans, his preaching was very scriptural and lucid. To that extent he never abandoned his Puritanism completely.

On the one hand Tillotson abandoned the use of medieval *exempla*, whilst on the other hand he rejected the pedantry of Andrewes and others, with their almost mechanical reiteration of terms and phrases. For both he substituted the appeal to reason and to common sense with its careful argument, solid, unhurried and unadorned.

Before taking orders in 1658 **Robert South** was a noted champion of Calvinism against Socinianism and Arminianism. He also showed a leaning to Presbyterianism, but under the Restoration his views on church government underwent a change. He was regarded by many as a time-server, though not necessarily a self-seeker. In fact he was a bitter partisan, and his distaste for the preaching of the sectarian groups of the time was matched only by his detestation of their politics.

South was by nature a controversialist, and embroiled himself in a number of controversies. A zealous advocate of the doctrine of passive obedience, he strongly opposed the Toleration Act, declaiming in unmeasured terms against the various Nonconformist sects. Spurred on it is said by a personal grudge, South in 1693 published *Animadversions on Dr Sherlock's Book, entitled a Vindication of the Holy and Ever Blessed Trinity*, in which the views of William Sherlock were anonymously attacked with sarcastic bitterness. Sherlock published a *Defence* in 1694, to which South replied in *Tritheism Charged upon Dr Sherlock's New Notion of the Trinity, and the Charge Made Good*. The controversy was carried by the rival parties into the pulpit, and occasioned such keen feeling that the king interposed to stop it.

In the history of the development of Anglican preaching, South is significant in that he marked a break with medieval preaching on the one hand and the Puritans on the other. In his work *The Scribe instructed to the Kingdom of Heaven (1660)* he attacked the pulpit style of Andrewes and others with their

> Rhyming cadencies of similary word, and all the treasured artifices of medieval pulpit oratory, with a *quid*, a *quo*, and a *quomodo* and the like...[10]

Many commentators consider that this formidable diatribe sounded the final death knell of medieval preaching.

But South's attack was double-barrelled. His attack on Andrewes and the metaphysical preachers in *The Scribe Instructed* was balanced by the attack on the pulpit style of Owen and the Puritan divines. His main accusation was that the Puritans misused Scripture in the cause of schematization and doctrine.

First they seize upon some text, from which they draw something which they call a doctrine. And well may it be said to be *drawn* from the words, forasmuch as it seldom naturally flows or results from them.   In the next place, being thus provided, they branch into several heads, perhaps twenty, thirty or upwards. Whereupon, for the prosecution of these they repair to some trusty Concordance, and by help of that range six or seven Scriptures under one head, which Scriptures they prosecute one by one, for some considerable time, until they have spoiled it...[11]

He followed this up with an attack on the Puritan use of jargon, indeed on the use of jargon as a whole, and campaigned for simplicity and honesty in the vocabulary of all preachers.

South's own sermons had a vigorous style and a homely and humorous appeal. His wit inclines towards sarcasm, and his quarrelsome temperament, getting the better of him so often, may well have prevented the promotion to a bishopric that his undoubted talent merited. He published a large number of his sermons singly, though later they appeared in a collected form in six volumes (1692), reaching a second edition in his lifetime in 1715.

18th Century Revivals

With the restrictions placed on the non-conformists and the parish churches in the hands of ministers who were better at hunting, shooting and fishing than shepherding the flock, it is not surprising that the spiritual state of the nation declined and morality followed in its train.

Revival was needed, and that came along in the notable preaching figures of John and Charles Wesley, George Whitefield and Charles Simeon.

Whilst the name of **John Wesley** (1703-1791) is historically connected primarily with Methodism, it should be remembered that for most of his life he was Anglican. He remained Anglican in sympathy all his life, and it was only the inability or refusal of the Church of England to develop in the way he wished and to adopt the innovations he thought appropriate that forced John out into other areas.

As a student at Oxford he lived a rigidly methodical and abstemious life. With his brother Charles and a few fellow students he formed the famous "Holy Club", derisively called 'Methodists' because of those methodical habits.

John left for Savannah, Georgia in 1735 with the intent of converting the Indians as well as deepening and regulating the lives of the colonists. His stay in Georgia was brief and unhappy, so that he returned to England just two years later. The one positive thing about his stay in Georgia was his contact with the Moravians, destined to play a large part in his later life. Their devotion and sense of inner peace, even in trouble, deeply impressed John. It was indeed at a Moravian meeting in Aldersgate Street, London that he had his famous 'heart warming' experience and found his life revolutionised.

Wesley had always been a fine preacher, but now his preaching work began to take on new shape. His American venture and his newer associations caused certain conventional Anglican doors to be closed to him, including some churches in Bristol. Encouraged by his friend George Whitefield, John began preaching in the open air at nearby Kingswood. This preaching was so successful that it became almost John's trademark. He moved on to preach at Epworth, more than once using his father's tombstone as a pulpit. He continued for fifty years - entering churches when he was invited, and taking the stand in fields, in halls, cottages and chapels when the churches would not receive him.

John's work drew considerable opposition from clergymen and magistrates, opposition that resulted in attacks in print as well as physical attacks from mobs. Such opposition however spurred him on all the more. Wesley regarded himself as commissioned by God to bring revival to the Church, and no persecution could prevail against the divine urgency or authority of this commission. Seeing that he and the few clergymen cooperating with him could not do the work that needed to be done, he was led to encourage lay preaching. In essence this meant that men and women who were not episcopally ordained were permitted to preach and do pastoral work. What became one of the main features of Methodism arose as the answer to a necessity, but it inevitably hastened Wesley's breach with the Church of England. This breach became wider still when John, impatient of the Bishop of London's refusal to ordain a minister for the American Methodists, proceeded to ordain ministers himself for Scotland, England and America. But though John rejoiced that the American Methodists were free, he advised his English followers to remain within the Established Church, as he did.

In his preaching John did not shy away from controversy, most notably in his opposition to the doctrines of predestination and election espoused by Whitefield and others. Nevertheless he laid great emphasis on the work and witness of the Holy Spirit in the hearts of believers. The witness of the Spirit was the inward impression on the soul of believers whereby the Spirit of God directly testifies to their spirit that they are children of God.[12]

John laid great emphasis in his preaching on sanctification. His name is associated with a doctrine of perfectionism, though this was not so much a concept of *sinless* perfection as perfection in love.

He also stressed in his sermons the importance of experiential faith. Truth would be verified in the experience of Christians if it were really truth. But important though experience is, every doctrine must be able to be defended rationally. He did not divorce faith from reason. Tradition, faith and reason were however all subject to Scripture.

Charles Wesley, younger brother of John, is remembered primarily for his hymn-writing rather than his preaching. Nevertheless he deserves to be set alongside his older brother John as well as Whitefield as one of the leading preachers of his day. This has become clear only lately with the recent publication of the content and analysis of his sermons. Yet, like his brother, he travelled widely as an itinerant preacher during the Evangelical Revival.

His sermons reflect an evangelical commitment to preach to slaves, prisoners and prostitutes and other "sinners". It should be noted that although he confessed an evangelical conversion on May 21, 1738, Charles did not abandon his identity as an Anglican Priest. Newport writes:

> Charles was and remained first and foremost a clergyman of the Church of England whose loyalty to the doctrines, creeds and traditions of the ecclesiastical body never wavered[13]

He persisted in relying on the standard theological resources for Anglicans: the Bible, the Homilies, and the Book of Common Prayer. However, he also borrowed from Greek and Latin Christian authors such as Justin Martyr, Hilary, Basil and Ambrose.

As was the case with John, the note of perfectionism rang through Charles' sermons. A precise definition of perfectionism is however difficult to pin down in either Charles' sermons or hymns. It worth noting that Charles' writes in his journal in 1740 that perfection is

> Utter dominion over sin, constant peace, and love and joy in the Holy Ghost: the full assurance of faith, righteousness and true holiness[14]

131

Again, like John, Charles adapted very easily to open air preaching, borne of necessity after finding Church doors shut to him, including the door of his own parish in Islington.

Charles' sermons were often short in comparison with those of his contemporaries. However he was flexible and adaptable, and was often known to add material *extempore* depending on the reactions of his audience. They were written in bold, evangelistic style. This boldness, and his desire to follow Jesus in reaching out to the outcasts and lower orders of society, including prisoners and prostitutes, often brought him into contention with his more affluent Islington parishioners, resulting eventually in their demand for his licence.

From June 24 through July 8, 1738, Charles reported preaching twice to crowds of ten thousand at Moorfields, once called "that Coney Island of the eighteenth century." He preached to 20,000 at Kennington Common plus gave a sermon on justification before the University of Oxford.

Charles continued to travel and preach, sometimes creating tension with John, who complained that "I do not even know when and where you intend to go."

George Whitefield was the most travelled preacher of the gospel up to his time and many feel he was the greatest evangelist of all time. Making 13 trips across the Atlantic Ocean was a feat in itself, for it was during a time when sea travel was primitive. This meant he spent over two years of his life travelling on water -- 782 days in all. However, his diligence and sacrifice helped turn two nations back to God. Jonathan Edwards was stirring things up in New England, and John Wesley was doing the same in England. Whitefield completed the trio of men humanly responsible for the Great Awakening on both sides of the Atlantic.

Although Whitefield is perhaps chiefly remembered for his revivalist work in America, he in fact spent most of his preaching life in England, spent about 24 years of ministry in the British Isles and only nine in America, speaking to some ten million souls.

On Sunday, January 14, 1739, George Whitefield was ordained as a priest in the Church of England by his friend, Bishop Benson, in an Oxford ceremony. Upon his return to London, he naively assumed that the doors would be opened and that he would be warmly received. Instead the opposite was the case. His successes, preaching, and connection with Methodist societies -- in particular his association with the Wesleys -- were all opposed by the Establishment, and therefore meant that many churches were closed to him.

He preached to as many churches as would receive him, working and visiting with such as the Moravians and other non-conformist religious societies in London.

He soon discovered that the buildings that were willing to host him rapidly became too small to hold the crowds that wanted to listen to him. Alternative plans had to be formulated. Whitefield discovered that Howell Harris of Wales was preaching in the fields, and wondered if he ought to try it too. He concluded that, as he was an outcast anyway, why not try to reach people this "new" way? He conferred with the Wesleys and other Oxford Methodists before going to Bristol in February. In due course the Wesleys would be compelled to follow Whitefield's example. Whitefield launched his open air preaching strategy just outside the city of Bristol in was a coal mine district known as Kingswood Hill. The first time about 200 came to hear him, but in a very short time he was preaching to 10,000 at once.

It is said his voice could be heard a mile away. His crowds were the greatest ever assembled to hear the preaching of the gospel before the days of amplification--and, if we might add, before the days of advertising. At an early age, he had discovered that he had a passion and talent for acting and the theatre, a passion that he would carry on through the very theatrical re-enactments of Bible stories that he told during his sermons. Unlike many preachers of his time, he often spoke extemporaneously, rather than reading his sermon from notes.

Whitefield's democratic speaking style was greatly appealing to his American audience. Benjamin Franklin once attended a revival meeting in Philadelphia and was greatly impressed with his ability to deliver a message to such a large audience. Franklin had dismissed reports of Whitefield preaching to crowds of the order of tens of thousands in England as exaggeration. When listening to Whitefield preaching from the Philadelphia court house, Franklin walked away towards his shop in Market Street until he could no longer hear Whitefield distinctly. He then estimated his distance from Whitefield and calculated the area of a semi-circle centred on Whitefield. Allowing two square feet per person he realized that Whitefield really could be heard by tens of thousands of people in the open air. He then became Whitefield's publisher and friend, though he never shared Whitefield's beliefs. Whitefield was also known to be able to use the newspaper media for beneficial publicity. His revolutionary preaching style shaped the way in which sermons were delivered.

More than 18,000 sermons were to follow in his lifetime, an average of 500 a year, or ten a week. Many of them were given over and over again. Less than 90 of them have survived in any form. Almost every one of Whitefield's sermons was marked by a fundamentally democratic determination to simplify the essentials of religion in a way that would give them the widest possible mass appeal. As it was in the days of Whitefield, so it has been in the two centuries since. The most visible evangelicals, with the broadest popular influence, have been public speakers whose influence rested on their ability to communicate a simple message to a broad audience.

Whitefield was unique in his time also because he was a staunch Calvinist, something that caused him to be at variance with

John Wesley, and believed quite strongly in election, whilst at the same time being one of the most passionate evangelists of the Great Awakening. Over against many who would deny the possibility, Whitefield is a great example of the fact that a firm belief in the sovereignty of God can sit alongside a strong conviction in the urgent necessity of men and women to respond to the preached Gospel. He reminded his contemporaries us to be passionate about preaching the Gospel, and to let nothing get in the way of answering the call of the Lord.

In stark contrast to the Wesleys and Whitefield, the life of **Charles Simeon** had a much narrower compass, based almost entirely in and around Cambridge. Nevertheless, Simeon's life and work is of great strategic importance in our story of the development of preaching in the Church of England.

It is important firstly because although the Evangelical Revival was taking place within the Church of England it was in danger of being driven into non- conformity by the caution of the Anglican leaders and hostility of many parish clergy. Simeon's genius is that he succeeded in maintaining and extending the benefits of the revival within the bounds of the Church of England itself. Where the Wesleys had been driven to the fringes, Simeon stayed at the centre. Simeon firmly believed in Church order and taught the young men under his influence to respect that order also. Though a convinced Anglican and convinced evangelical, he was not a man of party spirit, and was able to recognize and accept the gifts of men who did not always see things precisely as he did.

Simeon is remembered and revered not only for his own preaching but also for his burning desire to train other preachers for the greater benefit of the Church. As a preacher, he ranks highly in the history of Anglicanism. His sermons were unfailingly biblical, simple, and passionate. On the inside of the pulpit in Holy Trinity Church, where only the preacher could see, Charles had carved the words from John

12:21, when Philip brought the Greeks to our Lord, and they said "Sir, we would see Jesus." These words were a constant reminder to him that people came not to gaze on a great preacher or to admire his eloquence, but to seek Jesus.

One of his preaching innovations was the development of the idea of sermon "skeletons" or outlines to give order and direction to the sermon. In 1840 these outlines were gathered together and published in the form of *horae homileticae,* a publication that comprised a commentary on the whole Bible. These outlines became an invaluable resource tool for the preachers in training.

Ministering at a time when there was no formal ordination training, Simeon began teaching a fortnightly sermon class for those intending to be ordained, as well as hosting a weekly conversation party for all undergraduates. As the initial basis for his lectures Simeon used an essay entitled *An Essay on the Composition of a Sermon* by the French Reformed Minister Jean Claude, whose principles of sermon preparation Simeon had found to be identical to his own. It was this essay that gave the impetus to the eventual preparation of the *horae homileticae.*

He taught his students that the herald of the Gospel must never becloud his text, or treat it capriciously, or wander at will from it. Rather, he would say, "let it speak."

To this end the sermon, according to Simeon, must always be pointed, having a definite unity in its theme and message. It must be delivered from the heart to the heart, the preacher himself experiencing its truth before attempting to offer it to others. But the heat must balance the light of the sermon: it must be grasped by the average intelligent mind of the congregation, and above all delivered in an interesting way.

He meant to make out of his students intelligent and intelligible preachers. Imbibing biblical truth in the privacy of their study, they were meant to know their great and awesome responsibility in speaking on behalf of the King of kings.

Apart from his reliance on the Holy Spirit that assisted his preaching, Simeon was endowed with great wisdom and not a little common sense. Some of his preaching maxims are well-worth quoting.

Insisting of the primacy of audibility and articulation, he used to say,

bite your words

thus warning against the common mistake of slurring consonants and final syllables.

avoid a continuous solemnity; it should be as music, and not like a funeral procession.

In his all-embracing aim to penetrate to the soul, to render it willing to do God's will, he discouraged an over-decorous style. He said once to a consulting companion:

poetry is beautiful in itself but if you will come from the mount of God, you will find prose better suited for telling men about their golden calf.

He also discouraged theatricality and all sorts of gimmicks in the use of language. He said on another occasion:

great familiarity does not become the pulpit, but a monotonous solemnity is even worse. Seek to speak always in your natural voice. You are generally told to speak up; I say rather speak down. It is by the strength not by the elevation of your voice that you are to be heard.

A wise balance was aimed at concerning the preacher's manner in the pulpit:

> speak exactly as you would if you were conversing with an aged and pious superior. This will keep you from undue formality and from improper familiarity.

Simeon enjoyed great success in his training of preachers. But such was the situation in the Church of England that many of the preachers trained by Simeon had difficulty in finding positions of ministry both on the mission field and in the parochial ministry. Ever resourceful, Simeon solved the problem by using family legacies to purchase the Rights of Appointment in numerous parish churches, thus ensuring evangelical ministry in the parishes of the land. When Simeon died the Simeon Trust had the right to nominate the clergy to twenty-one Anglican positions. These were mainly in large towns such as Bradford and Derby. By 1820, one in twenty of the Anglican clergy were evangelical; by 1830 it was one in eight.[15]

Lord Macaulay had sufficient opportunities to be acquainted with Simeon and his work. He writes to his sister:

> As to Simeon, if you knew what his authority and influence were, and how they extended from Cambridge to the most remote corners of England, you would allow that his real sway over the Church was far greater than that of any Primate [16]

19th Century, Catholicism and Liberalism

A number of factors contributed towards the rise of the movement known as the **Oxford Movement**, or "Tractarianism". The so-called Enlightenment had brought a new fear of liberalism in theology and concern about the negative effect this would have on both nation and church.

This became combined with a romantic interest in medieval and primitive Christianity.

Nevertheless, whilst the movement is normally associated with ritual and liturgy, its key figures were also notable preachers. The movement as such began with a sermon by **John Keble**. In his celebrated Assize Sermon in Oxford in 1833 Keble attacked the decision by the Government to reduce by ten the number of Irish bishoprics in the Church of Ireland following the 1832 Reform Act, something Keble described as "national apostasy". Keble himself was not a particularly political figure, spending most of his ministry quietly in Hursley, Hampshire, where he settled down to family life and remained for the rest of his life as a parish priest at All Soul's Church. His lasting contribution lay in the field of literature, with the publication of devotional poems, *The Christian Year*.

John Henry Newman on the other hand, is the best-remembered figure of the Oxford Movement, striving in every way for its advancement and the extending of its influence. This he did in the publication of his *Tracts for our Times*, from which the nickname "Tractarians" came, reinforcing their message with his own series of Sunday afternoon sermons at St Mary's, the influence of which, especially over the junior members of the university, was increasingly marked during a period of eight years.

Newman later wrote that the influences leading him in a religiously liberal direction were abruptly checked by his suffering first, at the end of 1827, a kind of nervous collapse brought on by overwork and family financial troubles, and then, at the beginning of 1828, the sudden death of his beloved youngest sister, Mary. There was also a crucial theological factor: his fascination since 1816 with the Fathers of the church, whose works he began to read systematically in the long vacation of 1828. This he regarded as the second of three formative providential illnesses.

Becoming increasingly convinced that the Church of England's position was untenable as an apostolic Church, he was formally received into the Roman Catholic Church October 9, 1845 by Blessed Dominic Barberi, an Italian Passionist, at the College, Littlemore. In February 1846 he left Oxford for Oscott, where Bishop Wiseman, then Vicar-apostolic of the Midland district, resided; and in October he proceeded to Rome, where he was ordained priest by Giacomo Filippo Cardinal Fransoni and was given the degree of Doctor of Divinity by Pope Pius IX.

Pope Pius IX charged Newman with founding and heading the Oratory in England. The first house was established in a suburb of Birmingham, an industrial city; there, Newman would dwell, with occasional exceptions, for the rest of his life.

He continued to preach and to write. A series of Sunday evening sermons, and several series of lectures, drew great crowds of all kinds of people, and he effected many conversions. As a preacher Newman was formal in style, always using notes and never preaching extempore. He was not what we would call a "charismatic" preacher; he kept his eyes fixed upon his manuscript, never moving, looking at his congregation, or varying the tone or inflection of his voice.

This lack of a "pulpit presence" did not keep Newman from gaining a reputation as perhaps the most intellectually and spiritually gifted preacher of his day. Several hundred worshippers crowded into St. Mary's each week, attracted by Newman's eloquence and earnestness, his "piercing yet tender" voice, and his ability to not only "enter into the very minds of his hearers," but to lay "bare the inmost fibres of the heart" and soul as well[17].

Publication secured Newman's place in the first rank of Victorian preachers. In 1843, Rivington's issued *Sermons*

Bearing on Subjects of the Day, which contemporaries regarded as some of the most striking and beautiful sermons ever published. Another reviewer saw the volume as a literary and religious masterpiece; he called attention to its "eminently English" style and "calm, dignified" tone and declared that its publication marked the beginning of "a new era in our English theology".

In 1868, nearly 25 years after Newman's conversion to Rome, Rivington's published a new edition of *Parochial and Plain Sermons*, reviving memories among those who had heard him preach and making his Anglican discourses available to a new generation of readers. This series was also very well received.

Newman was considered by many to have, more than any other person, turned around England's view of Catholics and their religion. After Newman, no more would they be called intellectually inferior or morally depraved, just because they were Catholics.

Liberalism became a significant force in the Church of England largely through the work of **Charles Gore.** Gore himself came to prominence through becoming Principle of Pusey House in Oxford in 1884. As principal of Pusey House Gore exercised a wide influence over undergraduates and the younger clergy and it was largely, if not mainly, under this influence that the Oxford Movement underwent a change which to the survivors of the old school of Tractarians seemed to involve a break with its basic principles. Puseyism had been in the highest degree conservative, basing itself on authority and tradition and repudiating any compromise with the modern critical and liberalizing spirit. Gore, starting from the same basis of faith and authority, soon found from his practical experience in dealing with the doubts and difficulties of the younger generation that this uncompromising attitude was untenable and set himself the task of reconciling the principle of authority in religion with that of scientific authority by attempting to define the boundaries of their respective spheres of influence.

So far his published views had been in complete consonance with those of the older Tractarians but, in 1890, a great stir was created by the publication, under his editorship, of *Lux Mundi*, a series of essays by different writers, being an attempt to succour a distressed faith by endeavouring to bring the Christian creed into its right relation to the modern growth of knowledge, scientific, historic, critical; and to modern problems of politics and ethics. Gore himself contributed an essay on *The Holy Spirit and Inspiration* and from the tenth edition one of Gore's sermons, *On the Christian Doctrine of Sin*, was included as an appendix. The book, which ran through twelve editions in a little over a year, met with a somewhat mixed reception. Orthodox churchmen, evangelical and tractarian alike, were alarmed by views on the incarnate nature of Christ that seemed to them to impugn his divinity, and by concessions to the Higher Criticism in the matter of the inspiration of Holy Scripture which appeared to them to convert the impregnable rock, as Gladstone had called it, into a foundation of sand; sceptics, on the other hand, were not greatly impressed by a system of defence which seemed to draw an artificial line beyond which criticism was not to advance. For Gore personally the watershed came with his famous Bampton lectures of 1891. Taking the subject of Incarnation, he sought to explain the hitherto inconceivable notion that Christ could err by the developing the concepts of kenosis and accomodation. For Gore this meant that Christ, on his incarnation, became subject to all human limitations and had stripped himself of all the attributes of Godhead, including omniscience, the divine nature being subsumed by the human.

The Bampton lectures led to a tense situation which was relieved when in 1893 he resigned his principalship and became vicar of Radley, a small parish near Oxford. Gore, while retaining his office as Senior of the Community of the Resurrection, was made Canon of Westminster late in 1894, where his preaching attracted great crowds. When it was known that he was scheduled to preach, would-be listeners gathered outside the Abbey well in advance, and when the doors were opened the building filled like a lock in flood-time. In minutes, not even standing-room was to be found. In addition to his Sunday sermons, he also gave weekday lectures, many of them later collected into books, such as *The Sermon On the Mount* (1896), The Epistle To The Ephesians (1897), and *The Epistle To the Romans* (1898).

Gore's significance in Anglican history is that he was largely responsible for setting a trend which many would argue has been the dominant trend in Anglicanism ever since, that of seeking to find a compromise between Catholic/Evangelical conservatism on the one hand and liberalism on the other. For our purposes it should be noted that Gore's impulses were entirely pastoral, and that he is remembered as much for his vigorous preaching as for his championing of liberalism. He is a firm example of the fact that the two are not mutually exclusive.

However, the Victorian era saw the rise of a number of Anglican leaders, simultaneously noted preachers of the Gospel as well as eminent Biblical scholars, who would greatly aid the setting of this catholic/liberal synthesis, and prevent the Church sliding away from the historic faith. These included the great scholarly churchmen, **B.F.Westcott, F.J.A.Hort** and **J.B.Lightfoot**. In their roles as leading churchmen and Biblical scholars of the highest calibre, they ensured that preachers of the era could preach with confidence in the text of the Bible, in spite of the waves of liberalism that were washing around them. Although inevitably dated, their work is held in high regard even by modern New Testament scholars.

It is well worth noting that the great scholarship of these men did not cause them to become detached from the lives of ordinary people. In March 1890 for example **Westcott** was nominated to the see of Durham. The change of work and surroundings could hardly have been greater for him. The sudden immersion in the practical administration of a northern diocese rather than dissipating his scholarly energies, gave him instead new strength. He surprised the world, which had supposed him to be a recluse and a mystic, by the practical interest he took in the mining population of Durham and in the great shipping and artisan industries of Sunderland and Gateshead. On one famous occasion in 1892 he succeeded in bringing to a peaceful solution a long and bitter strike which had divided the masters and men in the Durham collieries, a success due in no small measure to the confidence he inspired by the extraordinary moral energy that arose from his personality, at the same time thoughtful, vehement and affectionate.

Amongst the figures that emerged towards the end of the Victorian Era, one of the most prominent was **John Charles Ryle,** the first Anglican Bishop of Liverpool, a new diocese carved out of the Diocese of Chester.   His appointment to Liverpool was at the recommendation of the outgoing Prime Minister, Benjamin Disraeli. The son of a wealthy banker, Ryle had been destined for a career in politics before answering a call to ordained ministry.

He was spiritually awakened in 1838 while hearing Ephesians 2 read in church. The story is that he was late arriving at Church, getting there just in time for the reading of the Second Lesson, from Ephesians. That passage, with its clear proclamation of salvation through grace, was the turning point for Ryle. He was ordained by Bishop Sumner at Winchester in 1842. For 38 years he was a parish vicar, first at Helmingham and later at Stradbrooke, in Suffolk. He became a leader of the evangelical party in the Church of England and was noted for his doctrinal essays and polemical writings.

Although he is largely remembered as a polemicist, fighting for evangelical doctrine at a critical time, he should be remembered also for his preaching. In his diocese, he exercised a vigorous and straightforward preaching ministry.

In his Foreword to the reprint of Ryle's *Holiness* Lloyd Jones writes

> He is pre-eminently and always scriptural and expository. He never starts with a theory into which he tries to fit various scriptures. He always starts with the Word and expounds it. It is exposition at its very best and highest. It is always clear and logical and invariably leads to a clear enunciation of doctrine. It is strong and virile and entirely free from the sentimentality that is often described as 'devotional'.

In his book *The Upper Room* there is a paper entitled "Simplicity in Preaching". It was a paper given to clergy much later in St Paul's Cathedral and is still worth reading. It expresses Ryle's mature views. He made five substantial points.

> First, "have a clear view of the subject upon which you are going to preach."
> Secondly, "try to use in all your sermons, as far as you can, simple words."
> Thirdly, "take care to aim at a simple style of composition."
> Fourthly, "use a direct style." [i.e. using "I" and "you" and not "we"]
> Fifthly, "use plenty of anecdotes and illustrations."

As far as his own preaching was concerned, Ryle aimed at all times for it to be Christ-centred. In the same volume he writes

If there is no salvation excepting by Christ we must not be surprised if ministers of the gospel preach much about him. They cannot tell us   too much about the name which is above every name. We cannot hear of him too much. We may hear too much about controversy in sermons, we may hear too much of works and duties, of forms and ceremonies, of sacraments and ordinances, but there is one subject which we never hear too much of, we can never hear too much of Christ."

He was also a faithful pastor to his clergy, exercising particular care over ordination retreats. He formed a clergy pension fund for his diocese and built over forty churches. Despite criticism, he put raising clergy salaries ahead of building a cathedral for his new diocese.

Ryle combined his commanding presence and vigorous advocacy of his principles with graciousness and warmth in his personal relations. His successor at Liverpool, Bishop Chavasse described him as

that man of granite, with the heart of a child

Vast numbers of working men and women attended his special preaching meetings, and many were led to faith in Christ.

One preacher to build on the solid foundations laid by Westcott, Hort and Lightfoot was Archbishop **William Temple.** A renowned teacher and preacher, Temple is perhaps best known for his 1942 book *Christianity and Social Order*, which set out an Anglican social theology and a vision for what would constitute a just post-war society. Also in 1942, with Chief Rabbi Joseph Hertz, Temple jointly founded the Council of Christians and Jews to combat anti-Jewish bigotry.

One of his more famous sayings (though it's hard to pin down a source) is that,

The Church is the only organisation that exists for the benefit of those who are not its members.

Temple is regarded by some as the most brilliant Archbishop of Canterbury since St. Anselm of Canterbury in the late 11th and early 12th century.

John Stott, born in London in 1921, is an evangelical Anglican, preacher, and teacher of Scripture. He was ordained in 1945 and for most of his years has served in various capacities at All Souls Church in London, where he carried out an effective urban pastoral ministry.

Whether in the West or in the Third World, a hallmark of Stott's ministry has been expository preaching that addresses not only the hearts but also the minds of contemporary men and women. His preaching became the model and inspiration for evangelicals in particular all over the world, as they sought to regain their confidence in sound, expository preaching and in the efficacy of the Scriptures when effectively proclaimed. So outstanding was Stott's preaching ministry that he began to receive and accept invitations to preach from all over the world, so that he became a worldwide leader in the revival of expository preaching.

As well as his preaching ministry, Stott developed an effective writing ministry also. In particular he wrote major books on preaching itself, most notably, *I Believe in Preaching* (London: Hodder, 1982) reprinted in the USA under the title *Between Two Worlds: The Challenge of Preaching Today*. His style is marked by thoroughness, attention to detail and the desire to present accurate exegesis of the passage. If sometimes a little pedestrian for the present writer's taste, there is no denying that Stott presents as accurate a model as one could find of what expository preaching is all about.

As well as being a fine preacher, Stott became a "Church Statesman" and *de facto* leader of the Evangelical Movement within the Church of England.

Equally significant, but in a different way was **David Watson** Watson became Curate-in-Charge of St. Cuthbert's, York in 1965 which was attended by no more than twelve at any service, and was twelve months away from redundancy. Eight years later, largely through Watson's sound Biblical preaching and his imaginative approach to liturgy, the congregation had out-grown St. Cuthbert's and an array of annexes resulting in an eventual move to St. Michael le Belfrey, York. Subsequently the congregation grew to many hundreds, in only a few years. He left St. Michael-Le-Belfrey in 1982 for London.

Watson's ministry is significant in that, unlike that of Stott, it combined sound, expository preaching with the open influences of the Renewal Movement. He overcame the fear that many Anglican Evangelicals had concerning Charismatic Renewal and embraced it wholeheartedly, with remarkable results. He demonstrated that the answer to liberalism is not staid orthodoxy. He was a regular contributor to *Renewal* magazine, a publication of the interdenominational charismatic movement which started in the 1960s. Watson's story is a tragic one, as he died of cancer on February 18 1984 after recording his fight with the disease in a book, *Fear No Evil.* John Gunstone remarked of David Watson:

> It is doubtful whether any other English Christian leader has had greater influence on this side of the Atlantic since the Second World War.

An Anglican Preaching Tradition ?

We have seen how, as we noted at the head of the Chapter, how the work of preaching has been shaped by the various movements that have in turn shaped the ecclesiastical environment in which preachers have pursued their calling. If we were to view it from another angle we might say that it is encouraging that each fresh movement of the Spirit in the Church has brought forward its notable preachers. And this would be true of all the different strands of the Church of England, whether Evangelical, Catholic or Liberal.

Is there the evidence from what has gone before to suggest that there has been a distinctively "Church of England Preaching Tradition ?". The answer, I suggest, is "yes". Just as there has been a "Methodist Tradition" or a "Puritan Tradition", so there has been a definable "Anglican Tradition", a style of preaching that has taken on board all the significant elements of the ecclesiastical setting in which it has taken place. Article XIX, "Of the Church" describes the Church as "a congregation of faithful men, in which the pure Word of God is preached and the sacraments duly administered, in accordance with Christ's ordinance." This places preaching right at the heart of the Reformation definition of the Church in England, a definition which, in the Reformation context, would scarcely include the Roman Church. The Anglican Church therefore, in its very conception, is a preaching Church.

It was Richard Hooker who first put forward the notion of the Church of England as a *via media* between Catholicism and Puritanism[18]. This position involved the assertion that reason and tradition had their place alongside the Scriptures as the means of establishing Christian Truth. The Bible was, after all, the product of specific historical circumstances, and needed to be interpreted in order to be understood. In Hooker's view words must be taken according to the matter whereof they are uttered.

This elevation of reason and tradition inevitably played its part in shaping the preaching style of Anglican preachers. We have already noted how preachers like Tillotson adopted a very reasoned and rational style, often devoid of emotion. This openness to reason has also inevitably meant an accompanying openness to Biblical criticism, which at its worst has led many preachers to lose confidence in the authority of the Word they preach. This is of course not an inevitable result of Biblical Criticism, but that it has happened in many cases is beyond dispute.

Another consequence of introducing reason into the equation has been that preaching in the Church of England is often characteristically cerebral, enlightening the minds of the hearers, but failing to stir their emotions. At its worst again, it causes the sermon often to be thought of as "dull", in spite of the preacher's best efforts. This association with dullness can sometimes be reinforced by the formalizing and ritualising of the sermon by placing it at the heart of what can often be a complex and highly refined liturgy. Spontaneity and improvisation can seem to be out of place in such a setting.

We shall see later that none of these things need be the case. For now we are grateful for the examples of all those in past ages whose pulpit oratory, prompted by the Holy Spirit, but moulded and shaped by the often tumultuous times in which they lived, that have been and continue to be an inspiration to preachers today.

CHAPTER THREE
ENDNOTES

[1] T.Birch, *The Life of Dr.John Tillotson, Lord Archbishop of Canterbury* (1752),18.
[2] Sermon before the Prior of Buckingham.
[3] Printed in eds. Gee, Henry, and William John Hardy, *Documents Illustrative of English Church History*, (New York: MacMillan

Press, 1896), 416.

[4] Printed in eds. Gee, Henry, and William John Hardy, *Documents Illustrative of English Church History,* (New York: MacMillan Press, 1896), 481,2.

[5] Printed in eds. Gee, Henry, and William John Hardy, *Documents Illustrative of English Church History,* (New York: MacMillan Press, 1896), 516-8.

[6] T.S.Eliot, *For Lancelot Andrewes Essays on Style and Order* (London: Faber & Gwyer, 1928),24

[7] Birch, op.cit. 18,19

[8] Smyth, C *The Art of Preaching:A Practical Survey of Preaching in the Church of England 747-1939* (London: SPCK, 1953), 114.

[9] Smyth, *op cit,* 120.

[10] preached in St. Mary's Church, Oxford on 29th July 1660, in *South's Sermons,* 4th ed., (Oxford, 1727), 46-8.

[11] *South's Sermons,* 4th ed., (Oxford, 1727), 49-53.

[12] cf. Romans 8.15,16.

[13] ed. K.G.C.Newport, *The Sermons of Charles Wesley: A Critical Edition with Introduction and Notes* (Oxford: O.U.P., 2001).

[14] John R.Tyson, *Charles Wesley on Sanctification* (Grand Rapids: Astbury Press, 1986), 177.

[15] ed. T.Dowley, Eerdmans' *Handbook to the History of Christianity* (Grand Rapids: Eerdmans , 1987), 513.

16 G. O. Trevelyan, *Life and Letters of Lord Macaulay, I., 67.*

[17] Wiseman, Nicholas. "Newman's sermons." Review of sermons bearing on Subjects of the Day, by John Henry Newman. Dublin Review 15 (1843),103,106

[18] *Of the Lawes of Ecclesiastical Politie* (1593 - 1662) Book IV.11.7.

4

THE PREACHER'S SOURCE

APPROACHES TO THE BIBLE

It has to be admitted that, considering that it is the preacher's primary source, the Bible is not the easiest book in the world to understand. It yields its treasures only to those who are prepared to spend time on excavation, that is, to do the hard work of study and investigation. Unlike a popular novel, its meaning cannot simply be read straight off the page. A preacher will therefore need to examine various mining techniques, to familiarise himself with the main ways the text of the Bible needs to be approached in order to bring those treasures into open view.

In particular, a number of descriptive questions will need to be asked of the text on which the preacher is proposing to preach, in order to discover for example what the text said to those who originally wrote and heard it, in order to discover what the text may have to say to those to whom the preacher is speaking. The following list of questions is not exhaustive, and it will not necessarily be the case that the preacher will need to ask all of them for every text. However, he will need to have a working knowledge of the areas of study and the disciplines from which the questions are drawn.

What do the words of the passage mean ?

Only the most superficial of Bible students would fail to realise that the Bible is an ancient book, written in ancient languages. There are some members of some congregations who would find it a great shock to the system to discover for example that the Lord's Prayer, taken from Matthew 6.5-15, was not originally given in Tudor English, but in an ancient Eastern language ! Happily by and large these people are now few and far between, and most members of our congregation recognise that the Bible they have in the pew in front of them is a translation of something written originally in another language or languages. The existence of a number of different translations today is a recognition also that the understanding of those original languages of the Bible has developed in recent decades, as well as recognising the fact that the English language into which it has been translated from time to time has also undergone considerable development.

The Old Testament was written in **Hebrew**, apart from a few passages written in the sister language of Aramaic[1]. It is a member of a family of languages known as "semitic", the predominant language group in the Middle East for the last 5,000 years. This means, in passing, that it is structured quite differently from Greek, the language of the New Testament. Many a student of Biblical linguistics, such as the present author, have struggled not only to master the written words of Hebrew, but to understand the underlying concepts on which the language is built. Tightening the focus even more, we should note that Hebrew belongs to the north west of the "semitic" area, being linked to Phoenician and the various Canaanite dialects of that region.

154

As previously mentioned, the New Testament was written in **Greek**. That statement is somewhat simplistic, however, since the Greek language appeared in several guises in separate areas. The Greek of the New Testament is not the Classical Greek of Homer and Plato, for example. It is sometimes referred to as "Hellenistic Greek", by which is meant the Greek spoken and written in Alexander the Great's Empire, a language often closely linked with the native languages of the various lands within that Empire. Such links are of great importance when it comes to looking at the language of the New Testament documents.

Many Jews of Palestine were bi-lingual[2]. In some regions Hebrew/Aramaic would be the primary language, whilst others would fall in with the use of Greek as the *lingua franca* of the Empire. Hellenistic culture had pervaded Palestine to a degree not recognised by scholars of a generation or so ago. In John 1.43 tells us that Philip, Andrew and Peter were all from Bethsaida, a Greek city on the shores of the Sea of Galilee. If so, Greek would almost certainly have been their first language, which means that the group of disciples of Jesus (and perhaps Jesus Himself ?) were bi-lingual.[2] If this idea is sound then it challenges the general consensus that the Gospels are a translation of something spoken originally in Aramaic.

Some passages in the New Testament undoubtedly exhibit a greater semitic flavour than others, although the topic has not yet generated a consensus. We have already observed that the Acts speeches for example, have a greater semitic flavour, as direct speech, than the surrounding prose[3]. A great deal of study has gone into the question of to what extent the Gospels of Matthew and John preserve original Aramaic idioms[4]. The debate is far from settled, but for our purposes it flags up the point that reading the Bible, written originally in languages that are fluid and in a constant development flux is no simple thing.

It is often pointed out also that the standard of Greek in the New Testament varies from author to author. Luke the Doctor writes in quite elevated Greek, whilst the author of Hebrews writes some of the most complex Greek of the New Testament. The writer of the Fourth Gospel on the other hand, by comparison writes relatively unsophisticated Greek, a point which has been used by some engaged in the above discussion to indicate that for the writer Greek was not his first language. Paul's Greek, the language of a man travelling widely throughout the Empire, falls somewhere between the two.

Older linguistic studies, particularly those of the New Testament, focussed largely on etymology, on the derivation of words. So the debate on the method of baptism in the New Testament Church was often illuminated by the observation that βαπτιζω was a word originally used in the dyeing industry, whilst επισκοπος was a word which, in secular Greek denoted an "overseer", someone who had charged of others, in many different industries. Many an otherwise dull appeal for increased giving has had its tone lifted by the observation that "cheerful", as in the sentence "The Lord loves a cheerful giver" is in Greek ιλαρος, from which we get our English word "hilarious" (2 Cor.9.7). Such lexical studies are for ever associated with the names of Moulton and Milligan, Liddell and Scott, Adolph Deissman and Abbott and Smith.

In more recent years however, encouraged by the work of scholars such as James Barr, attention has moved from the question of derivation, that is, looking at where the Biblical writers got their words from, onto the question of how the writers actually *used* those words[5]. A whole new science has grown up, that of "Modern Linguistics", a discipline scholars have not been slow in applying to the Biblical Text.

This science looks for example at *phonology*, how the sounds of a language contribute to meaning; at *morphology*, how words are formed; at *syntax*, the way words are combined to make sentences; at *structure*, the logical relation of the propositions embedded in a sentence or paragraph; and *discourse*, or how texts and contexts create meaning. Thus modern linguistics is a thoroughgoing and exacting discipline, aiming to become descriptive of every aspect of a text. It does not obliterate or render useless the earlier lexical studies, but seeks to complement them with additional, new insights.

Amongst the basic principles of modern linguistics is the observation that the basic meaning of a word is actually arbitrary, and based on convention and use. Thus by convention and use the sound "tree" comes to describe something with branches and leaves. There is nothing inherent in the sound "tree" to denote the reality, since people in other countries denote exactly the same reality by means of other sounds. We learn to associate sound and meaning by communication with others around us.

A further principle is that of "synchronicity". What matters is not so much the derivation of a word as the meaning it carries at any given point in time. This principle cautions against too readily establishing the "general sense" of a word for a particular author. A particular word, such as αγαπη, "love", may carry a different sense even for the same New Testament author when he uses it in different contexts. In each separate context the use of the word needs to be examined. A visitor to the United Kingdom from another country researching the word "coach" for example might well be in for a degree of confusion. Having read in a history book that a "coach" was a vehicle pulled by horses in which people travelled, he may well be startled to read in his newspaper that so-and-so has been appointed "coach" of the local Football team. He may well wish to enquire as to how one meaning has led to the other. The etymologist and the modern linguistics exponent would do well to work together, the former identifying contexts in which the term occurs, the latter elucidating the dynamics of the use of the word in those contexts.

The third principle, related to this, is the observation that structure influences meaning, so that it is the way a word is used in relation to other words that will help illuminate what the word means. At a number of points in the New Testament this becomes important. In John 1.1, a lively debate with Jehovah's Witnesses and others turns on whether the statement ο λογος θεος ην means "the Word was God" or "the Word was *a* god", determined by the absence of the definite article which normally precedes nouns in Greek. On "Colwell's Rule", named after the philologist E.C.Colwell, John 1.1 can be taken as an example of the omission of the article before a predicate noun in order to distinguish precisely between subject and predicate[6]. Further study shows that this is one example of a pattern for such use in John's Gospel[7]. The dynamics of word use is relevant to other passages such as Romans 9.5, where Paul speaks of "Christ, who is God over all, blessed for ever". Word order and use leads the consensus of translators to prefer this rendering to the one which sees "God over all, blessed for ever" as an isolated eulogistic burst on the part of Paul.

Although the subject of linguistics is a fascinating one, the average preacher may well find it beyond his scope to delve deeply into it. Of course this is not necessary. What is necessary for every preacher is to use commentaries that are modern, that take seriously the advances in the understanding of the way language is used, and to be aware of the general principles that underlie such use.

What kind of passage is it ?

In society, people interact with each other by using conventional, repeatable patterns of speech. Without these speech patterns social life would not flow smoothly. This applies within the Church just as much as it applies outside it. When we attend a service of worship for example we take part in a known liturgical pattern that incorporates numerous recognisable types of material (creeds, hymns, prayers, etc).

Over the years scholars have learned to identify within Biblical Literature these recognizable patterns, classifying them according to specific formal types or genres. When reading the New Testament we will not appreciate what is going on within biblical texts unless we recognize the operative genres and their specific uses.

The word "genre" may be defined as *a conventional and repeatable pattern of oral and written speech that facilitates interaction with people in a specific social situation.*

The rhetorical impact of using a specific genre depends therefore on the way the genre pattern is employed and the kind of social setting in which it is used.

Martin Dibelius and Rudolph Bultmann were early pioneers of what is known as **Genre Analysis**, with their application of form critical procedures to identify certain literary forms in the Gospel text (pronouncement stories, etc) and the setting in the early church that caused the material to be cast the material into these forms. Their analyses tended to produce small, fragmented units, whereas contemporary scholars have refined their work and identified larger units in the Bible text, sometimes comprising whole books (ancient letter, apocalypse, biography, etc).

As interpreters of the New Testament, we engage in genre analysis every time we seek to understand the character and function of any text, whether it be short or long, simple or complex, originating in an oral or literary environment. The process is complicated by the fact that longer texts will sometimes incorporate more than one literary genre. When

Paul writes for example, he uses the genre of a Hellenistic letter, but modifies it by building in other shorter genres, such as household codes, ethical instruction and advice (*paranesis*), liturgical and hymnic forms.

The preacher, when looking at the text in front of him, will therefore seek to ask "what type of literary genre(s) is/are represented in this text ?" as a way of understanding and applying it.

Sometimes the English Bible itself helps the preacher out by the way the text is sometimes indented. This is the case for example in Old Testament passages that employ the Hebrew genre of *parallelism*. Parallelism is itself often divided into sub-genres:

Synonymous parallelism - the thought of the first half of the sentence is repeated, using different words

Antithetic parallelism - the opposite of part one is set out in part two.

Synthetic parallelism - the thought of part one is enhanced by the statement

in part two.

Although the Old Testament is a rich treasury of examples of Hebrew parallelism, such forms are to be found in the New Testament also, particularly in the Gospels. So in Luke 1.46,7 we read

My soul magnifies the Lord,
And my spirit rejoices in God my Saviour.

This is fairly easy to detect, being in an obviously poetic passage. Less easy to spot, but just as striking is John 6.35

He who comes to me shall not hunger,
He who believes in me shall never thirst.

Both are examples of synonymous parallelism. Antithetic parallelism is found in the familiar words of John 3.18

He who believes in Him is not condemned
He who does not believe in Him is condemned already.

An example of synthetic parallelism is the key saying of Jesus in John 8.44

You are of your Father, the devil
And your will is to do your Father's desires.

Another important area in which genre analysis illuminates the text is the interplay between narrative and dialogue in the Gospels and Acts. So, within one literary unit may be found narration, dialogue, monologue, summary pronouncement, parenthetical explanation, and so on. The New Testament is a very rich source of literary genres, and it follows that full understanding of a text will not come until all literary avenues have been explored.

Genre analysis dovetails neatly with other forms of biblical analysis, relying as it does for example on the historical investigation of the social and cultural factors that led to the development of these characteristic literary patterns. It depends also on the understanding of the development of rhetorical and narrative patterns in the ancient world. Despite these dependencies, Genre criticism is an essential and valuable tool for the preacher, guarding against some of the worst excesses of Biblical interpretation that arise from treating the text as something which in fact it is not.

In what circumstances was the passage written ?

Preachers will need to recognise that the text they are using came to birth in a particular context, a context to be described in both historical and literary terms.

The preacher will therefore wish to understand where the text belongs in the sweep of historical events that cover the millennium within which the Bible was written. The Biblical authors were people who belonged within that sweep of history, who were influenced by it and who in there turn influenced it to a certain degree. The Gospels for example were written in a period of great political ferment, amid the political and religious currents that would lead to the Jewish War of a.d. 66-70. They could not fail to reflect some of the issues of the day, although the extent to which they do so is a matter of great debate. In addition, the particular circumstances of the author went some way to shaping the texts he wrote. The relatively calm and reflective nature of Ephesians, for example, could be all the better appreciated when it is understood to have been written by an author languishing in prison. The Book of Revelation, with all its complexities, must first of necessity to be set within the author's perception of the inevitable clash between the Kingdom of God and the kingdom of satan as represented by the Roman Empire.

Much confusion will be engendered by a failure to place Old Testament texts in their correct relationship to on the one hand, the split of the Jewish Nation into the Northern Kingdoms of Israel and Judah, and on the other to the dramatic events of the return from Exile. The religion of the Jews was markedly different after the Exile to Babylon from what it had previously been, a difference that may be very crudely characterised as a change from Temple/sacrifice based religion to a religion of the Torah. As we shall have cause to remark later, the reluctance of many preachers to preach on texts from the Old

Testament often stems from the necessity of having to sketch in the historical background of each text being used.

In similar fashion the relationship of New Testament documents to the dramatic events surrounding the Fall of Jerusalem in a.d. 70 is one of the keys to their proper understanding. Again differences of opinion exist. The scholarly consensus dates all the Gospels after the Fall of Jerusalem, although it has to be acknowledged that the traditions that were put together to form the Gospels come from much earlier. J.A.T. Robinson threw a spanner into the scholarly works in 1976 when he wrote *Redating the New Testament,* in which he dated virtually all the New Testament documents before a.d. 70[8]. Although Robinson failed to shake that scholarly consensus, the present writer feels that the strength of Robinson's arguments have not been taken sufficiently seriously in the world of New Testament scholarship.

Historical criticism of the Bible goes of course much further than simply the illumination of the historical setting of the Biblical texts. By on the one hand setting them alongside extra-biblical historical sources and on the other by looking at the intrinsic probabilities within the text itself, it attempts to offer an assessment of the historical value of that text. So the Old Testament accounts of the Exodus are set against what is known of the history of Egypt at that time from extra-biblical sources. Whilst direct evidence from archaeology for these events is relatively scarce, discoveries do at least show the degree to which the Bible story fits into the historical and cultural background of the times.

In the New Testament, the work of the Gospel authors and Acts is often set aside accounts of the same events in non-Christian writers such as the Jew Josephus and the Greek Thucydides. At times the comparison is unfavourable, Josephus being regarded as the "objective" writer of history, whilst the New Testament writers are "slanted" in their accounts, subordinating history to their theological and literary concerns. In passing we may note that in fact Josephus is just as open to the accusation of "spin" as any other writer, composing an account of Jewish history that was favourable towards his Roman patron Vespasian.

Yet it is undoubtedly true that the New Testament writers did have their theological motives in writing their accounts of the events concerning Jesus, and that these motives have to be taken into account when assessing the historical value of what they wrote. This does from time to time lead to some very negative assessments of that historical value from some New Testament scholars. There are, however, not a few who are very willing to concede that it is perfectly possible to combine history with theology. Given the relatively short time between the events being covered and the publication of the Gospels, it is most unlikely that any writer would contemplate publishing an account that did not correspond generally to known facts. Very recently Richard Bauckham has published *Jesus and the Eyewitnesses*, a ground breaking work that establishes the eyewitness tradition very firmly at the centre of the process of composing the Gospels[9]. So far the work has been given a favourable reception by those in the mainstream of New Testament scholarship.[10]

Where historical criticism threatens to lose its objectivity is the point where scholars seek to make judgements on the internal consistency and inherent probability of events recorded in historical passages. Because the motives of the New Testament writers are often not *merely* historical, they fail to give enough information to answer many of the questions a historian might wish to ask of the text. There are tantalising gaps in the New Testament accounts which makes the reader ask almost in frustration, "I wonder what happened in between events A and B ?". These gaps make historical judgements notoriously hazardous. There is so much we are simply not told. So when a scholar such as Haenchen argues that Luke's accounts of Paul's time in Ephesus (Acts 18-20) are unreliable because Luke could not have had access to direct information about them, we are bound to reply "how do we know he didn't ?"[11]. The information is simply not there.

Haenchen is rather negative in his assessment of the historical value of much of the material in Acts, arguing that it contains many inherent improbabilities. However, Ian Howard Marshall's *Acts: An Introduction and Commentary* (Leicester: IVP, 1980), in the Tyndale Commentary series, is written to be set alongside Haenchen to deal with many of the questions he raises, and to show that historical scepticism is not the only possible outcome of applying criticism to Biblical narratives. The assessment of "intrinsic probabilities" is an area where objectivity can all too easily be lost.

The process of historical study has several refinements. There is for example a study of the **history of the traditions** (German: *traditionsgeschichte*) on which the Bible was based. The various Biblical books were not of course written down at one sitting directly out of the author's head *de novo*. Often the books are a condensation or distillation of information, stories and ideas transmitted from person to person, sometimes from generation to generation, over long periods. The prophetic books were collections of the prophet's sermons drawn from within identifiable historical periods, but sometimes over a period representing their entire ministry. The Gospel writers in similar fashion wrote down stories about Jesus passed on within the Early Church, most probably orally initially, but also in written form.[12] Even the Epistles, documents one would think would come straight out of the author's head, contain "traditional" materials, that is, material passed on within the Church. Within Ephesians, for example, the use of the Old Testament, the use of "Household Codes" (German: *Haustafeln*) as well as the list of vices and virtues have all been identified as traditional materials. It is more difficult in some books to distinguish between the author's own thinking and material he is simply passing on. The Gospel of John is a notorious example of this difficulty. The very obvious difference between the structure and content of the Fourth Gospel from that of the Synoptic Gospels was for ages accounted for on the basis that the author, whether John the Apostle or not, was a "lone genius" who wrote from his own distinctive viewpoint, based on personal reminiscences of Jesus in many cases, and then sometimes on material that was derived from external Greek or even Persian sources. The ground-breaking work of Gardner Smith, taken up and developed by C.H.Dodd and Barnabas Lindars, identified a process of tradition, similar to but independent of the Synoptic tradition, as the basis of much of the material in the Fourth Gospel.[13] This contributed to what J.A.T. Robinson described as a "new look" at the Fourth Gospel, a new look that gave it a place as of the same genre as the other canonical Gospels. However, unlike the Synoptics, where the authors' sources can to a degree be identified, there has never been a general consensus as to what sources contributed to this Johannine tradition, so that the extent to which the Fourth Gospel represents his own thinking as distinct from traditional material he is using remains problematical.

But that traditional material has been shaped in its transmission is readily recognised. In some cases a key factor in shaping the tradition was the theological viewpoint of the author himself. These authors did not merely pass on the tradition, but shaped and adapted it for their own purposes in the process. The most accessible examples of this come in the use made by Matthew and Luke of material from the Gospel of Mark. They remain faithful to the material they use, but often tweak the details in order to make a particular point. For example, in his use of the story of the Stilling of the Storm, Matthew changes the Markan *"Teacher,* do you not care that we are perishing ?" to "Save us *Lord,* we are perishing", to bring out a point about faith.[14] The issue for Matthew is not so much the power of Jesus over the elemental forces of nature, though he reflects that in his account, as the question of how far those who already acknowledge Jesus as Lord put their trust in Him. The discipline known as **redaction criticism** seeks therefore to scrutinize the role played by the authors of the Biblical books in setting the final form of the material they record. This is part of the recognition that whilst Christians believe the Holy Spirit to be at work through the whole process of the compilation of the Bible, the work is done through the agency of human authors, with their distinctive personalities and distinctive viewpoints.

What needs to be recognised in the historical approach to the Bible is that the Bible has its own sense of history. So the Book of Genesis begins with the dramatic pronouncement, "In the beginning God created the heavens and the earth" (Gen.1.1). The Fourth Gospel begins in similar dramatic style when it declares "In the beginning was the Word", the Word that subsequently "became flesh and dwelled among us" (John 1.1,14). Ephesians pushes the boundary back even further when it declares that the work of God in election took place *"before* the foundation of the world" (Eph.l.4). If the Bible is concerned with the beginning of things, it is also concerned with the end, when human history will be brought to a conclusion and all things brought to their rightful unity in Christ (Eph.1.10). As the Psalmist declares, over the whole process of time, "from everlasting to everlasting you are God" (Psalm 90.2).

Punctuating this sweep of time are the great saving Acts of God: the making of the Covenant, the Rescue from Egypt, the Giving of the Law, the Return from Babylon, the Sending of the Prophets, the Birth, Death, Resurrection of Jesus, the Sending of the Spirit, the Mission of the Church and the Final Consummation. None of these are isolated events, but are part of God's Plan for His work in the world, part of what has come to be known as **Salvation History** (German: *Heilsgeschichte*).

167

Yet a further refinement of historical study comes in what has been referred to as the **History of Religions** (German: *Religionsgeschichte*).[15] This form of study acknowledges the fact that both the People of Israel and then the Early Church lived their lives amidst other peoples who had their own religious practices and beliefs that were sometimes organised into highly organised religious systems. The natural syncretistic atmosphere of the cultural and religious mixes of the Ancient Near East meant that interchange and interaction between those religious was inevitable and unavoidable. The Biblical scholar and expositor will be on the lookout therefore for possible influences on the Biblical text from the religious communities that surrounded the Judaeo-Christian community in which the Bible was written. The Old Testament specialist will be aware of the possibility of influence on the Bible texts from the religions of Egypt, Babylon, Persia, Greece and Rome. Within the New Testament scholarship community the key issue for decades, still not totally resolved, was the possible influence of Gnostic religions and myths on the development of the Bible text. Such consensus as exists leans to the idea that the New Testament was born in a situation where elements of Gnostic thought existed, but that the developed Gnostic religious systems post-date the New Testament. The same could pretty much be said for the Mystery Cults, many of which flourished throughout the Roman Empire. That they and the New Testament communities inhabited the same religio-philosophical community is recognised, but that there was direct cross-fertilization between the New Testament and the Mystery Cults is the subject of much less agreement.

The community in and around the city of Ephesus provides an interesting test case for this type of study. Increasing attention is being placed on the prominence of Roman Religion in the area, and in particular the Cult of the Roman Empire. More and more it is being argued in recent times that New Testament documents such as Ephesians were written to counter the increasing claims being made for the Emperor.[16] So the supremacy of Christ set out in such passages as Eph.1.10 & 1.20-22 is set out in contrast to such claims. What is overlooked in such studies is that Ephesus already had a strong and vigorous local cult, the Cult of Artemis, before ever the Roman Imperial Cult arrived in the city. It is equally arguable therefore that the Christology of Ephesians is formed over against the Artemis Cult rather than that of the emperor.

Although, as in the case of the other disciplines outlined, work is continuing and no widespread consensus is as yet established. What is important, however is the recognition that the religion of the Bible did not arise out of a vacuum. Religious groups already existed, sometimes in highly developed forms. Jesus was a Jew; Paul was a Jew.   Once recognised, the examination of Jesus and Paul against their religious backgrounds opens up all sorts of new panoramas and vistas that greatly enrich the preaching task.

One final aspect of the historical approach to the Bible text comes with the application of the **Social Sciences** to the Bible. By "Social Science" we understand the disciplines of sociology, social (or cultural) anthropology and psychology. These disciplines have the potential for throwing light on the world behind the text (the world of the author), the world within the text (the narrated world of characters, intentions and events), and the world in front of the text (the world of the reader).[17]   This study emphasises that the people of the Bible were real people living in communities, and that their experience of living in community shaped the way they transmitted the Biblical material.

A very obvious example of this stems from the fact that Jesus spent the great part of His ministry in the rural, seaside community of Galilee, amidst relatively hard-working but poor and unsophisticated provincials. Much of the Gospel teaching therefore involves stories taken from farming and fishing. Although the note of controversy is by no means absent, it does not take on the heated dimension it has once Jesus arrives in urban Jerusalem.

In similar fashion there is much New Testament teaching about servant hood and slavery, something that becomes all the more understandable when we remember that many of the Early Christians were from the lower reaches of society.

The social science approach is concerned not so much with the people of the Bible as individuals as people in community. It will be concerned therefore with the dynamics of the change of Israel from a tribal federation to a nation under a King. It will examine the later adjustment to life without the Temple in the post-exilic period, and how the Torah became the new representation of Jewishness. It will look not only at which groups the New Testament Christians belonged to, but at how these groups functioned. It will want to look at the beliefs, rituals and symbolic universes that gave the groups their identity and enabled them to maintain that identity.

We may look at an example. Great interest has focussed in recent years on the community that lies behind the Fourth Gospel, the so-called "Johannine Community"[18]. Brown and others argue that the Fourth Gospel was written in part to strengthen the work of a particular Christian community with its own distinctive beliefs and practices.[19] Some scholars have taken this point much further, and argued that the Johannine Community was in fact a sectarian group, involved in a concerted withdrawal from other Christian communities on the one hand and the world on the other.

Wayne Meeks notes the symbolic language of the Fourth Gospel and argues that this is the "code language" of a closed group[20]. This language in Meek's view comprises an "in language", comprehensible only to those inside the group and therefore preserving the group's distinctive identity.

The language of the Fourth Gospel in the view of Meeks represents

A closed system of metaphors, clear to the initiated but opaque to the outsider[21]

Meeks reinforces this observation by arguing that the Johannine Community uses the Gnostic Myth of the "Man from Heaven", coming down as Revealer but being rejected by those to whom He came, as a means of expressing their own sense of rejection. The Johannine Community is a community therefore well down the road of sectarian withdrawal, and all their beliefs, as attested by the Fourth Gospel, should be seen in this light.

Against this it should be pointed out that this is not the only way, nor the most helpful way, of approaching the Fourth Gospel. Craig Koester, for example, convincing demonstrates that the symbolic language of the Gospel, far from being designed to hide the truth from the initiated, is designed to widen the appeal of the book and make its meaning accessible to a wide spectrum of readers.[22] The symbols serve to create interest in Jesus on the part of the reader. The symbols, pointing to basic concepts such as darkness, light, bread, water, life, etc serve to draw the reader in to a fuller understanding. To be sure, further understanding will come once the enquirer is within the community, but he does not by any means need to be an initiate before any understanding comes.

Then again, alongside language that could be interpreted as representing rejection of the world and other communities comes very striking Johannine language about mission. The theme of mission runs through the Gospel from end to end, from the dramatic beginning, with the assertion that light has come into the world, to the conclusion in which Jesus tells His disciples "As the Father has sent me, so I am sending you" (20.21), and the end reminder that "these things are written that you might believe" (20.31).[23] No matter to what extent the Community was battered by the world around it, and no matter what the temptation was to withdraw, the Community retained its divinely-given sense of mission, so that there is every justification for seeing the Fourth Gospel as an evangelistic document.

This is just one of many examples of how social science study opens windows of understanding of how the Bible was written, as we note all the interfaces between the Bible communities and the communities around them.

Is the passage telling a story ?

A significant part of the Bible text comes in what we might style "propositional" form, where the prophets and the letter writers for example make specific statements about reality, we cannot fail to notice that much of the text comes in narrative form. The scholarly discipline known as **Narrative Criticism,** sometimes referred to as Reader-response Criticism, focuses on the stories in the Biblical literature and attempts to read these stories with insights drawn from the secular field of modern literary criticism. The goal is to determine the effects that the stories are expected to have on their audience.

In New Testament studies narrative criticism is practised with primary reference to the four Gospels and the Book of Acts. Until relatively recently the focus was completely on what the text contains rather than the way the details of the text were related. It is perfectly possible to see the Gospels as the record of significant history, whilst at the same time seeing them as comprising stories that were intended to fire the imagination and provoke a response. It is a very useful way of understanding narrative criticism as a discipline intended to illuminate how the writer seeks to involve the reader in the setting forth of eternal truth.

Certain elements are important in the literary analysis of a particular narrative text

The Implied Author - this is not necessarily to be assumed to be the same as the actual, historical author. By "implied author" narrative critics mean the perspective from which the work appears to have been written, a perspective that must be reconstructed by readers on the basis of what they find in the narrative. This concept is of particular importance to those scholars who regard some of the New Testament documents as pseudonymous, i.e., written by someone other than the named author.

The Implied Readers - the concept of the implied reader parallels that of the implied author. The implied reader is one who actualises the potential for meaning in a text, who responds to it in ways consistent with the expectations that we may ascribe to its implied author. The concept of the implied reader allows the critic to distinguish between his own responses to a narrative and those the text appears to invite.

The narrative critic has to take seriously the world in which the implied reader lives. In the famous Lukan parable for example, the writer assumes that the readers understand who and what a Samaritan is, the antipathy that existed between Jews and Samaritans, and the worth of a *denarius*, for example.

The story is accepted as a whole. Historical or literary nitpicking of individual elements of a story will destroy the impact of that wholeness. The narrative only works if the writer can assume that his readers share the thought world and value systems that he seeks to generate by his narrative. We have already observed how the focus on the Bible as story spawned the new style of preaching we named as "narrative preaching". Names such as Robert W. Funk, Amos Wilder and John Dominic Crossan, have made important contributions in the area of rhetorical and narrative approaches to preaching from the Bible. Their various contributions to the field include the idea that form and content cannot be separated; what the text *does* is as important as what it says. They argue that texts don't just have a past, they have a present and a future through their readers and hearers, as the preachers use the material to construct an alternate world.

Recent studies of the Fourth Gospel have highlighted the theme of the Kingship of Jesus within it, particularly in the Passion Narrative.[24] They point out that this would have particular meanings as particular resonances for the largely Jewish audiences that Jesus had when the words were spoke, but quite different resonances for Gentile readers at the end of the First Century, when the Cult of the God/Emperor was in development.

It need to be remembered that the approach to the text as story, like the other methods we are listing, is only one tool amongst many to use in approaching the biblical text, and has very real limitations. The biblical narratives are not always stories as we might wish to tell them. Very often the story outline is skeletal, and there are many details missing, many questions we would like to ask unanswered, and many things we would like to know not mentioned. How readers would long to know exactly what happened in the early hours of that first Easter Day for example.   It is very noticeable that film-makers and others that have attempted to dramatise the Bible for the media find themselves inevitably having to fill in the blanks, and write extra dialogue and action to created dramatic effect. This is something for which they are often criticised, but is at the same time a necessity in order to construct a connected narrative.

A further complicating factor in the case of the Bible text is that proposition and narrative are not always easily separated. It is simply not possible to maintain the distinction between the two to the extent that someone like Lowry would like to do. So the *narrative* of the call of Zacchaeus, in Luke 19.1-10, ends with the *proposition* "for the Son of Man came to seek and save the lost". In much the same way the vivid and dramatic narrative of the paralysed man healed at Capernaum is told to illustrate the truth that "the Son of Man has authority on earth to forgive sins". They are examples of what the early Form Critics such as Vincent Taylor used to call *pronouncement stories,* narratives told with a revelatory "kick".

Then again, in Matthew and Luke's editing of Mark the details that are omitted in the transmission are often those colourful, descriptive details that would colour the narrative aspect of the material, suggesting that for them the narrative aspect was not always the most important aspect. Furthermore, this approach does not answer historical questions, nor does it allow scrutiny of those elements within a text that may be considered objectionable by the modern reader. What is does do is to allow the preacher to study biblical stories on their own terms - as stories, rather than just sources for historical and theological reflection.

What does the passage mean for us ?

As we said at the beginning of the Chapter, we have by no means exhausted the list of questions that could be asked of the Bible passage in view by the preacher. We have noted the main ones. For a full treatment of the subject see *Hearing the New Testament,* edited by Joel B. Green (Eerdmans: Grand Rapids, 1995). A balanced approach to a text will involve asking most, if not all, of the above questions. Rarely will a single approach suffice, although for particular texts some questions may be more important than others. If doing a combination of things simultaneously may seem a daunting task, then we can perhaps reflect that learning to drive offered us a similarly terrifying prospect. Now doing several things at once behind the wheel is second nature to us, and in time this multi-faceted approach to the Bible text will become natural also.

When all is said and done, and the Bible text has been interrogated in the different ways outlined above, the most important question the preacher will want to ask is "what will this text mean to my hearers on Sunday ?". Different elements of a passage will resonate and ring bells with different types of congregation. Jesus' teaching on love, for example, will mean something special to a congregation torn apart by internal strife. Those who have been through the agony of suffering will listen with special attentiveness to what Paul has to say on the subject in 2 Corinthians. Many other obvious examples could be given.

Equally obvious is the statement that the preacher should know his congregation and know where they are in their spiritual pilgrimage. His message will be targeted in the nicest possible way. But just because it is obvious doesn't mean it is easy, and so we turn our attention next to what such targeting involves.

CHAPTER FOUR
ENDNOTES

[1] Jeremiah 10.11; Daniel 2.4- 7.28; Ezra 4.8- 6.18; 7.12-26 and two words in Genesis 31.47

[2] See S.E.Porter, "Did Jesus ever teach in Greek ?" *Tyndale Bulletin,* 44 (1993), 199-236.

[3] Wilcox, *The Semitisms of Acts* (Oxford: OUP, 1965); D.F.Payne, *Semitisms in the Book of Acts,* in eds. W.W.Gasque & R.P.Martin, *Apostolic History and the Gospel: Essays presented to F.F.Bruce,* (Exeter: Paternoster, 1970), 134-150;

[4] C.K.Barrett, *The Gospel of John and Judaism,* (London: SPCK, 1975).

[5] Barr, *The Semantics of Biblical Language* (Oxford:OUP, 1961)

[6] E.C.Colwell, "A Definite Rule for the use of the Article in the Greek New Testament ", *JBL 52* (1933), 12ff; discussed in C.F.D.Moule, *An Idiom Book of New Testament Greek* (Cambridge:CUP, 1963), 115-117.

[7] see also 1 John 4.17 "God is love".

[8] J.A.T.Robinson, *Redating the New Testament* (London: SCM, 1976)

[9] R.Bauckham, *Jesus and the Eyewitnesses: The Gospels as Eyewitness Testimony* (Grand Rapids: Eerdmans, 2006).

[10] See reviews by J.Schroter and C.Evans, with Bauckham's response in *JSNT* 31 (2008), 195-235.

[11] E.Haenchen, *The Acts of the Apostles* (ET Oxford: OUP, 1971), 558-579.

[12] The relationship between oral and written tradition is one of the key issues in Bauckham's book.

[13] See P.Gardner Smith, *St. John and the Synoptic Gospels* (Cambridge: CUP, 1938); C.H.Dodd, *Historical Tradition in the Fourth Gospel* (Cambridge: CUP, 1963); B.Lindars, *The Gospel of John* (New Century Bible, Oliphants, 1969)

[14] Mark 4.35-41; Matthew 8.23-27.

[15] In the New Testament Studies this work is associated with such people as W.Bousset and R.Bultmann. Bousset resisted the idea of clear demarcations between the Christian religion and the surrounding cults, cf. W.Bousset, *Kyrios Christos*, (Nashville: Abingdon Press, 1970). Bultmann saw the Gnostic Redeemer Myth as particularly influential in the formation of New Testament Christology. Cf. R.Bultmann *The Gospel of John: A Commentary*, (Westminster John Knox Press, 1971). There were of course other strings to Bultmann's theological bow !

[16] See for example N.T.Wright, *Paul: Fresh Perspectives,* (London: SPCK, 2005), 69-79. Other names associated with this trend are R.Horsley, *Paul and Empire: Religion and Power in Roman Imperial Society* (Harrisburg: Trinity Press International, 1997), esp.10-24; *Paul and Politics* (Harrisburg: Trinity Press International, 2000); D.Georgi, *Theocracy: In Paul's Praxis and Theology* (trans. David E. Green, Philadelphia: Fortress Press, 1991); J.D.Crossan, with Jonathan L.Reed, *In Search of Paul: How Jesus' Apostle opposed Rome's Empire with God's Kingdom.* For criticism of this view see S.Kim, *Christ and Caesar: The Gospel and the Empire in the Writings of Luke* (Eerdmans: Grand Rapids, 2008).

[17] Two names associated with the pioneering phrase of this study

are Max Weber, *The Sociology of Religion* (ET Boston: Beacon, 1963) and *The Theory of Social and Economic Organization* (New York: Free, 1947; along with Bryan R.Wilson, *Religious Sects: A Sociological Study* (London: Weidenfield and Nicholson, 1970) and *Magic and the Millennium* (London: Heinnemann, 1973). Ben Witherington III has produced a whole series of commentaries on the New Testament books from a social science point of view. Bruce J. Malina is another notable scholar who follows this approach.

[18] For a thoroughgoing description and working through of the "Johannine Community Hypothesis" see R.A.Brown, *The Community of the Beloved Disciple* (London: Geoffrey Chapman, 1979); see also O.Cullmann, *The Johannine Circle* (London: SCM, 1976); R.A.Culpepper, *The Johannine School*, (SBL 26, Missoula: Scholars Press, 1975).

[19] Note that more recently Richard Bauckham has criticised this view, arguing that all the Gospels were written for the whole Christian Community. Cf. R.Bauckham, *The Gospel for All Christians :Rethinking the Gospel Audiences* (Edinburgh: T & T Clark, 1998). Bauckham has indeed succeeding in making many "rethink", though he has yet to arrive at a convincing theory to explain the distinctiveness of the Fourth Gospel.

[20] W.A.Meeks, "The Man from Heaven in Johannine Sectarianism" in *JBL* 91 (1972), 44-72.

[21] Meeks, *art.cit.*, 68. Bruce Malina takes a similar view. He sees the language of John as having a degree of artificiality, with new words devised for familiar concepts, and new meanings given for familiar metaphors. It is an "anti-language" devised for an anti-social group. Cf. B.J.Malina, *The Gospel of John in Sociolinguistic Perspective* (California: Berkeley, 1985).

[22] Craig Koester, *Symbolism in the Fourth Gospel: Meaning, Mystery and Community* (Minneapolis: Fortress Press, 1995)

[23] It is just possible that πιστευσητε "that you might believe" could be understood as πιστ ε ητε "that you might continue to believe", I.e. a statement addressed to Christians; but most mss. and translators take it in its former sense.

[24] See for example, W.Carter, *John and Ephesus: Initial Exploration* (New York: T & T Clark, 2008); also W.Salier, "Jesus, the Emperor and the Gospel of John" in ed. J.Lierman, *Challenging Perspectives on the Gospel of John*, (Tubingen: Mohr Siebeck, 2006), 284-301.

5

THE PREACHER'S AUDIENCE

PREACHING TO PEOPLE WHERE THEY ARE

As a Governor of a local school I am only too aware how often the word "targets" appears in educational discussion. Modern educationalists are target-orientated almost to the point of obsession. The modern preacher will have definite aims and objectives in everything he does, but will use the word "target" in a slightly different sense. For the preacher the targets are the recipients of his message. The sermon is not a treatise delivered in a vacuum, but is a message from a real person to real people. And the nature of the preachers' targets will play a big part in deciding the shape of the message.

We ended the previous chapter by suggesting that the situation of our listeners will largely determine which questions to ask of the Bible text we are using. To a degree it will also determine the answers we give. Given the importance of this, therefore, we must look in general terms at least at what the setting of our congregations is likely to be. It will of course

179

vary from congregation to congregation, but there is enough common ground to make the investigation worthwhile.

In his book *Preaching to a Postmodern World*, Graham Johnston entitles his opening chapter "Toto, we're not in Kansas any more", quoting Dorothy's famous line from *Wizard of Oz*[1]. On arrival in the Land of Oz, Dorothy realises immediately that it is not the safe, predictable and familiar world in which she grew up. She is going to have to adjust to new people, new ways and new demands if she is to survive in the new circumstances into which fate has delivered her.

This illustration points to the equally obvious truth that the world in which we preach today is not the world of the Bible. We are removed from that world by two millennia of time, but also by many changed languages, ideas and customs. This poses an immediate problem for us as preachers, for we cannot assume that our twenty-first century listeners will have any significant grasp of the conceptual background of the truths we seek to preach. The Cross of Jesus for example gains much of its theological significance from being located against the background of the Jewish sacrificial system, a system alien to sophisticated western society. Without giving his hearers some understanding of that system, the preacher will have great difficulty in getting them to grasp the truth of atonement, and its significance for them.

That particular example could be repeated several times over. Concepts such as "sacrifice", common enough in the Biblical world, are in many ways alien to our contemporary society.

Johnston wishes to go further still, of course. He points us to the equally obvious truth that our modern world is in flux, that ideas and concepts taken as axiomatic a generation ago are now in danger of becoming unfashionable and expendable. He very capably describes how the Modernism that grew out of the Enlightenment, dominated by scientific rationalism, has given way to something called *"Post*modernism", dominated by the desire of people disillusioned by the dryness of modernism to seek out answers for themselves. We would add that there are signs that even postmodernism may, in some instances, have run its course and be in danger of being itself superseded.

All this is by way of saying that the "target" at which the preacher aims - his listener - is essentially a moving target. Through the media he or she is constantly being exposed to new ideas and new ways of thinking. Keeping abreast of the conceptual currents that are shaping his listeners' thinking may at times feel like attempting to run up a down escalator, and yet it is something he must continually be doing.

What we have said already might seem to present the preacher with a Herculean task, that of making a book written in an ancient, largely alien culture relevant to listeners in a unstable and constantly shifting modern culture. Before rushing to the conclusion that this is indeed an impossible task, it might be as well to note one or two things that reduce the difficulty of the task slightly.

The first point is the recognition that, whilst there are many points of discontinuity with the Biblical world and ours, there are many points of continuity also. The two worlds are not *totally* different. A preacher might wish to present a discourse on God as Father for example. He will point to the twin foci of fatherhood in the Ancient World as being *loving care* and *discipline*. He will suggest that a father's loving care will be shaped by what is best for the child, and may well quote Jesus as saying, "Which of you fathers, if his son asks for a fish will give him a serpent ?"[2]. He will go on to point out something that the Israelites sometimes forgot, that a father is responsible for discipline also, and will be expected to pull his children up short when they set off on wrong paths. The listeners' personal experience of fatherhood will of course vary from person to person, but all these ideas will ring bells with them very clearly.

Nationalism, perhaps one of the strongest forces in our modern world, responsible for many atrocities and for great bloodshed, is a concept firmly embedded in the biblical tradition. When the Jews themselves were beguiled by nationalistic desires all entered into political alliances with other nations, they placed themselves in conflict with God. Their desire to be like other nations, to have a king and all the associated political institutions, constantly moved them away from the centre of God's purposes for them. It led them to disaster and occupation by a succession of foreign armies, culminating in the Romans in the time of Jesus. As many commentators have noted, nationalistic currents flow through the social climate of the Gospels. To what extent they shaped the Gospel material itself is hotly debated of course, but without some understanding of First Century Jewish nationalism it is impossible to appreciate fully what is going on in the ministry of Jesus. But then this is good, because it presents another promising link between the world of the Bible and ours.

On a lighter note, we suggest that, whilst the tax collectors of Jesus' day operated in ways different from today, they evoke the same basic emotion as when we view our own tax assessments today. The unpopularity of tax collectors is very close to being a universal truth !

The next point of encouragement to note is that the process of *crossing cultural and philosophical barriers* can be observed within the pages of the New Testament itself. Migration was a constant feature of the Ancient World. Particularly on the Eurasian land mass, whole peoples were constantly on the move. As they moved they took with them their language, cultures and gods, often blending them with the cultural and religious phenomena they discovered in their new place of settlement. The whole history of a region such as Anatolia (Turkey) a recognised land bridge between Europe and Asia, is a history of migration and resettlement. If the implications of these population movements are drawn to their logical conclusion, it could be argued that in many, if not most, regions there is no such thing as a truly indigenous population and culture. Virtually everything in a local culture, if we press back far enough, probably came from somewhere else. It means also that no local culture will be a pure culture, but will be a blend or amalgam of originally separate elements.

Take Palestine, the Land of Jesus, as an example. The ancestors of Jesus' Jewish contemporaries migrated there under Moses and Joshua. When they arrived we are told the land was already occupied, so that settlement in the land inevitably involved a degree of cultural compromise. After the collapse of the two kingdoms, the people and the land came under a series of conquests by foreign armies - the Babylonians, the Persians, the Greeks, and finally the Romans. Each left their mark culturally and made their contribution to what became known eventually as "Palestinian Judaism".

The most notable of these contributions was of course that made by the Greeks. Hellenism, aggressively sponsored by Alexander and forced onto local populations everywhere within his empire, became the most significant cultural feature of the period. In some areas it was not imposed without resistance, such resistance being one of the major factors that led to the Maccabean Revolt. In spite of such resistance the Hellenizing movement was so successful that old, simplistic distinctions between "Palestinian Judaism" and "Hellenistic Judaism" have had to be abandoned, and recognition made to the reality that Judaism in Palestine was thoroughly Hellenised by the time of Jesus. Hengel, in his short but perceptive study argues that "Hellenism" should no constitute any meaningful differentiation in terms of the history of religions within the history of earliest Christianity.[3] In spite of this it may still be possible to trace streams of tradition that stem from Hellenistic and pre-Hellenistic times.

In addition the various attempts to blend together the various cultural layers of Palestine spawned a whole series of fringe Jewish movements, such as that which plagued the Church at Colossae, as well as the much-debated and highly complex movement referred to as "Gnosticism". The latter is commonly regarded as the ultimate end of the process of the hellenization of Judaism highlighted by Hengel.

The genius of Paul, and his major contribution to New Testament Theology, was his ability to cross cultural barriers and interpret the Gospel of Jesus Christ to new people in new situations. In Athens he begins where his philosophically minded hearers are and goes on to the declaration of Judgement and Resurrection; in writing to Phrygian Colossae he gives the most wonderful portrait of the exalted Christ (Col.1.15-20); in writing to Anatolian/Greek Ephesus he declares Christ's superiority to all powers (Eph.1.20-22).

This is a rather long-winded way of saying that the process of relating Bible truth to changing culture is not a new one. It is as old as the Bible itself. We have been seriously misled in the past by suggestions that the Biblical world was uniform and static. Rather it was diverse and constantly in a state of flux. The task of the preacher is to identify such "fixed points" as there are and move from there to the new, less familiar territory.

Today's Cultural Barriers

What features of our modern culture threaten to isolate us from the world of the Bible and thereby pose problems for the preacher ? Again, we do not pretend to have produced a exhaustive list, but we may without too much difficulty identify a few.

The Enlightment, with its emphasis on scientific rationalism as the basis of understanding the world, had a great influence on proponents of the Christian religion. As the pace of scientific discovery increased, so the conviction grew that science was the key to everything, and that scientific truth was the only reliable kind of truth. The notion of "spiritual" truth was similarly sent into retreat, and emphasis placed increasingly on the material realm as the basis of reality. The Church found itself under attack from science, from rationalism, from "Darwinism" and the new realisation that Christianity was far from unique within the range of world religions and philosophies.

These various attacks spawned a whole series of defenders of Christianity. Christian apologists responded by engaging with science and rationalism, in the worthy attempt to show that the Christian Faith was in fact reasonable, and based on reliable evidence, whilst people such as Gore tried to blend the new philosophies with traditional Christianity. Essentially however they were "playing the game", and defending Christianity, not on its own terms, but on the terms dictated by their opponents. From the post-Enlightment conflict was born, for example, *The Modern Churchman's Union* in 1898, with its slogan, "Liberal Theology in a Changing World". Its role was to demonstrate that the Christian Faith was intellectually respectable to people caught up in the scientific revolution. But these demonstrations, though well-intentioned, were not without cost. Often the Christian Faith would be stripped of its supernatural trappings, miracles being deemed problematical to the modern mind. The most famous instance of this is of course the famous (or infamous) *Honest to God*, published by Bishop Robinson in 1963. To this extent Robinson and others were following in the footsteps of Gore, but like Gore they found themselves giving licence to those who would take their speculations much further than they intended, spawning such children as Hick's *The Myth of God Incarnate* and Dom Cupitt's *Sea of Faith* amongst others.

There will be people in our congregations therefore who have been brought up in and affected by this general atmosphere of scepticism. They will want to be assured therefore that the preacher knows his stuff, that he has been well trained, and is able to present evidence for statements that he makes about God. This is not to resort to "playing the game", as mentioned above, but is simply aimed to reassure the listener that the preacher's work is securely founded on knowledge and understanding.

Postmodernism

Some readers might argue that the previous section was unnecessary and irrelevant. They would graciously point out that we have moved beyond modernism into a *post*-modern era. In general terms they would be correct: there are many indications that scientific modernism has had its heyday, and that people have moved on.[4] Yet it is worth mentioning, since, in any given congregation there will be those who have not moved on with everybody else. In some cases they may lag well behind in embracing the latest trends in philosophy, science and theology, while in other cases they may be well ahead. Keeping ourselves up to speed with the latest trends is fine, but is no substitute for knowing the thinking of the individuals in our congregations. People simply may not be where the generalizations of the learned journals say they should be.

Proponents of postmodernism do have a point when they suggest that the earlier optimism that scientific progress would solve all the world's problems and give us a complete understanding of the world around us has dissipated somewhat. University after university confesses to be having difficulty filling up places on pure science courses. That

186

could of course be for many reasons; but it inevitably gives an indication that young people today are not exactly filled with wild enthusiasm by the prospects of what scientific progress offers. Disciplines like medicine and medical research tend to be exceptions to this, for pretty obvious reasons.

What is now referred to as postmodernism is difficult to define. It is somewhat amorphous, and tends to mean different things to different people. The average person doesn't have any idea what that means. All he knows is he's pretty much free to think and do whatever he wants. That's how postmodernism filters down to the guy in the pew. It's not a philosophy—it's a lifestyle. The above-mentioned average person just knows that the culture doesn't care what he does. The movies he sees don't make a moral judgment on anything except racism or somebody's intolerance. So he's free to do whatever he wants in the society, and nobody can tell him what to be or what to do, and the bottom line is that he should feel good about himself. That's what filters down. But all this goes completely against the grain of his conscience and his reason, and ultimately what he knows to be true. The unbeliever's conscience is a reality, and even reason tells him that there have to be some absolutes.

It is probably better to speak of a "postmodern age" with certain definable characteristics. These characteristics include **the rejection of the concept of a world view**, by which is meant a single principle that overarches everything. This inevitably involves the theistic view of the world espoused by the big, world religions, and even by modernism itself, which presented science as the single key to everything. In addition there has been **a rejection of the concept objective truth and a suspicion of authority.** In the postmodern world nothing is universally true, and all truth is relative. "It works for me" is the slogan so often heard. The notion of objective truth is regarded as an illusion, since truth cannot be divorced from our perception of truth, and that perception is the product of a sometimes long interpretative processes that involves our mind, emotions and will. The logical application of this is that one person's truth is as good as another's. This may well mean that the postmodern person is not inevitably hostile to Christian Truth. It sees it as true for those who follow the Faith. But as a universal truth it has no greater claim than any other philosophy or religion.

People will not settle for being told what to do, nor what is true. They want to think for themselves and participate in the discovery of what is true. We have already noted this as a valuable insight latched onto by the proponents of the New Homiletic, and been forced to concede that traditional expository preachers have tended to be over prescriptive and not allowed people that independence of thought.

Statements made by authoritative figures of all kinds are therefore regarded with suspicion since such statements are assumed to be clothed with the interpretative garment of the authority figure. It will not be too difficult for people to point to the interpretative framework within which authoritative biblical statements are made. The preacher will have to take careful account of this framework when presenting "Bible Truth", and beware of insensitively making authoritative statements. Saying that something is true simply because the Bible says it is true will not be sufficient for the postmodern person. "Jesus loves me this I know *for the Bible tells me so*" will be greatly reassuring for some, but will cut no ice with others.

Another characteristic of the postmodern age is the questioning of consensus statements about history. How many times do we see books or television programmes entitled "What really happened at...... ?". Nothing is accepted at face value - which may be no bad thing.

Johnston gives the helpful illustration of Christopher Columbus at this point.[5]

> All of us will have been brought up on the notion of Columbus as a courageous explorer and great liberator. Even though it became common knowledge that indigenous peoples lived there when Columbus arrived, he was nevertheless credited with opening up a new world.   More recent studies, especially by the native peoples themselves, see Columbus more as a villain, triggering off the exploitation and rape of a true paradise.   One moment's thought will bring us the realisation that America was not discovered by Columbus or anybody. It had always been there, with its peoples and its rich culture long before he arrived.   It is simply that we have been conditioned by our assumptions to see Columbus' exploits from a Western point of view only.

Another characteristic of this approach is **the blurring of morality into expediency.**   The removal of the notion of objective truth in general, when applied to the field of morals, has had the effect of reducing the latter to pragmatism. The first product of the process is the notion that no-one has the right to condemn anyone else, and comes perilously close to saying that no-one has the right to exert authority in the field of morals on anyone else.   Even the Law itself, which does have that right, finds its boundaries being pushed further and further back.   We find ourselves living in a society with fewer and fewer moral taboos and restraints.

The factors that have brought about this situation are not difficult to identify.   Roy Jenkins, one-time Home Secretary famously declared, "the permissive society is the compassionate society".   It is not enough for example to punish people for taking drugs.   One must at the same time seek to show compassion and minimise the suffering involved in their drug habit.   Drug takers needed helping, not simply punishing. Nothing that anyone could object to in that. The problem was that this led to a steady process of decriminalising an increasing number of behaviours, not just in the field of drugs, but in many other areas as well, in the name of compassion. We might add that it is a thoroughly Christian impulse to care for the person concerned, whilst disapproving of and seeking to change their behaviour.

The main difficulty is that the process worked too well. In almost every case, liberalisation of laws related to particular forms of behaviour led to an increase in that behaviour. The 1967 Abortion Act is of course a classic example. No-one, certainly not this writer, would want to go back to the situation that prevailed prior to 1967, but it has to be acknowledged that a change in the law designed to prevent a relatively small abuse, has led to an open situation, with abortions for purely non-medical social reasons multiplying. When one has said everything about those trapped with unwanted pregnancies, that fact remains. It is a genuine dilemma, and it is not easy to know what the answer is, how to care for people caught up in behaviours (such as homosexuality) that the Bible seems to regard as wrong, without lapsing into moral relativism and expediency such as that which seems to characterised our postmodern society of today.

Whenever and however precisely the postmodern age began, without doubt the dominating factor is **the media**, and television in particular. If the written word could be said to have dominated post-Enlightenment modernism, then TV shapes the postmodern age. Whilst books, now on supermarket shelves, continue to sell in encouraging numbers, in the thinking of many we are in a visual rather than literary society. The all-powerful visual image as seen on TV dominates and shapes our thinking to a tremendous degree. "Yes, it's true, I saw it on the telly" presents the media almost as the new standard of truth. Actually appearing on TV, even if only for a few seconds, becomes the ultimate ambition.

The quality of TV varies enormously. The advent of satellite broadcasting and digitalization have greatly increased the *quantity* of television output, but without necessarily producing a corresponding increase in *quality*. Some programmes still seek to inform people, and stimulate them to think, whilst others unashamedly seek the lowest common denominator, and present only entertainment. So-called "Reality Television" programmes, cheap to make, make voyeurs of us all, intruding into the tiniest nooks and crannies of human life. The combination of television and the computer mean that in television we not only have a new standard of truth, but a new fantasy world in which we can live vicariously. This hi-tech combination threatens to blur the whole distinction between reality and fantasy. As one commentator puts it:

> Film and video can now render the wildest fantasies and make them seem realistic. Real events, by the same token, are fictionalized. It's little wonder that the TV generation has a hard time distinguishing between truth and fiction.[6]

This of course is not all bad news for the preacher. It means he will preach to people more open to ideas of what is possible, less dismissive to the claims of the supernatural in the Bible. The success of programmes such as the X-Files indicates the willingness of people to consider the existence of something beyond the here and now.

There again, television has built-in limitations. The need to constantly change the visual image means that sometimes arguments and thoughts cannot be developed as well as they ought. And then there are the all important ratings, things that dominate a director's work and on which his or her livelihood will ultimately depend. The pressure to sacrifice integrity in the interests of what makes "good television" and will therefore pull in the viewers (and push those ratings up) is a constantly pressure on that director.

One factor that has always been there but has come to the fore in recent postmodern times is **the search for community**. Many of our contemporary listeners will have suffered from the breakdown of traditional patterns of community life, especially those based on the family. Some will themselves, or have seen their parents go through divorce, will all its implications for the children.

Once again television is seen as the villain of the piece. One of the negative implications of the growth of television is that people can become isolated. It is not necessary to go out to view the outside world - through television the outside world, or an alternative virtual world, is brought into the home. People can go through a full range of experiences vicariously on the television screen. Through television they can even walk on the moon. The cinema, theatre or concert hall become irrelevances to the average person since all the entertainment they provide is brought into our home. Even the traditional "take away", involving curry, pizza, fish and chips, is transfigured into "delivered to your home".

It becomes increasingly difficult therefore for churches to tempt people out of their homes, especially on dark winter's evenings to come together to worship and learn about God. Interestingly enough, this is not just a problem for churches. The traditional British pub, for so long the Church's main rival, especially in reaching men, is under great pressure from falling numbers. A steady stream of pubs close down every week. Increasingly pubs have to diversify, by including food and entertainment, in order to draw people from their homes. The tremendous range of alcoholic drinks now available in supermarkets means that people will no longer go out "simply for a drink". Cinemas and theatres have experienced similar crises, and have responded positively by increasing the quality of the product and the diversity of the environment in which it is presented. Many other social, participatory clubs and societies continue to struggle for members.

Yet it remains true that community is a basic need, and in our postmodern age is as strong as ever. When an important soccer match is being shown live on Sky TV in the local pub, men put on their team shirts and stream down to the pub, infinitely preferring to watch it with their mates rather than sitting at home with a wife or partner who may have little interest in football. And community is something the Church can, and always has been able to provide. For the Church *is* community, community in Christ. Postmodern man asks the Church to present community in an attractive, contemporary way that meets his or her needs. In this way, as in many other ways, postmodernism becomes a friend as well as an enemy of a Church seeking to present the ageless Gospel of Christ in the contemporary age.

Postmodernism therefore, as well as presenting a stiff challenge to the Church by questioning its absolute, historical values, also presents new opportunities by means of a greater openness. In a visual age for example the challenge is to use a greater variety of visual symbols, from the world of art or music. It is a challenge to respond to, not run away from. It is a call not to do entirely new things (that we may or may not be good at), but to traditional things better and in more imaginative ways.

We suggested earlier that one of the things that characterised traditional Anglican preaching was its cerebral nature. However, proponents of postmodernism suggest that many people today **function on a non-cerebral level.** This is a million miles away from saying that they are dullards, or "thick", but is simply pointing to the fact that people are a complex combination of mind, emotions and will. More often than we would care to admit we operate at feelings level, rarely thinking about what we do at all. In practice we will do the right thing, not when we are convinced intellectually that it is right, but when we come to *feel* it is right. One of our major tasks as preachers is precisely to bring about a unity of mind, emotions and will in our listeners. We cannot assume that, because we present a convincing argument from the pulpit, people will be convinced and will change their behaviour. And of course as preachers we understand there is the spiritual dimension also. Paul reminds us that Christian Truth is *"spiritually* discerned" (1 Cor.2.14). The preacher's task is "interpreting spiritual truth to those who are spiritual" (1 Cor.2.13).

Nominalism or formalism is a problem as old as the Old Testament itself. "These people honour me with their mouths, but their hearts are far from me" (Is.29.13) describes people who are very adept at saying and singing the right things, but who have failed to grasp the inner, spiritual meaning of what they are saying and singing. To some degree this is true of all of us at certain times in our Christian walk, but is a particular problem in a formal, liturgical situation. Whilst by no means exclusive to them, it is particularly the curse of churches whose worship is liturgical in character.

Now I am an Anglican by conviction, and as such I believe in liturgy as the best way of ensuring truly common worship. But I do acknowledge that it is all too easy in an Anglican context (and in a Roman Catholic context too I would imagine) to hide behind the form of words without their meaning fully coming home to us. It is not sheer repetition that is the problem. Repetition can be helpful. It is empty or *vain* repetition Jesus warns us against (Matt.6.7).

The preacher, confronted by formalism, will experience the frustration of preaching to people, often for years, who do and say the right things, but for whom, in spiritual terms, the penny never seems quite to have dropped. And it is nothing incidentally to do with intelligence. These people often will be highly intelligent and knowledgeable, but never quite latched onto the change of heart necessary to bring about true spiritual understanding.

A simplification of the message will not therefore bring about the required result. What is necessary is persistence, and the immersion of one's whole preaching ministry in prayer. When we preach kingdoms are clashing, and the enemy's defences will be destroyed only by prayer.

I well remember a lady, Margaret, in one of my congregations. On the street one day she announced that she was thinking a not coming to church any more because she was "getting nothing out of the services". Now I knew that she had been attending worship not merely in my own church, but in the town where she had previously lived. Her problem was that she had faithfully worshipped for years, but never come into a personal relationship with the God she worshipped. To cut a long story short, she took that step of faith in Jesus and found that all her problems about worship disappeared. The analogy might be reading a novel having personally met the author, or listening to a piece of music having come to know the composer. The difference is beyond words.

Some ground rules for 'targeting' the message

So we are stressing the importance of understanding the intellectual currents that affect our listeners, but we are gently warning against overstressing them and unhelpfully pigeon-holing our congregation. What pointers can we have that will help us ensure our message is as appropriate as possible to those in the pews ?

Listen to our Congregations

In this particular exercise listening comes before speaking. We might dryly comment that if we all did a little more listening before speaking, we would avoid making many of the mistakes that trouble our memories. For the preacher it is an absolutely vital exercise.

The process of preaching begins with the preacher listening to the text on behalf of the community, bringing their eyes and ears with him. He listens to their fears, anxieties and hopes. He listens *with* the congregation in order to listen *for* the congregation, to what God would say to them through his preaching. He listens even as he preaches, for lots of things are being said verbally and non-verbally in that moment.

For the preacher listening means gaining as intimate a knowledge of his congregation that he possibly can. He will want to know where they live, and how their family life is constructed. He will want to know where they work, and whether they are happy or unhappy in their job. He will want to know about their pastimes, for often these play a great part in shaping the lives of our listeners. "Which football team do they support ? How is that team doing ?" he will ask, (remembering that these are questions to be put to the ladies as well as the men !).   He will want to know which clubs or associations they belong to in the local community. More delicately, he will enquire about political loyalities, always remembering the great British privilege of keeping to ourselves how we actually vote.

Having gathered this basic information, the preacher will maintain open channels of communication with his congregation to monitor changes in the data, as well as being aware of extraneous factors that may come in and affect the way they are feeling in their day to day lives.

Andy Capp and Flo are coming out of Church, Andy looking rather glum. "Not uplifted then?", Flo enquires.   "With that bore ?", And snorts. Flo looks sympathetically out at the reader and says, "he never mentioned pigeons, darts or billiards in his sermon once !"

I had that cartoon on my vestry door for years, the last thing I saw before going into Church to begin the service. It was a reminder to me that I had no automatic right to be heard or listened to by the congregation. I had to earn that right, and I did so by showing that I valued the things they valued in their everyday lives. It is all part of affirming them as people, and of *showing* that I cared about them. Once people can see that (and it can take years in some communities to bring it about), then they will listen gladly.

Be flexible and adapt, but without compromising the message

We have had occasion to note earlier that the Gospel was born in a situation of great cultural flux. Within a relatively short time of the death and resurrection of Jesus it was carried into new geographical and cultural territories. It was the ability of Paul and the other missionaries to adapt that enabled the message to survive and grow in the way it did.

This adaptation involved isolating those elements of the Gospel message that were permanent and non-negotiable from those that were non-essential and expendable. The ability to compromise on non-essentials is a necessary requirement of leaving peacefully in any community, especially one with diverse cultures and values. Where people are not able to compromise at all, conflict arises. Because in Britain we have been thought to be living in a predominantly Christian country, compromise for Christians has not been a major problem. The growth of secularization and multiculturalism has caused us to revise that opinion. For Christian groups who are minorities in non-Christian countries, it has always been a problem.

Amongst the non-negotiable truths we would of course include the basic elements of the apostolic κερυγμα, referred to in more detail in an earlier chapter. Without these elements – death, resurrection, future judgement, etc – there simply is no Gospel. The challenge in each generation is to present these truths in new and challenging ways, according to the needs of our particular congregations. Prophets like Ezekiel showed great versatility and imagination in their presentation, but without compromising the essential message.

It is worth saying, however, that there are limits to what adaptation can achieve. The Gospel, because it is ageless, in another sense belongs to no one particular age. There will always be a sense it which it doesn't fit our particular culture, in which it is counter-cultural, and we should accept this. The complexities of our contemporary age therefore, as outlined above, should not cause us to lose confidence in the Ageless Word.

Develop good communication skills

Paul dramatically refers to the "foolishness of what we preach" (1Cor.1.21), and compares it unfavourably with the polished professional style of Greek orators. He reflects that it is the power of the Spirit and not human skill that renders that preaching effective. Many of us have had the strange experience of seeing what we would regard as our less worthy efforts bearing unexpected fruit.

Yet it would be utterly wrong to draw the conclusion from that that the development of good communication skills is unimportant or even unnecessary. Things like audibility, clarity, speed of delivery remain as important as ever.

While these skills are universally important, it is important to develop them particularly in relation to the congregation with which you are working and to which you preach regularly. What switches your congregation on will not be the same as that which switches on the neighbouring congregation. Learning this will involve developing the listening skills referred to above, as well as carefully monitoring the response (or lack of it) to the preaching each week. At the end of the day preaching is a very personal business, and the most effective preaching will come from a preacher who knows his congregation well, and who in turn know him well.

I remember well listening to a drama critic, speaking at the Greater Manchester Drama Federation Awards Dinner some years ago. He made the memorable point, in a drama context, that there was no such thing as a bad audience. If a specific audience on a particular night is not responding to the jokes as well as the audience the night before, it is not *their* fault. It is not because they are slow or thick. It is because those operating on stage have not yet found the key to unlocking their particular emotional responses in the way they did the previous evening.

It is a point well made. One of my personal strong dislikes is a comedian who scolds his audience for not laughing at his jokes, instead of searching for the right way in for that particular audience. He imagines that scolding them will cover up his own inadequacies. A preacher must at all costs avoid falling into this trap, and must avoid all expressions of disapproval. It will not endear his congregation to him one little bit, and will certainly not make them any more receptive to his message. The problem is probably in him anyway. An apparently unresponsive congregation is a challenge to be faced, a problem to be solved. It will be solved only by patience, imagination and sensitivity on the part of the preacher.

Accept a relatively low level of Biblical knowledge on the part of the congregation

A sad feature of modern life is that people will in general have a much lower level of basic Biblical knowledge than would have been the case just one or two generations ago. Most will have a basic understanding of the difference between Old and New Testaments; most will know the more familiar Bible stories, though they may have difficulty in locating them

199

within the Bible's own time-line; they will have some grasp of the main facts of the life of Jesus. But there will be many gaps, gaps the preacher will be challenged to fill in.

This has obvious implications for the preaching of the Old Testament, and is a part explanation of why many preachers avoid it. So much time has to spent in filling in the historical background that there is scarcely enough time left for practical application (though the skilful preacher will combine explanation and application as he goes along).

There is a strong argument for saying that a good starting point with many congregations is, instead of ranging far and wide over the full spectrum of Biblical narrative material, to build up a central stock of representative Bible stories, chosen from both Old and New Testaments, that will, over a relatively short space of time, give the congregation a good basic grasp of the Bible's message and its application. This will enable the congregation to give what David Wilkinson, Principal of St. John's College, Durham calls "the nod of recognition" to the material when it is introduced by the preacher. Over time this builds confidence and strengthens the bond between preacher and congregation.

What the preacher must constantly guard against is the making of casual assumptions about his or her congregation. Care must not be taken to assume the congregation knows things they don't in fact know. At the same time the preacher mustn't assume that the reason they are not in possession of certain facts is that they are half-wits and fail to measure to his standards. "Talking down to the congregation" is one of the great pulpit taboos. Filling in the gaps in people's knowledge and understanding without being patronising is one of the most important of the communication skills referred to above, a skill that all good preachers possess. The maxim

Never *over*estimate your congregation's knowledge, but never underestimate their intelligence remains a good one for all preachers to remember.

Going back to chapter one, almost the first comment made referred to a concern amongst many senior clergymen today concerning the standard of contemporary preaching. One of the factors not listed in that opening chapter, left out for fear of alienating readers right at the outset, is a lack of knowledge of the Bible on the part of *preachers* themselves. I am extremely reluctant to criticize theological colleges and seminaries, most of whom do sterling work in training clergy. But observation tells me that the courses are so crammed with the wide-ranging skills needed in ministry today that often basic Bible knowledge is squeezed out or minimalized. In response they might argue that a minimum level of knowledge of the contents of the Bible should be presumed before training starts. It is an interesting debate, and I am keen to sympathise with the task of the colleges. But I think it would well nigh impossible for them to defend the proposition that contemporary ordinands do not have as firm a grip of the Bible and its message as would have been the case a generation ago. I think that the non-residential courses, with the additional demands of time on their students, would have an even harder time fending off the above accusation.

I am not speaking here of hermeneutics and principles of interpretation. The extent to which parish priest's will be able to take on board and apply the various approaches illustrated in the previous chapter will vary according to his ability and time. What I am talking about is a basic working knowledge of the *contents* of the Bible. That working knowledge means being able to move beyond "it says somewhere in the Bible" to having the ability to turn to specific parts of the Bible to find texts and passages that relate to specific matters under discussion. It goes without saying that no-one can be an effective expository preacher without a solid, working knowledge of the Bible.

Don't confuse Authority with Dogmatism

We have already noted how postmodern people have an inbred suspicion of authority. So the preacher who is dogmatic about everything and will tolerate no alternative viewpoints will pretty soon find himself in hot water. Of course, as we have argued, the sermon is an authoritative discourse, its authority stemming from the Word of God being preached rather than the person preaching it. It follows then that the preacher's authority relates to his statement of biblical truth, and does not stretch to his personal opinions on extraneous matters. I may have a good grasp of the prophetic message about social justice for example, and may be effective in communicating this message to my congregation; but that doesn't entitle me to tell them how to vote at a General Election. That is not within my sphere of authority. I may state my opinion from time to time; but it will be no more than that – my opinion.

Then again, some aspects of the Gospel stand out more plainly in the Bible than others. The apostolic κηρυγμα, with its insistence on the central importance of the death and physical resurrection of Jesus are (to the majority of preachers) beyond dispute. But on other matters such as the Ordination of Women, there are different discernable approaches based on the teaching of the Bible. The wise preacher will not be slow to express his own view of course; but it will be his own view, and honesty will compel him to acknowledge other approaches and other views.

The clearest example of all is the problem of suffering and evil, a problem that has troubled thinkers from the dawn of biblical time down to the present day. How can a good, omnipotent God allow suffering on the scale we see it today ? All those involved in pastoral ministry are constantly struggling with this. There are of course positive things we can and do say in the light of this problem, but any preacher bold enough to claim to have found the answer will soon be humbled by experience. The honest and best way is to encourage our congregations to hold onto the things they can hold onto, whilst acknowledging the struggle we are all involved in this particular area.

Many of us will remember our early mathematics lessons when we were urged by the teacher to "show your working". When we are led to make statements authoritative it is no bad thing the share with our congregations the thought processes that have led us to the conclusion they have. It is a way of enabling them, and helping not simply to believe in, but to articulate Christian truth. Faith is of course much more than "process", but the process itself has an important part to play in Christian teaching.

Present your message boldly, but sensitively

One of the key points in the Johannine Passion Narrative is the point where, in reply to Jesus' claim to have come "to bear witness to the truth", Pilate dismissively asks "what is truth ?" (John 18.37,38). Many commentators have noted how this ends Pilate's discussion with Jesus, and that he does not wait around to debate the issue. In an age where there is a suspicion towards anyone who claims to speak of *the* Truth and argues that a true understanding of reality is whatever each individual makes of it, the preacher still has the task of proclaiming the uniqueness of Christ and the inadequacy of all pluralistic understandings of the world.

It is a task, as we have noted, that Paul did not shrink from. It was in the context of those great, cosmopolitan homes of pluralism, Ephesus and Colossae, that he gives us his most sublime statements about the supremacy of Christ to all powers and authorities, and of the inadequacy and redundancy of all other claimants to truth.

It is interesting to note how Paul approaches this task. He rarely targets opponents directly. That the identity of his opponents at Colossae have remained a mystery for so long stems from the fact that Paul does not identify them directly or attack them directly. He contents himself with drawing his wonderful portrait of Jesus in Col.1.15-20, as the one in whom "all things hold together", and in whom "all the fullness of God was pleased to dwell". He leaves his readers to draw their own conclusions about the inadequacies of all other approaches to the truth. The more his readers eyes are focussed on Christ, the more easily they will come to understand the truth about God without him having to spell it out for them.

The wise preacher will follow in the steps of Paul. Sadly, we find all too many occupants of our pulpits who seem to gain a perverse delight in denouncing and condemning what they perceive as diversions from the truth as they see it. One can all too easily see this as meeting a constant psychological need for self-affirmation on the part of the preacher. Such denunciations will often sound impressive to the congregation, who at a superficial level are impressed by the preacher's erudition and learning. It can so often, however, push the sermon into the realm of polemics, and actually make the congregation less amenable to the word that God wants to speak to them. Sometimes it can actually backfire on the preacher calamitously, as for example when he gets his facts wrong, or when the view he is attacking is seen by the congregation as an obvious Aunt Sally of the preacher's own construction. A patently unfair attack on someone else's viewpoint will actually create sympathy for that viewpoint and lead to entrenchment rather than capitulation.

Where a direct attack from the pulpit on someone else's stance *is* required (and that will be less often than one might suppose) it should always be done sensitively, and out of a very obvious desire on the part of the preacher to promote the best interests of his listeners. At this point pastor and preacher will be one and the same. What the preacher must never lose sight of is that people and their beliefs cannot be separated. In attacking somebody's beliefs or practices, the preacher can so easily be see as attacking the person himself. Of course, the preacher will plead, "No, I am not doing that; I am abstracting the belief/practice without attacking the individual". Unfortunately nine times out of ten that is not how it will be perceived. Someone finding their sincerely held views attacked from the pulpit can be inflicted with wounds that are extremely difficult to heal. As someone once said to me , "there has been more trouble caused in churches by the attempt at 'speaking the truth in love' than anything else."

It goes without saying that the greatest sensitivity of all will be required when dealing with modern issues such as homosexuality, divorce, abortion, or the many other personal issues that cause so much contemporary debate. The spirit of the contemporary age is inclusion, and the preacher who aims to isolate people on grounds of their beliefs and practices will find himself under great pressure, and even hostility. More importantly still, some of the positions he is tempted to attack may be represented, unknown to him, by people among his listeners. When going on the attack, the greatest possible caution is advised. The ill-considered word and the slightest hint of a judgemental approach can irretrievably scar the lives of listeners, and make the preacher's subsequent pastoral task extremely difficult.

This is not of course to say that controversial matters should not be tackled from the pulpit. On the contrary, the truth of the Gospel should be proclaimed in all its fullness if our congregations are to grow, and related to the lives they actually live, day by day. To use Lowry's terminology, a preacher who studiously avoids every issue that is delicate or sensitive and constantly plays safe may well be thought to be "scratching" where people are not "itching". It is a tough world out there, a world in which people often get hurt, and our congregations are thoroughly immersed in it. They need to know that they can be sure of guidance and help from their parish priest.

What we are saying however is that our primary task as preachers is always to lift up Jesus, that He may draw others to Himself, and that all our preaching, especially in controversial areas, must be shaped by a sensitive and caring pastoral heart. As He Himself said, "I, when I am lifted up will draw all men to myself" (John 12.32). Our task as preachers is to do the work of lifting up, that He may do the drawing.

CHAPTER FIVE
ENDNOTES

[1] G.Johnston, *Preaching to a Postmodern World: A Guide to Reaching Twenty-First Century Listeners* (Leicester: Inter Varsity Press, 2001), 13.

[2] Luke 11.11.

[3] M.Hengel, *The Hellenization of Judaea in the First Century after Christ* (London: SCM, 1989), 53.

[4] cf. S.Marsh, *Christianity in a Post-Atheistic Age* (London: SPCK, 2002)

[5] Johnston, *Preaching*, 32.

[6] G.E.Veith, Jr., *Postmodern Times: A Christian Guide to Contemporary Thought and Culture,* (Wheaton: Crossway, 1994), 81-2.

6

THE PREACHER'S SETTING

WORSHIP AS THE CONTEXT OF PREACHING

Preaching does not take place in isolation. People do not turn up to Church each Sunday just to hear a sermon. They expect other things to happen as well. They expect to sing; they expect to pray; they expect to receive bread and wine in communion; and they expect to participate in expressions of fellowship with their fellow Christians. They expect to listen to and receive God's Word in the sermon, but not to the exclusion of any of these other elements. The delivery of the sermon has to be placed within the context of worship, and has to bear a creative relationship to all its basic elements. Precisely what this relationship is will be the subject of our discussion in this chapter.

Worship and Word in the Life of Israel

The link with what we might style the "ministry" of the Word, that is the reading and explanation of the Word, and worship runs right through the life of Israel as depicted in the Old Testament. We may trace it from the dramatic events surrounding the renewal of the Covenant reported in Exodus. The pattern we see is of Moses receiving the Word of the Lord, passing it on with explanation to the people, and the people making a concerted (liturgical) response. So in 19.6 Moses is told "these are the words you are to speak to the Israelites". In v.7 Moses goes and "sets before the people" those same words, and in v.8 the people, having been informed of the practical implications of the words, respond by saying "we will do everything the Lord has said".

The pattern is repeated in chapter 24, except that in this case the people are responding to the whole Law, as delivered to Moses in chapters 20-23. Their response to the Word is cemented by the building of an altar the next morning, and the erection of the 12 pillars, the latter representing the fact that the response of obedience is being made by the whole people of Israel, the whole 12 tribes. In the course of the consequent sacrifice on that altar first the altar and then the people are sprinkled with the blood. The sprinkling of the people takes place in the context of the reading of the Book of the Covenant (24.8). Thus Covenant renewal and blood are indissolubly linked together, a link made real by the recital, and explanation where necessary, of the covenant demands. The process is tied together with the classic words

> This is the blood of the covenant that the Lord has made
> with you in accordance with all these words.
>
> *Exodus 24.8*

All this is happening in the context of worship - the obvious awe that the dramatic outward signs of Sinai would inspire, as well as the response inspired by the words of God themselves.

The link between Word and Worship is further demonstrated by the close link between priest and prophet in Israel. Traditionally they are thought of as two distinct, if overlapping, roles. The priest is there to supervise the altar and execute the sacrifices made on it, whilst the prophet is there to provide the Word from God. There is in fact a blurring of roles, especially in the early part of the Old Testament. Remarks made to the Tribe of Levi in Deuteronomy 33 include:

> He teaches your precepts to Jacob and your law to Israel;
> He offers incense before you and whole burnt offerings on your altar
>
> *Deuteronomy 33.10*

The Levites are therefore to be *both* prophet *and* priests. Pulpit and altar are not mutually exclusive, but complementary. In his depiction of the failure of the nation's leaders, a failure that has brought them to brink of exile, Jeremiah rounds on both priest and prophet with substantially the same accusation:

> The priests did not ask, "where is the Lord ?".
> *Those who deal with the law* did not know me;
> The leaders rebelled against me,
> The prophets prophesied by Baal, following worthless idols.
>
> *Jeremiah 2.8*

Both priest and prophet have essentially the same task, that of bringing the Word of God to the people.

This dual role of priest-prophet is typified by the work of Samuel. Samuel as a boy is given a word from God, concerning the sons of Eli, a word he passes on only with great reluctance (1 Sam.3.1-18). He continues to give prophetic leadership to the tribes right through the traumatic metamorphosis into nationhood, choosing both Saul and then David as kings. As the writer tells us "Samuel's word came to all Israel" (1

Sam.4.1). He inherits Eli's priestly functions, although his own sons turned out no better than Eli's. At Mizpah Samuel intercedes for the people prior to the recapture of the Ark from the Philistines (1 Sam.7.5), as well as offering sacrifices on behalf of the people (v.9,10). Saul is condemned for his impatience in offering sacrifice without waiting for Samuel, the only one presumably authorised to offer such sacrifice (1 Sam.13.13). Samuel is not typical in that in addition to this role he exercised the role of judge, the secular leader of the tribes (1 Sam.7.15). It appears that Samuel's *de facto* leadership of the tribes (1 Sam.7.6) was based on this ability to exercise the dual role of speaking to the people on God's behalf, as well as speaking to God on behalf of the people.

If we are to make any kind of distinction between prophet and priest, we could say that the prophet brings *new* revelation from God, whilst the priest "deals with the law", that is, he elucidates revelation *already given*. The role of giving divinely-authorised elucidation and interpretation is what puts him closest to the role of the modern preacher.

What is important to note in addition is that the prophet's work was not done in isolation from the worship life of Israel. Whilst there may not be enough evidence to argue conclusively for the prophets as a class of cultic prophets, as earlier Old Testament scholars did, it is not too difficult to show the close link between individual prophets and the various cultic centres in Israel, such as Ramah, Gibeah, Jericho, Gilgal, Bethel and so on. This does not mean they were part of the cults there, but that they exercised their prophetic gifts within a liturgical context.

It has sometimes been argued that prophets like Isaiah, Jeremiah and Amos were so critical of Israel's religious practices that their approaches amounted to a rejection of the cult altogether.

"the multitude of your sacrifices - what are they to me
?" says the Lord, "I have had more than enough of burnt
offerings, of rams and the fat of fattened animals; I have no
pleasure in the blood of bulls and lambs and goats."

Isaiah 1.11

However, it is recognised that what they are speaking about
is not the cult as such, but the abuses of the cult, the religion
that is outward show only, and which does not come from
the heart. "Reasoning together" with the Lord will bring
forgiveness and a new start (v.18,19).

Word and Worship in the Psalms

The Psalms also link together the worlds of prophecy and
worship. Since the classic work of Mowinckel it has been
recognised that the psalms, whilst designed for use in worship,
were in many cases drawn up by a process analogous to
prophet inspiration.[1] In Psalm 21 for example, after rejoicing
in the victories God gives, the psalmist suddenly launches
into what sounds like a prophetic oracle:

> Your hand will lay hold of all your enemies;
> your right hand will seize your foes.
> At the time of your appearing
> you will make them like a fiery furnace.
> In his wrath the Lord will swallow them up,
> and his fire will consume them.
> You will destroy their descendants from the earth,
> their posterity from mankind.
> Though they plot evil against you and devise wicked
> schemes,
> they cannot succeed;
> For you will make them turn their backs
> when you aim at them with drawn bow.

Psalm 21.8-12

Psalm 110, a psalm made so much of in the New Testament, reads almost entirely as something constructed in the style of the prophetic oracle.

The Lord said to my Lord,
"Sit at my right hand until I make your enemies a footstool
for your feet;
The Lord will extend your mighty sceptre from Zion;
you will rule in the midst of your enemies."
Including the classic prophecy
The Lord has sworn and will not change his mind
"You are a priest for ever after the order of Melchizedek."

Later Developments: Ezra and the Synagogue

Later Israelite history sees the locus of worship moving from the ruined Temple to the synagogue. The prototype of synagogue worship is seen in Ezra's reading of the Law to the people as recorded in Nehemiah 8. Although the need for such a reading was dictated by circumstances, and the task of re-identifying the nation in the light of the trauma of Exile, the situation here is highly structured. Ezra stands on a specially constructed wooden platform, built specially for the occasion, flanked by named community leaders (v.4). He opens the book in the sight of the people, and at the sight of this action the people stand up (v.5). When Ezra praises the Lord, the people respond with *words* - "Amen, amen", and with *actions* - lifting their hands and bowing their heads towards the ground (v.6). The whole ceremony has the ring of a liturgical occasion, with principles and practices that must have been in place for some considerable time.

In the worship of the Synagogue, the Early Church has its nearest antecedent. The earliest disciples continued to worship in the synagogue, taking such opportunities the synagogue presented for reading and preaching the Word. At Nazareth we read how Jesus himself accepts the invitation often given to visitors to read from the Scriptures[2]. The normal custom in the Synagogue was to have a reading from the Torah followed by a reading from the Prophets (NABI'IM). The reader stood to read and then sat down to give the explanation and/or interpretation, usually on the Torah passage. Jesus instead speaks on the prophetic reading, from Isaiah 61. We do not know whether this happened to be the set passage, or whether Jesus himself chose it. His elucidation, and even His application of the passage to Himself charms the audience. It is only when some begin to reflect on Jesus' pedigree that dissent creeps in.

The significance of the reading and exposition of the Scriptures in the Synagogue is that it places such exposition within a set liturgical sequence. To be sure that sequence was relatively uncomplicated, but it was firmly fixed nevertheless.

The liturgical sequence had five basic elements:

1. The *Shema*, "Hear, O Israel, the Lord your God is the only Lord". This dramatic opening statement served as a defining statement of what it meant to be an Israelite, and was followed by the command to love God and neighbour.

2. The *Shemoneh Esreh*, the so-called Eighteen Benedictions, a comprehensive prayer cycle.

3. The reading of *Torah*, often (but not always) followed by a reading from *Nebi'im*, the writings of the prophets.

4. The sermon, the explanation and interpretation, usually of the reading from the Torah.

5. The blessing (*berakah*).

After the formal business, informal discussions would often take place in or around the Synagogue.

From time to time surprise is often expressed as to how the Early Church managed to get its act together so quickly and establish a secure base for its organisation, mission and worship. The answer is that he early church did not therefore construct its organisation its worship in a vacuum. It inherited a well established and developed system from the synagogue. It is no coincidence for example that the earliest church leaders were called (πρεσβυτεροι), bishops (επισκοποι) and deacons (διακονοι), all the titles of synagogue officials.

For our purposes it is important to note that the Early Church inherited a fixed tradition by which Word and Worship were very intimately linked, and that the tradition of reading and preaching of the Word with which the Church's earliest leaders were most familiar was transmitted in a liturgical context.

The Interdepence of Word and Worship

The strong connection between the Word of God and worship should come as no surprise. This is because the Word of God is revelatory. God makes Himself known through His Word, His Word revealed in the scriptures, and pre-eminently in His Word Incarnate, Jesus Christ. Without such revelation worship remains superstition. In Athens Paul was impressed by the genuine religious spirit of the Athenians, but saddened that their religion amounted to groping in the dark and was unenlightened by revealed truth.

Worship cannot be real therefore unless it is based on word. It follows therefore that any act of worship, even Christian worship, that does not include at least the reading of the Scriptures, if not exposition, will be deficient to a degree, no matter how well intentioned. Worryingly we do from time to time encounter people in churches, often of the charismatic flavour, who exhibit the tendency to regard worship as being confined to singing and prayer. The reading and teaching of the Word are regarded as supplementary to worship, as optional extras. The biblical tradition does not countenance such an idea.

But if it is true that worship needs the Word, so it is also true that the reading and teaching of the Word necessitates an opportunity for response on the part of both listener *and* preacher. Within the Biblical tradition revelation is always followed by response. To hear and receive a Word *from* God is to receive a revelation *of* God, and the only appropriate response is that of worship.

We may take as a very clear and well-known example the experience of Isaiah in the Temple, as recorded in Isaiah 6.1-9. Whilst involved in a routine visit to the Temple, Isaiah breaks through into the presence of God and receives a new, dynamic vision of Him. He hears the angels crying

Holy, holy, holy is the Lord Almighty, the whole earth is
full of His glory

This dramatic insight into the holiness of God causes Isaiah to fall down in mortal fear, confessing his unworthiness to be in the presence of such a God.

He then receives further revelation, as the angel performs the ritual action of touching his lips with a coal, and he hears

See this has touched your lips; your guilt is taken away and
your guilt atoned for.

Isaiah therefore learns not only about God's holiness but about God's mercy and forgiveness. When the further Word comes therefore

Whom shall I send, and who will go for us ?

Isaiah is able to complete his response of worship with his self-offering

Here I am, send me

So we see in this passage confirmation of the close link between word and worship. The two of necessity go together. The sermon, as we shall see again later, is not an academic lecture, but rather a ministry of the Word of God which seeks to reveal God in a new way to the listeners and thus to bring about a response of worship and service. It is perfectly natural therefore that the delivery of the sermon should end with a prayer, either a liturgical response or (preferably) an *ex tempore* prayer delivered by the preacher and tailored to the subject matter of the sermon. It is to be hoped that this will not be the only worship response to the sermon, but it certainly represents the bare minimum.

In current Church of England practice Common Worship offers the Nicene Creed as an immediate liturgical response to the Word. The Word encourages us to reaffirm both our belief and our standing as Christians through the communal recital of beliefs. Not too far behind is the Peace, which gives us the opportunity to reaffirm one another, in the light of what we have heard from the pulpit.

In attempting to determine the relationship between preaching and liturgy when planning a service, it is as well to avoid two obvious extremes. The first is that the liturgy is so full and so packed out that too little time is left for the sermon. Because the length of the sermon is variable, it can all too easily be squeezed by other things to the point where too little time is left to do the Bible text justice. The opposite extreme is to emphasise the sermon to such an extent that too little time is left for worship, either as a preliminary to the sermon or as

216

a response.   As in so many things, a point of balance has to be reached. But how do we determine this point of balance ? In this section we will suggest one or two ways in which this balance may be achieved.

Approaches to the sermon in worship

There are two major discernable approaches to the place of the sermon in worship, following the main Catholic and Protestant streams.

In general Protestants are anxious to show that preaching is a legitimate enterprise to be placed alongside, but not replace, the sacred ministry of the Church, whilst Roman Catholics are equally determined to demonstrate the sacramental nature of preaching itself and to restore respectability to the Catholic tradition[3]

Both traditions, approaching the matter from opposite ends, come to the conclusion that there is a proper balance between "Word and Table".

Catholic Approaches

Here we include both Anglo- and Roman- Catholic approaches as both giving a high value to the liturgy of the Church.

In spite of what some church histories may from time to time have implied, preaching of one kind or another has always been important in the Roman Catholic Tradition.   Medieval debates would often surround who should be allowed to preach and what they should preach, but the principle of preaching at Mass was not in dispute.

From the ninth century on, the proclamation of the Gospel became one of the functions of the local parish priest. Prior to that monks and other lay people were free to preach.

Preaching became more and more connected with the church, that is the building, and with the Sunday Eucharist, and thus with the responsibilities of the parish clergy. The relatively low level of education and theological knowledge amongst those clergy however, meant that bishops could not leave them to their own devices, but had perforce to prescribe what should be preached or read. The preacher's diet tended to be the homilies of the early (mainly Latin) Church Fathers. The bishops became conscious that alongside the straight readings of the Fathers, a rudimentary catechetical and ethical teaching needed to be given. To make this task easier, the homilies were often translated into the vernacular.

The Council of Mainz (AD 847) spells the new obligation out:

> Every bishop should have homilies containing the necessary admonitions by which their subjects may be taught, i.e. *de fide catholica,* so that they can grasp about the eternal reward of the good and the eternal damnation of the bad, and also of the coming resurrection and the last judgement, and by which works to merit the blessed things, and by which to be excluded. And that someone should publicly study to transfer the same homilies into the rustic Roman language or into the German that all may more easily understand what is being said.

This settled situation was threatened however by the expansion of the monastic abbeys in the tenth and eleventh centuries, leading to constant friction between preachers sponsored by the bishops and those sponsored by the abbots. Monks often preached against the decadence of the clergy, which not surprisingly led to some popes imposing a ban on preaching by monks. Other popes however defended monastic preaching because the monks were supporters of papal reform programmes. But at least homiletically instruction of the people had some degree of regulation and systematization. In principle at least preaching was a priestly function and especially a function of the parish priest.

The growing sophistication of people at the end of the medieval period is reflected in a desire for more adequate, regular preaching. One response to this was the foundation of Preaching Orders, the most notable of which was the Order founded by St. Dominic. Dominic sought to establish a new kind of order, one that would bring the dedication and systematic education of the older monastic orders like the Benedictines to bear on the religious problems of the burgeoning population of cities, but with more organizational flexibility than either monastic orders or the secular clergy. Dominic's new order was to be a preaching order, trained to preach in the vernacular languages but with a sound background in academic theology. Rather than earning their living on vast farms as the monasteries had done, the new friars would survive by begging, "selling" themselves through persuasive preaching.

Dominic established a religious community in Toulouse in 1214, to be governed by the rule of St. Augustine. The founding documents establish that the Order was founded for two purposes -- preaching and the salvation of souls. The organization of this Order of Preachers gained the approval of Pope Honorius III in December 1216.

The Council of Trent, remember chiefly for its systematic response to the new Reformation teachings, also made a significant contribution to the development of preaching within the Church. It roundly condemned the teaching of the Reformists, but agreed with them that the preaching of the Gospel was an urgent necessity for the Church:

> But seeing that the preaching of the Gospel is no less necessary to the Christian commonwealth than the reading thereof; and whereas this is the principal duty of bishops;

the same holy Synod hath resolved and decreed, that all bishops, archbishops, primates, and all other prelates of the churches be bound personally--if they be not lawfully hindered--to preach the holy Gospel of Jesus Christ. But if it should happen that bishops, and the others aforesaid, be hindered by any lawful impediment, they shall be bound, in accordance with the form prescribed by the general Council (of Lateran), to appoint fit persons to discharge wholesomely this office of preaching. But if any one through contempt do not execute this, let him be subjected to rigorous punishment.

On Original Sin. Second Decree, Chapter 2. (1546)

Nevertheless, Trent urged that such preaching should have a catechetical element, to oppose contemporary errors and lay the foundation for the Counter Reformation.

As one writer points out, the sermon was not considered to be really part of the liturgy. It wasn't even in Latin ! The celebrant when preaching was acting in his capacity as teacher, rather than priest, and would often remove his outer garment, the chasuble, to indicate that what he was doing was an *interruption* of the liturgy, and not part of it. The separation of preaching and liturgy had become as complete as can be between two things happening on the same occasion. Indeed, the sermon could be at the end of Mass for the convenience of those with pressing engagements elsewhere !⁴

As Hendrie points out,

> Preaching is one of those areas - perhaps indeed the only one - of which it can be unqualifiedly correct to say "Vatican II" changed all that.⁵

It was recognised that the dynamic of preaching is such that it changes the life of the parish. Hendrie goes as far as to argue that "this is where church happens".

Vatican II made the homily normative, and linked it to the readings. The advent of the new lectionary greatly assisted the process of integrating preaching and liturgy. The Liturgy of the Word was seen to flow into the Liturgy of the Eucharist, so that together they form one act of worship. As with the other liturgical elements, the sermon is seen in a real sense as sacramental. The sermon is viewed not as words *about* Christ, but the Word of Christ Himself. In the preaching of the Word Christ becomes really present in His Church.

> Since it is Christ who speaks when the Holy Scriptures are read in Church, the Scriptures become an effective sign of the presence of Christ, and our speech about God (i.e. the homily) is God's speech to us.[6]

Such an understanding links the Word very closely to the Sacrament, and leads naturally from one to the other. As Schillebeeckx puts it

> What is begun in the Word is perfected in the Sacrament[7]

As Hendrie picturesquely puts it, "the river of preaching in the Catholic Tradition remains unbroken although it has had its meanders."

As was the case in the medieval times, as mentioned above, there is a real desire within the Roman Catholic Church that the river should come to full flood tide, and that the standard of preaching should constantly improve.

One observer comments that the sermons he hears are not that bad, but are not as good as they could be had the preacher been better taught.

> It's like a fiddler who hits all the right notes, but doesn't know how to keep time - because, one suspects, he learned the fiddle from an accordian player.

Taking a more positive view, Bishop Kicanas of Arizona, addressing a conference of Catholic bishops argues that, with a global, concerted effort to improve preaching,

The new springtime for Christianity could burst forth and bloom throughout our church.

It is worth noting that one of the most significant movements in the Church in recent decades, the Liturgical Movement, began in the Roman Catholic Church. Although its origins can be traced to the early part of the 20th Century, its main effects were not felt until after the Second World War. One of its major fruits was a "back to the Scriptures" theme, recognising them as our earliest witnesses to the centre of the Christian Faith, Jesus Christ. This impulse brought about reform of the lectionary, introducing an Old Testament reading and linking Old Testament, Epistle and Gospels together in a single theme. Associated with this was the designation of Sundays in between the main Christian Festivals as "Ordinary Time", offering the possibility of extended, continuous readings of particular books. The success of this reform is measured by the fact that the principles on which this lectionary reform were based have been adopted by all the major Anglican and Protestant churches in Britain. As Wainwright aptly puts it

> In general, the Scriptures are being allowed to bear their own witness within the liturgical context more clearly than had long been the case[8]

In addition, it is well acknowledged that the role within the ministry of priest and prophet are complementary, not mutually exclusive. This is a reflection of the aforementioned blurring of roles between prophet and priest in the Old Testament. In Catholic thought, both Roman and Anglican, the sacred ministry is both prophetic and sacerdotal. Its normative role is that of the apostle, the messenger- witness of the resurrection, a role that transcends and combines those of preacher and sacramental ministrant.

The point may be underlined by the historical observation that the Oxford Movement, a movement representing the apex of Anglican Liturgy and Ritual, as well as restoring the grandeur and mystery to the Liturgy, also produced great preachers, in the form of Keble, Pusey and Newman amongst others. Their work has inspired, and continues to inspire many within the Catholic Tradition.

Yet, in spite of these encouraging developments, it remains true that in the Word/Table balance, the Catholic emphasis still remains on the Table. In the Roman Catholic Church a sermon is required only on Sundays. Daily Mass is still often celebrated without a sermon, as would be true also within the Anglican Tradition. Still, the movement towards greater emphasis on the proclamation and exposition of the Word within the Liturgy is to be welcomed.

The Protestant Tradition

Here the issue is approached from the opposite end of the spectrum. That stream of worship that is distinguishably Protestant sees the Word as its centre. So, alongside the Eucharistic we can see various types of "Services of the Word", where the reading and exposition of Scripture are the key elements, with liturgy kept to a minimum. This tendency was developed to its extremes within Non- conformism, classically in the "hymn sandwich". Everything that precedes it seems no more than a prelude or introduction to the sermon. The sheer length of the sermon makes it the dominant element of the service. Everything else becomes subservient to the sermon, rather than standing in its own right as worship. In general the leader of worship tends to be the preacher, and he or she is thought of as the latter rather than the former.

Churches built to reflect this form of worship tend to have large, central pulpits, with a much smaller table placed somewhere in front of it. No doubt the architecture reflects to a degree the architecture of the Synagogue, where the reading and exposition of the Torah is the central activity. Certainly in churches it reflects very clearly the relative priority given to Word and Sacrament. Another corollary is that the relative lack of space for movement by the congregation tends to encourage passivity on their part.

For Anglicans the major turning point came with the advent of the Parish Communion Movement. Alan Hayes notes that from the 1560's to the mid- 20th century the principal worship service in most Anglican churches were the Prayer Book services of the Word, Morning and Evening Prayer, centred on the reading of Scripture. By the end of the 1970's however the so-called "Parish Communion Movement" had persuaded most Anglican churches to adopt the Eucharist as their principal Sunday service.[9]

This Movement is normally traced to the publication in 1937 of a collection of essays edited by A.G.Herbert, entitled *The Parish Communion*.[10] All the essays were written on the conviction that the Eucharist was central to Christian life, and fundamental to the nature of the Church. The appeal of the movement was that it promised to heal the divisions between evangelicals and catholics.

The evangelical world signalled acceptance of its objectives in the final statement of the National Evangelical Anglican Congress at Keele in 1967. This contained the statement that evangelicals would work towards weekly Holy Communion as the central corporate service of the Church. The Eucharistic Liturgy maintains the balance between the two wings by being divided into two main sections, The Service of the Word, with reading of 3 lessons and an obligatory sermon, and the Service of the Table. Provision is made for the retention of services of the Word, but their profile has been lowered, and there is a common emphasis on the Eucharist as that which creates and sustains the community, and an expectation that it will be the principal weekly service.

Time has passed, and a feeling has grown that establishing the Eucharist as the central service is very far from having solved the Church's problems. Because in its very nature it is exclusive, as a service only the baptized can participate in, it is sectarian in its nature. Outsiders and seekers cannot feel entirely at home in it, because of the level of Christian commitment it assumes. Michael Marshall, in his book *Renewal in Worship,* goes as far as to say that the Parish Communion Movement

> Has done more than any other single movement to unchurch the people of the United Kingdom.[11]

Kenneth Leech comments that because of the increasing profile of the Eucharist the Church is in danger of becoming a eucharistic sect. While acknowledging that the Eucharist is at the very heart of Christian worship, it is not all there is. The Church needs to develop or recover ways of worship that allow other sources of life to surface.[12]

From the point of view of our study, we could argue that the shift from Morning and Evening Prayer to Holy Communion has placed increased restrictions on the sermon. It has of course placed greater restrictions of time, since a sermon of any significant length will inevitably make the whole service unacceptably long. Morning and Evening Prayer left the preacher with a tremendous degree of freedom and scope that is simply not there when it is part of the Eucharist. There has therefore been a move back in many churches to a situation where there was great flexibility in determining what the focus of worship would be on any particular Sunday.

Liturgy as proclamation

As the Anglican Liturgical Commission began its work of developing new liturgies alongside the Book of Common Prayer, there were encouraging signs that Evangelicals, inspired by such figures as Colin Buchanan, were prepared to play a full part in this process and in so doing rediscover the value of liturgy. This rediscovery stemmed from two factors. There was the recognition that the Bible itself contains liturgical material, shaped and used by the developing New Testament Church. Alongside this was a new realisation that the Liturgy is itself for the most part a proclamation of the Word of God.

The Psalms of the Old Testament are the Bible's primary liturgical material. They were used widely in Temple and Synagogue, and Jesus and His disciples would have been very familiar with them. At the end of the Last Supper we are told that Jesus and His disciples "sang a hymn" (ὑμνησαντες) before moving out to the Mount of Olives (Mark 14.26). If the meal were in fact a Passover Meal, then what they sang would almost certainly be from Pss.114-118, the Passover *hallel*.[13] Paul exhorts the Ephesian Christians to address each other in *"psalms,* and hymns and spiritual songs (Eph.5.19). There is a broad consensus that texts such as Phil.2.5-11, Col.1.15-20 and 1 Tim.3.16 are liturgical passages or hymns, possibly pre-dating the documents in which they are contained. The New Testament reflects Early Church creedal formulae, especially the very earliest, the Aramaic *Marana Tha* "come Lord" in 1 Cor.16.9. The formula of 1 Cor.15.3f, concerning the death, burial and resurrection of Jesus 'according to the Scriptures' has the ring of a credal formula about it, especially as Paul explicitly describes it as tradition he is passing on. Paul assumes that prayer in the Church will be corporate as well as individual, and this is made explicit by the description of the early activity of the members of the Church as including devotion to *"the* Prayers" (Acts 2.42). In his discussion of the

Lord's Supper in 1 Corinthians 11, Paul insists that in what he says he is not innovating, but discussing a worship practice that stems back to the Lord Himself, a practice that included the reciting of the Words of Institution over the bread and wine. There is no shortage of evidence therefore to suggest that the worship of the New Testament Church involved practices that in a primitive form could genuinely be described as liturgical.

The Scriptural content of the Book of Common Prayer was of course well known, but the peculiarities of ancient language, as well as its provenance being a cauldron of theological controversy caused this to be lost sight of. The new focus on liturgical development brought to life a new understanding of how the Word of God could be proclaimed in the Liturgy.

In addition, realisation came that this method of proclamation had one distinct advantage over the sermon: repetition. Worshippers were hearing the same passages of Scripture, declaring God's great acts of Salvation, week by week, and could therefore absorb them into their spiritual lives almost without realising they were doing it.

This can be illustrated by a quick skip through the Order One Eucharist of Common Worship:

Liturgy as Proclamation: The Eucharist as an Example

The Gathering

- *The Greeting*

- *Collect for Purity* - God is present and God knows our thoughts. A reminder of John 4.24 - "God is spirit, and those who worship Him must worship Him in Spirit and Truth".

- *Confession* - Summary of the Law, the *Shema* (Matt.22.37-40/Mark 8.29-31). A summary of God's demands upon us. The prayer of confession and absolution are based on the assumption of God's forgiveness for penitent sinners, cf. 1 John 1.9.

- *Gloria.* An ancient liturgical text. Combines the twin thoughts of God's holiness and grace. God is "God in the highest" - He is our heavenly King. The contemplation of this reminds us of sin. At the same time Jesus is the Lamb of God who takes away the sin of the world.

- In the Triune God glory, holiness and mercy are perfectly blended together as an assurance to the penitent sinner.

- *The Collect for the Day.* Anglican collects are classically teaching vehicles, always beginning by teaching the worshipper something about. They typically begin with "God, who…..".

The Liturgy of the Word

- *Bible Readings.* This section offers the option of 3 Bible Readings plus, for those with stamina, a psalm as well. Constraints of time will limit most churches to just 2 readings, an OT or Epistle plus a Gospel portion. Often the block of readings will be broken up by a hymn (Gradual).

- *The Sermon* follows the Gospel Reading immediately. For that reason the temptation is virtually irresistible to preach on the Gospel reading, in the interests of continuity. It goes without saying that this temptation must from time to time be resisted, or an unbalanced preaching ministry will result.

- *The Nicene Creed.* Following on the sermon, the reciting of the Creed offers an immediate opportunity for making an initial outward response to the Word of God. The weekly recitation is a constant reminder to the congregation of the Biblically-derived truths on which their faith rests.

- *The Peace.* There are a number of New Testament texts that serve as alternatives to the default text of 1 Corinthians 12, all serving to remind the congregation of their oneness in Christ. Having received a fresh revelation of God's love through the Ministry of the Word, the people renew their expression of oneness in a new way.

The Liturgy of the Sacrament

- The key focus of this section is the Eucharistic Prayer, of which Common Worship offers 8 alternatives. All of them however have the same basic structure.

- *A recital of the Mighty Acts of God,* truths made familiar of course through the Scriptures.

- *The Words of Institution,* as recorded in the Gospels and 1 Corinthians.

- *An Epiclesis,* a prayer for the Holy Spirit to apply the benefits of taking part in the Eucharist in the lives of the people.

The Dismissal

Reception of communion leads very abruptly to the end of the Service and the sending out of the congregation into the world, following the Trinitarian blessing. The double aspect of worship, offering and service, as reflected in Romans 12.1 are linked together in the dismissal.

Whilst it is arguable that the Sermon remains the central part of the ministry of the Word, and the main teaching vehicle within the Eucharist, it is by no means the only instance in the service where the Word of God is proclaimed to the congregation. The whole liturgy, either employing words of Scripture directly, or using truths based on the Scriptures is a teaching vehicle from beginning to end.

As was mentioned earlier, the very repetition of the liturgy, far from being inimical to the absorbing of Christian truth, is an extremely effective means by which that truth is absorbed and retained. I have on many occasions met elderly worshippers who, whilst having the utmost difficulty in locating the books of Nehemiah or Habbakuk, can recite verbatim collects and prayers from the liturgy learned many decades earlier.

To their credit, most evangelical Anglicans have long recognised the didactic value of the Liturgy. The challenge is on for those who play down the value of the liturgy and seek to replace it with other things to demonstrate that their alternatives have the same teaching value.

"Charismatic" Approaches to the Word in Worship

The word "charismatic" is deliberately placed in quotation marks to denote a style of Anglican worship that is *derived from* the movement of charismatic renewal, but which does not necessarily include those doctrines of the Holy Spirit that characterise that movement. To many Anglicans the word "charismatic", especially in Catholic circles, denotes simply "non-liturgical".

An increasing number of Anglican churches, generally in the Evangelical tradition have replaced traditional liturgy with more informal forms of singing and praying. In these instances liturgy is relegated to a number of "pieces", posted on a printed service sheet or displayed by an Overhead

Projector/Power Point system. Often these pieces will include a Confession and/or Creed, or other such items as the Minister sees fit for the congregation to join in with. This approach nods in the direction of liturgical worship, but no longer sees it as the basis of corporate worship. In some evangelical churches (as I have myself observed) there is not even a nod, and scarcely anything, apart from the building, that identifies the worship as Anglican at all ! We have already noted the unfortunate tendency in such churches is to describe the singing of worship songs and choruses as *the* worship time, leaving other elements, including the ministry of the Word, as accompaniments of worship, rather than worship itself.

Now it must be said at once that it is by far preferable to have a beautiful worship song sung by a talented Music Group than a traditional psalm or canticle sung badly by an ageing choir. Very few people would give an argument on that one. The question is whether modern worship songs contain the same didactic value as we have seen that the traditional liturgy has. The answer is that it varies from song to song. Some modern worship songs are based solidly on Scripture and do convey a biblical message. The works of Graham Kendrick come to mind here. In other cases some songs, whilst arguably having a place in worship, contain only minimal didactic value. It is argued that they have great value in creating a warm worship atmosphere, in stirring the emotions in a way that traditional liturgy does not, and in creating an atmosphere of receptivity in the congregation. The question is whether *in the long term* they provide a sufficient diet for a congregation seeking to grow both in devotion and maturity.

Many older readers will recall the pre-charismatic days of Scripture Union and CSSM choruses. They were no more than Bible verses put to music. That music was, by today's standards, extremely unsophisticated. And yet, as those older readers will readily confirm, they allowed Bible texts to be absorbed in an effortless and painless way, so that they became part of the singer, and are capable of being called to mind very readily many decades later. One might question whether many contemporary worship songs will have the same longevity.

Where does this leave the sermon ? Have the waves of the Charismatic Movement washed it up onto a bright new shore, or left it high and dry ? The answer is that the Renewal movement has done both. Church historians tell us that every movement of revival and renewal down the ages has led to an upsurge of effective preaching. Our earlier discussion of the Wesleys and Whitfield provided ample evidence of that. The present movement is no exception. Many people testify to a renewed interest in expository preaching in the Church today. Many of the Anglican Theological Colleges today are producing detailed, effective courses to meet this new enthusiasm for preaching the Word. It is worth commenting that these courses are all much more comprehensive than the present writer received in his training !

The picture is patchy, however. In some Anglican Renewal circles renewal has undoubtedly led to a downgrading of the sermon in favour of other aspects of worship. There are two basic influences on this downgrade. The first is the aforementioned tendency to restrict "worship time" to the singing of worship songs and to prayer. Because of the high emotional content of these sessions there is the feeling (usually unspoken) that "this is what the people have really come for" and consequently to squeeze out activities like the sermon and Bible readings as being activities that are conceived of as more cerebral, and therefore lacking the same emotional value. The extreme of this tendency is to have worship times with virtually no ministry of the Word at all.

Writing more than 40 years ago, D. Martyn Lloyd Jones has this perceptive comment:

232

You have now a 'song leader' as a new kind of official in the Church. He conducts the singing and is supposed to produce the atmosphere (for the sermon). But he often spends so much time in producing the atmosphere that there is no time left for preaching in the atmosphere ! This is a part of the whole depreciation of the message.[14]

The other element of Renewal that impinges on the sermon is the renewed interest in prophecy, and the subsequent setting of prophecy *over against* preaching. In this context prophecy may be defined as "a spontaneous speaking from God that contains an element of revelation".

Thus a careful distinction is made between prophecy and preaching/teaching, based on such texts as Ephesians 4.11, where prophets and teachers are listed separately amongst the gifts of the ascended Christ. The Corinthian letters speak of prophecy as an activity within the congregation that clearly could not be confused with preaching.

Such distinctions are maintained today. Preaching is seen as the delivery of a carefully constructed monologue, based on scripture, delivered to a passive audience. Prophecy, on the other hand, is seen as a spontaneous, dramatic activity that arises often from within the congregation itself, which brings new revelation and is closely related to the circumstances of that congregation. For this reason it is sometimes valued more highly than the sermon itself.

Assessing the value of this prophetic phenomenon for the Church today involves a number of considerations. In the first instance, it involves making a judgement on how far these New Testament phenomena form a pattern for today's Church. What is often lost sight of is the fact that the New Testament Church is an emerging and developing Church. Its patterns, such as they are, are not set in stone. As part of this development it is a diverse Church also. The categories of ministry seen at Ephesus are not seen at Philippi for example, where only bishops and deacons are mentioned (Phil.1.1). Orders of ministry are not seen in the Johannine Church at all according to the New Testament. There is simply not enough evidence in the New Testament to support the idea that the prophet is a separate category of ministry, intended to be part of the continuing Church of today. Of course the prophetic voice desperately needs to be heard in today's Church, and it risks being lost if it is confined to one category of person only. This certainly applies to the preacher. One hopes that preaching will be truly prophetic. But only the most foolhardy preacher will assume that the prophetic voice is confined to his own ministry. God's voice will be heard most clearly within the Church when it is realised that the whole congregation, both in its speaking and listening, needs to be prophetic.

If we are to look for prophetic patterns within the Church of today a more secure source is to be found in the Old Testament prophets. The prophetic voice in the Old Testament is heard *both* in the spontaneous utterances of prophets caught up in historical events, *and* in their carefully constructed written oracles. This combination of inspiration and systematisation is seen reflected in the New Testament most clearly in the Book of Revelation. The book claims very clearly to be a prophecy (1.3) and, by extension, its author a prophet. It's very title 'Revelation' (αποκαλυψις) implies a "drawing back of the veil" to reveal the truth of God. The author issues the work as a consequence of "being in the Spirit on the Lord's Day" (1.10). And yet far from being an ecstatic utterance it shows a schematization so sophisticated as to have baffled multitudes of commentators and exegetes down the ages. Although undoubtedly possessing all the hallmarks of prophecy, it is without doubt also a literary work, built on carefully hermeneutical principles, especially those principles reflected in the Old Testament.

Both inspired utterance and carefully prepared sermon need to be recognised as genuine representations of prophecy within the Church today. To make distinctions between them, or to attempt to rank one above the other is to risk doing justice to neither.

Worship built on the Word of God

The average worshipper's experience in Church can often seem like a merry-go-round. You drop a token in the collection box as you come in, and it is a good ride. There's music, and lots of motion up and down. The ride is carefully timed and rarely varies in length. Lots of good feelings are generated, and you can be sure that everything is sufficiently well controlled that there is no danger from the experience. But although you spend most of your time feeling as though you are going forward, in fact you get off exactly where you got on.

This was not true of the worship demonstrated within the pages of the Bible. Worship centred on the Word of God was dynamic, exciting, and above all, challenging to the worshipper. He could not be same leaving the assembly as he was when he walked into it.

Worship in Old Testament days was centred on the cult and the Temple, though by no means limited to them. Acceptable worship in Old Testament terms involved homage, service and reverence, demonstrated in the whole of life. Rituals associated with the Tabernacle, Ark and Temple were simply the cultic means of demonstrating what is universally true - God is present in power in the midst of His people. When the tumults of their history deprived them of these outward symbols, the people recovered their identity and unity in the Torah, the Word of God.

In the New Testament Jesus inherits and accepts the Old Testament traditions and symbols of worship, but presents them in a new and dynamic way. The Temple built of stone would be lost, but would in time be replaced in His person and work. "Destroy this Temple and I will rebuild it in three days", the saying recorded in John 2.19 that puzzled both friend and foe alike, is the cryptic way of pointing to Himself as the new symbol of the constant presence of God.

In reply to a question about the true locus of worship, Jesus points away from Jerusalem and Gerizim to discover those who, regardless of their geographical location, would worship Him in spirit and truth (John 4.21-24). Worship from beginning to end must be built on the truth of God revealed in the Word of God. Any attempt at worship therefore that diminishes or minimizes the importance of the Word of God risks damaging this Spirit/Truth balance and becoming weak and flabby. Worship that breaks the link with truth altogether soon descends into superstition.

As one writer puts it,

> We confess the greatness of God by making God's Word the centre of our activities - by reading it, preaching it, making it the basis of exhortation, and even by setting it to music in hymns and praise.[15]

The reading and exposition of Scripture is an important way therefore of ensuring that our spiritual worship is thoroughly imbued with the truth of God. It ensures that the truth to which Jesus referred is right there at the heart of our service of worship.

But, above and beyond those parts of the liturgy that make up what we are pleased to call "The Ministry of the Word", we have the responsibility to ensure that the whole offering of worship is structured on the basis of the Word of God, and that praise, repentance, intercession and self-offering are the vital building bricks of that structure.

Worship that is built on the Word of God will be God-centred, and in the case of Christian worship will be no less Christ-centred. It will be trinitarian in character, focussed on the self-revelation of God in Jesus Christ and empowered by the Holy Spirit. It will be a true response to the wonder of that revelation. The vision of God drives us, like Isaiah, to our knees in holy terror. But our lips will be touched and cleansed by the realization that the God who is both Creator and Judge is also Redeemer. Worship by the Word will be bathed in the experience of the love of God demonstrated by the Cross. The vision of God will be seen and appreciated through the lens of Calvary.

True worship will be a corporate experience. Although the plaintiff cry, so often heard by parish priests, "I can worship God without going to Church" is technically true, it is the theological equivalent of sticking a toe in the water instead of plunging in. There are so many depths that may be explored in the holy company of brothers and sisters in Christ. Although, as Carson points out, corporate worship by no means exhausts everything the New Testament has to say about worship, there is a sense of authenticity and a realisation of the presence of God in the gathering together of His people.[16]

The New Testament tells us that we are not to neglect the gathering of ourselves together is that the purpose of such gatherings is the mutual edification or building up of the Body of Christ (Eph.4.11-16, 29; 5.19,20). We build one another up as we teach and exhort one another on the basis of the Word, using the gifts that the Spirit has distributed to us. Even our casual conversation is to be edifying. This doesn't mean of course that we have to be earnest and deadly serious all the time, but that we must not waste words in unprofitable ways.

Edification is not of course a purely human activity, for God is at work amongst His people as they minister in this way.

Edification is the prime responsibility as Christ as the Head, but He achieves His purpose as the various members of the Body, not least the preacher, are motivated and equipped by Him to play their part. This mutual edification will happen most effectively when worship in both form and content breathes the atmosphere of the Word of God. The Preacher has an indispensable role in ensuring that this is the case.

As David Peterson points out,

> Christians of every tradition need to be regularly exposed to the breadth and depth of the Bible's teaching on worship and to understand how it relates to evangelism, edification, faith and obedience. Above all, they must come to grips with the New Testament perspective that acceptable worship is an engagement with God, through Jesus Christ, in the Holy Spirit - Christ centred, gospel-serving, life-orientation.[17]

Lastly but by no means of least importance, it is essential to ensure that our worship, seen as an encounter with God of the sort we see many times in the pages of the Bible, has its proper biblical outcome in mission. Isaiah's response in the Temple must always be our response. We take off our shoes to enter the holy presence and stand on the holy ground. As we go out we put on our shoes, take our staff in our hands, strengthened by our encounter of spirit and truth to do serve the purposes of the Kingdom of God.

CHAPTER SIX
ENDNOTES

[1] S. Mowinckel, *Psalmenstudien III: Kultprophetie und prophtische Psalmen*

[2] Luke 4.14-30.

[3] D.E.Babin, "Towards a Theology of Liturgical Preaching", *Anglican Theological Review* 52 (1970), 228.

[4] Taken from Robert Hendrie, "Preaching in the Roman Catholic Tradition" in *Finding the Voice,* magazine of the College of Preachers.

[5] Hendrie, "Preaching.."

[6] C.Noren, "The Word of God in Worship: Preaching in relation to Liturgy" in eds. C.Jones; G.Wainwright, E.Yarnold,S.J., P.Bradshaw, *The Study of Liturgy* (London; SPCK, 1992), 38.

[7] E.Schillebeeckx, "Word and Sacrament in the Church " *Listening, Winter 1969),* 62.

[8] G.Wainwright, "The Continuing Tradition of the Church" in *The Study of Liturgy,* 556.

[9] Alan L.Hayes, "The Service of the Word: Historical Considerations" in ed. A.L.Hayes & J.Webster, *What Happened to Morning Prayer ?* (Toronto: Wycliff College, 1997), 7.

[10] Published by SPCK.

[11] Hayes, 11.

[12] Marshall, 62.

[13] K.Leech, *The Sky is Red: Discerning the Signs of the Times* (London: Darton, Longman & Todd, 1997), 180.

[14] So says C.E. Cranfield, *The Cambridge Greek Testament Commentary* (Cambridge: C.U.P., 1963), 428.

[15] D.M.Lloyd Jones, *Preaching and Preachers,* (London: Hodder & Stoughton, 1971), 17.

[16] R.Doyle, "The One True Worshipper", *The Briefing* (1989), 8.

[17] D.A.Carson, "Worship under the Word", in ed. D.A.Carson, *Worship by the Book* (Grand Rapids: Zondervan, 2002), 11-163, esp. 49.

7

THE PREACHER'S PREPARATION

We have quite rightly spent a lot of time theorizing about preaching and looking at the theology behind it. This is right and proper because good practice can only be built on the foundations of solid principle. But now we turn to the nitty-gritty of preaching, to see how the task must be approached and implemented. Someone might point out that preaching is a personal and individual thing, and that there almost as many approaches as there are preachers. But there nevertheless are general principles which all preachers without exception need to take on board, so that, after adaptation for personal use, they may form the solid basis for an effective preaching ministry.

Deciding what to preach on

Many preachers will confess, present company included, that in the early years of their preaching career at least this was the hardest task. Once I was happy in the choice of subject, my experience was that the going got considerably easier. When the kernel at least of the message I believed God had given had formed, it was only a matter of time and effort before that idea was translated into a sermon. But those initial stages of wrestling with God for His message were often very testing. Now there are so many aids to the developing preacher that the task may be said to have become somewhat easier, though not to the extent that wrestling is completely excluded.

The assumption of Common Worship is that the sermon will be based on a biblical text. This is the point of placing the sermon within the Liturgy of the Word section in Holy Communion. There may be (extremely) rare occasions where a different approach is indicated, but generally the principle will hold. I vividly remember three members of a family in one of my churches being tragically killed in a road accident. The accident happened on a Saturday afternoon, when my original sermon had already been prepared. But the atmosphere in Church the following morning rendered that original sermon obsolete. It just seemed natural to stand and talk about the family and what had happened. The Bible was involved of course, but in this instance it was not the primary impulse to the sermon. Happily such occurrences are rare, and generally speaking the preacher will begin at least with a Bible text, made up of a single verse or a connected passage.

But how is that text chosen? Out of the vast treasury of material offered to us by the Scriptures, how do we chose the gem that will enrich the life of the congregation on this forthcoming Sunday?

The Use of a Lectionary

To some extent in the modern Church of England the text is chosen for us in the shape of the Revised Common Lectionary readings for the day. Three readings are made available each week, although a realistic assessment would suggest that the proximity of the Gospel reading will ensure that this will form the substance of the sermon in most cases. The really imaginative preacher will find a link between all three readings and incorporate them all into his address. But as such a link is sometimes difficult to spot, the result risks appearing contrived and artificial.

The RCL offers a number of advantages to the preacher:

- There is the opportunity of preaching continuously through portions of Scripture, especially in the Gospels.

- There is consequently the opportunity of speaking on passages and subjects that would be most unlikely to be chosen in any topical scheme, and thus allowing the preacher to develop a more complete ministry. My experience is that passages that often at first sight appear unpromising yield unexpected delights on further investigation.

- There is the opportunity through the Lectionary of linking our worship and our preaching to that of the wider Church.

As far as the limitations of the Revised Common Lectionary go we might say that like all lectionaries it has a limited field of vision. The scheme may not cover all the subjects a preacher may feel important to meet the particular needs and circumstances of his congregation, so that there may be the need from time to time to break away from it.

'As the Lord leads'

The legendary Baptist Preacher, C.H.Spurgeon, in his book *Lectures to my Students*, recounts how he would sometimes change his mind at the very last moment, perhaps on his walk up to Church, inspired by something he might catch a glimpse of by the wayside.[1] Now a careful, life-long study of the Bible, an equally careful study of the local and international news scene, a sharp insight into the coming and goings of daily life and a close walk with God could all make it possible to arrive at Church each Sunday with a fresh sermon based on a combination of all these factors[1]. It would be foolish and precipitate to rule this out completely. But it would be even more surprising indeed to find many preachers, even latter-day Spurgeons, adopting a completely spontaneous approach such as this. Spurgeon himself would argue that inspiration and planning are not mutually exclusive, and that such spontaneity as that described above was confined to very rare occasions. The problem with spontaneity is of course that on some days the inspiration simply is not there. The extreme danger is that, without inspiration, we go on with something half-baked and unworthy of God. There is no worse feeling for any preacher to have that to arrive at Saturday evening with no clear idea of what to preach on the next morning that will glorify God and feed His people. Whatever limitations a preaching plan might have, it is worth its weight in gold if it delivers the preacher from the dreaded "preacher's block".

The other danger with the "inspiration" model is that, over the weeks the preaching pattern ranges up hill and down dale, without any discernible pattern. It would be a bold preacher that attributed to God such haphazard behaviour !

Whilst every preacher should be sufficiently open and flexible to deal with a "Spurgeon Moment", there needs to be a closer link made between divine inspiration and human planning.

Where our emphasis on inspiration is valuable, however, is that, in the preparation of any sermon there should be what I call a **moment of recognition**. Recognition is a term closely akin to revelation, but has a slightly different nuance. By "recognition" I mean the discernment that the text in front of the preacher is the message from God for the congregation for that particular occasion. This can come in a flash or be a growing conviction as preparation of the sermon and engagement with the text takes place in the days leading up to its delivery.

Prayer and a sense of receptivity are important factors in coming to this recognition. What sometimes we substitute for this is the choice of texts which most easily break down into a hermeneutical structure (such as three points). The preacher in his humanity tends to assume that because a text easily yields a structure for his sermon, it must be the right text. This is of course not necessarily the case. That a text has a message that needs to be communicated must first be recognised by the preacher. Then, and only then, should his thoughts turn to structure.

Sometimes this recognition of God's message comes out of a clear blue sky, and it is very thrilling and exciting when it does. I remember vividly reading Isaiah in my daily reading one day when Isaiah 43.17,18 hit me between the eyes

> Forget the former things, and do not dwell on the past.
> Behold, I am doing a new thing, says the Lord.
> *Isaiah 43.17.18*

For me, twelve months after my wife's death, it was a very personal message. But then it led onto the thought that doing new things is what God is *always* doing. He doesn't want His people constantly looking backwards and longing for past days of supposed glories; He wants to lead them on to new heights and new victories. To me it was a word straight from God. The sermon virtually prepared itself, and when Sunday came I fairly raced up the pulpit steps !

The DIY Preaching Plan

It should not be beyond the wit of most parishes, especially where there is a shared ministry, to devise a preaching plan themselves for their congregations. This can be especially feasible where the Church leaders have sound Bible knowledge and theological insight. Such a scheme offers the obvious advantage of enabling the preacher or preachers to tailor their ministry to the situation of their congregation as they see it, to discern what needs should be met and what challenges they should be encouraged to face. In the three months leading up to my retirement for example I departed from RCL and devised a preaching scheme based on the nature of the Church, especially as the Body of Christ, with the specific intent of preparing and equipping the congregation for the impending interregnum.

Where the minister is solo in the parish he should encourage his church wardens or other leaders to be involved in the process of drawing up the preaching plan. The meeting at which this plan is drawn up then becomes the most important meeting in the Parish Diary, far more important than the PCC, for it stands to shape the life of the congregation and parish in a very fundamental way.

How far ahead the Preaching Plan should look is a matter of opinion. I would suggest that the preacher or preachers should have a general idea of what to preach on stretching forward two or three years. That length of vision gives the opportunity of ensuring that the congregation gets a balanced diet. As far as a *detailed* plan goes however, then three or six months may well be sufficient, allowing for the possibility that events may lead the congregation in an unforeseen direction, a direction to which the preacher needs to respond.

The preaching plan need not of course be entirely DIY, and a careful dovetailing of such a plan with RCL would ensure the best of both worlds. The danger of an entirely self-devised plan is the obvious one of selectivity. The plan reflects the likes, dislikes and ability of the preachers rather than what Paul terms the whole Counsel of God. We have already acknowledged however that this danger cannot be avoided, no matter which plan or lectionary is used. It simply becomes a case of who is operating the principle of selectivity.

An awareness of the danger takes us half way to avoiding it. In general, the more broadly based a preaching plan (e.g. in holding the balance between Old and New Testament texts) lessens the risks of subjectivity and selectivity. But these dangers are always present.

The Revised Common Lectionary

Preaching on the Old Testament passage

Most preachers, if asked, would admit to a relative neglect of the Old Testament. In the Eucharist, where time can be a problem, it is most often the Old Testament lesson that is jettisoned. This is a great pity, for a number of reasons.

For example, **the Old Testament gives us a much fuller picture of God than can be gained from the New Testament alone.** In the very first few verses of the Old Testament we are presented with a blockbuster - a picture of God as *creator* and *sustainer* of the universe. The Book of Isaiah, especially in the central chapters, amplifies this picture. As creator, he holds all the nations in His hands. The strongest human power is nothing compared to God. The creatorship of God underlies all His relationships with men and women.

The Old Testament introduces us to a God who *acts,* not only in creation, but in the everyday affairs of men and women. He delivers the righteous, and punishes the wicked. The prophets constantly warn that human actions, both good and bad, will bring an active response from an Almighty God.

His actions are not arbitrary, however. The Old Testament tells us that *God makes covenant* with His people, and puts His actions in line with that covenant. He binds Himself to His people, and delivers them when oppressed, first from Egypt, then from Babylon. The Isaiah vision reminds readers that God is a God of holiness, and makes demands on His people. So His covenant relationship sometimes leads Him to punish His people when they fail to reflect that holiness, but these are the actions of a loving father, wishing to bring them back to Him.

Following on from this we see that **the Old Testament helps us understand who Jesus is.** There is so much about Jesus and His earthly life we would fail to understand were it not for the Old Testament. The Infancy Narratives for example need to be set against the background of Old Testament prophecies, especially those of Isaiah, in order for us to understand why people saw the birth of Jesus as significant.

Christopher Seitz argues that it is not a case simply of the New Testament looking back to the Old: rather it is the case of the Old Testament, and the prophets in particular, reaching forward to the New Testament.

> Israel's history, as depicted in the Twelve Prophets, is a type or figure of a larger history, a history that takes two Testaments to tell. Amos for example is one man among the twelve, and the twelve are related to one man - Jesus Christ.[2]

The whole debate about Jesus' messiahship, as reflected in the Gospels, is incomprehensible unless we understand something of Old Testament messianic prophecy and the expectations Jesus' Jewish contemporaries consequently had. "Who do people say that I am ?" (Mark 8.27 *and parallels*) needs to be answered by an understanding of the Old Testament.

Titles given to Jesus in the New Testament, such as *Saviour* and *Lord* gain their meaning from the Old Testament. "Lord" (κυριος), whilst used in the New Testament on a number of levels is on the highest of those levels the term that translates

ADONAI, one of the Hebrew titles for God, in the Septuagint, the Greek version of the Old Testament.

Furthermore, **the Old Testament helps us understand what the Church is all about.** Although 'Church' (εκκλησια) is very much a New Testament word, the concept of the People of God goes way back into early Old Testament days. The concept of the called-out community (Heb: QAHAL) is seen in seed form in the conversations with Abraham in Genesis, when the Covenant Promise, "you will be my people, I will be your God" is made, but then in reality in the dramatic events at Sinai, when the people are bound to God in that Covenant. At Sinai they are called to be "a kingdom of priests and a holy nation"[3.] In the Servant Songs their role, to be as Servant of God, and a "light to the nations" is spelled out.[4] Time would see them fail in their God- given task, and for them to land in exile as a result. God's faithfulness brings them out, restores them, and gives them the assurance that their destiny as His people would yet be fulfilled, through a new act of God and through a New Covenant.[5] What is seen demonstrated in the church of New Testament days is not something novel, but is the continuation through the crucified and risen Christ of what was prefigured in the Old Testament.

The simple fact that the Old Testament was **the Bible used by Jesus**, by which He guided His life and from which he frequently quoted in the course of His teaching, should place us under a certain obligation to delve into it if we had no other reason.

The point needs no further labouring. Our preaching would be so much the poorer through neglect of our Old Testament heritage.

Preaching from the Old Testament is however not without its **difficulties**. Memories of bloody battles, lists of kings, repetitive words of doom from the prophets, miracles that strain the imagination and a pre-scientific cosmology all daunt even the most determined preacher, and threaten to drive him back to the relative safety of the Gospel passage. Yet, as we have sought to show, the congregation risks losing so much of value if the preacher continually paddles in the familiar and less demanding waters of the New Testament.

Yet the challenge of preaching on the Old Testament should not be underestimated. Its teaching for example is set in a convoluted historical context. The People of God begin with Abraham in Canaan, passes through the ups and downs of life with the Patriarchs, before arriving in Egypt. At this point they have a basic tribal structure. After deliverance through Moses they arrive back in Canaan, where events, under the leadership of Saul and David, mould them into nationhood, with their own kings and national institutions. In time that Kingdom is split, the two halves each in turn coming under foreign domination. The former southern Kingdom of Judah is taken into exile in Babylon, with many of those institutions, particularly the Temple, destroyed. The community that returns from exile is a very different one, with the Law becoming of increased importance. Most importantly their life is now dominated by eschatology, and the promise of a coming future kingdom.

Such a sketch of Old Testament history would be commonplace and even simplistic to an Old Testament scholar. But to the average member of an Anglican congregation it would, I suspect, be revolutionary ! Much of the Old Testament preacher's time is therefore of necessity dedicated to explaining how the individual piece he is examining fits into the picture as a whole. As a consequence relatively little time can be left in the sermon for application.

Then again, cultural background of the Old Testament people is obviously very different from that of the congregation. Those people are an Eastern people, with a world view and life style in many respects at variance from listeners in the comfortable, scientific west of two or three millennia later. Skilful elucidation by the preacher will be needed to help his congregation see the relevance of what he is trying to say that is hidden by the cultural layers in the material.

There again, the meaning of the Cross, so central to the Christian Faith, can be fully appreciated only by some understanding of the Old Testament system of sacrifices, and the consequent salvific significance of blood. The significance of that same cross lies partially hidden in the language of Covenant, a term with which our congregations are familiar in only its most narrow legal sense.

For the more committed and serious student one way into the task of preaching the Old Testament would be a study of how the New Testament speakers and writers themselves used Old Testament texts. Jewish writers such as Paul, as well as Jesus Himself, inherited a rich tradition of rabbinical use of the Old Testament. Gentile writers like Luke on the other hand, had access to more Hellenistic preaching practices. We do not have the space here to discuss this in any detail, though there are several excellent works available on the subject.[6] What we can say here is that the Old Testament is used by the New Testament speakers and writers in surprisingly flexible and imaginative ways. They were not interested in mechanically recycling old, familiar texts. For them the Old Testament was a living thing, a powerful tool for evangelistic and didactic preaching, to be used in creative and imaginative ways. One classic example is the flexible way the famous saying from Habbakuk 2.4,

- "the righteous will live by faith" is used by both Paul and the writer of the letter to the Hebrews.

- 'My righteous one will live by faith', says Hebrews 10.38,

- "the righteous will live by faith" (Rom. 1.17; Gal.3.11).

In the New Testament usage "faith" (πιστις) has a specifically Christian content, that is, it is faith in God through Jesus Christ. Paul makes this the centre piece of his argument in the early chapters of Romans. In Habbakuk, however, the word is more akin to "faithfulness", and describes the character of the righteous, rather than their attitude to God. This is no deterrent to the New Testament writers however, who use their Old Testament material, without violating exegetical rules completely, in ways that support their own missionary purposes. So the Old Testament is not a trackless desert. There are guidelines and tracks to help the preacher, though he has to show diligence in following them.

The preacher's main difficulty remains the relative unfamiliarity of the Old Testament to his hearers. And yet this is it is a symptom of the main problem itself. It is a self-fulfilling prophecy. Neglect of the Old Testament by preachers has led in its turn to ignorance and unfamiliarity on the part of the congregation. And this neglect is often the consequence of the unwillingness of many preachers to do the hard work of instructing themselves in the historical, cultural and theological background to which I have been referring. Many treasures we assume are buried deep in the Old Testament soil turn out to be surprisingly near the surface. They remain hidden often simply for want of digging.

In spite of its negative social impact, television is actually an effective ally in attempting to bridge the cultural gap between the world of the Old Testament and our modern world. In recent years there have been regrettably regular broadcasts from war zones such as Israel/Palestine, Afghanistan and Iraq. Add to these broadcasts related documentaries and news programmes, and you find that Middle-Eastern culture has quite a lot of coverage on the small screen, not just of urban areas but more often of more traditional, rural communities. Given also the great popularity of holidays in countries like Turkey, and the preacher may discover a greater understanding of the culture of the Biblical Lands on the part of the congregation than he may have dared to suppose.

Preaching on the Epistle

Some of the points made in connection with the Old Testament readings could be made about the reading from the Epistle. We have earlier noted the close relationship between Paul's letters and his oral preaching. If the thesis we outlined there is correct, then the passage set for the Epistle needs to be taken seriously as the basis for our sermon. It means also that the words of the epistle cannot simply be lifted off the page, but must be investigated in exactly the same way we investigate any part of the Bible.

We will for example want to look at the **situation to which the passage is being addressed.** When Paul writes, he writes as a pastor, seeking to give guidance, and particularly to address various problems that have arisen in the churches. All his letters, without exception, started life as responses to problems that had been brought to his attention by one means or another. Sometimes there are very specific problems connected with individuals, as in 1 Corinthians; at other times the problems are more general, but nevertheless urgent, as in Ephesians. Sometimes the situation is personal to Paul, such as when he writes to Timothy, conscious of being near the end of his life, to pass on his last will and testament. In still other cases imprisonment sharpens Paul's thinking. The preaching represented by Paul's letters characterises the relevance of his thinking and its practical application. The same sort of things could be said about the letters of Peter and John, set less frequently as the Epistle Reading than the letters of Paul, but nevertheless encountered by the preacher in the Revised Common Lectionary. Peter writes against the background of growing pressure on the Christians in central

Anatolia, whilst John writes his letters to address a situation of serious schism within the Johannine Church. The preacher on the epistle needs to explore these situations and see what common denominators they have with the situation of the Church today.

The preacher will need to investigate not only the historical context of the passage in view, but its **literary setting** also. Nearly all of Paul's letters have two main sections, a theological section followed by a practical section (paranesis). The transition is often marked by the use of "therefore" (ουν, Rom.12.1). The preacher will need to note in which section the text appears, to see how it functions within the text.

He will also need to identify which **rhetorical device** Paul uses to clothe the text. Is Paul saying something to be taken literally, or is it part of a rhetorical device Paul is using for effect ?

For example, in the key passage concerning submission to the ruling authorities in Romans 13.1-7, Paul begins by making a perfectly normal imperative statement in the third person:

> everyone must submit himself to the governing authorities
> *Romans 13.1*

But then in verse 3 he suddenly changes to the second person and the use of the rhetorical device of *diatribe*:

> Do you want to be free from the fear of the one in authority ? Then do what is right, and he will commend you. But if you do wrong, be afraid, for he does not bear the sword in vain.

The preacher will need to be aware therefore of Paul's use of these devices and of how quickly he can switch from one to the other.

Some understanding of **Pauline theology** will also be necessary if the preacher is to understand the text properly. Here the difficulties he will face should not be minimised, for the range of treatments of Paul's thought are legion. It would appear that almost daily books appear which purport to present us with a "fresh look" at some aspect or other of Paul's thought. Two examples that come readily to mind are James Dunn's *The New Perspective on Paul* (Grand Rapids: Eerdmans, 2007), and *Fresh Perspectives on Paul* by Tom Wright (Philadelphia: Fortress Press, 2009). Both are excellent works, as are many others that could be mentioned. The only caution for the reader is to beware thinking that any one of them gives the last word. Paul, bestriding several cultures as he does, defies being pinned down too exactly.

We can say two things about Paul and his theology can that confidently be agreed. The first of them is to beware of thinking of Paul as the archetypal systematic theologian. He was no such thing, and very often logical connections between different statements that he makes are not easy to identify.

The other important point is one that many scholars are agreed on, namely that we should beware of seeing Paul only through the lens of Reformation debates between sin and grace. Without doubt Paul's teaching is highly relevant to those debates, and Augustine, Calvin, Luther and others all stumbled on something vital when they identified grace as the heart of the Gospel. However, Paul did not write with those debates specifically in mind, and his writings should be viewed for what they are - the writings of a First Century Hellenistic Jew, and set against the debates that were current in his time.

One particularly good thing about preaching on the Epistle is that the Epistles often serve as a quarry for memorable texts and phrases.

For all have sinned and come short of the glory of God
Romans 3.23

Is a text well familiar to anyone who has been a counsellor in a Billy Graham Crusade, as is

If anyone is in Christ he is a new creation; the old has passed away, the new has come
2 Corinthians 5.17

The danger of course is to take these texts out of their context and giving them a meaning the author did not intend. But, once that danger has been recognised, there is much to be said for giving the congregation, brought up very much on media sound bytes the opportunity for memorising simple yet profound Bible texts. In our visual media dominated society we minimise the value of memory at our peril. Once the effort is made to memorise Scripture, it can remain part of our system for ever, and come to our aid in all sorts of situations. The risk of decontextualizing a text is a risk well worth taking.

Another factor that inhibits some preachers from using the Epistle is the feeling sometimes that the words of men like Paul, Peter and John don't *seem* to carry the same weight as words of Jesus Himself. Although part of the New Testament Canon as a result of the Holy Spirit guiding His Church, and passing the crucial test of "apostolicity", some preachers don't approach them with the same respect as other parts of the Bible. The danger is that once the humanity of the author is emphasised, it is all too easy to dismiss difficult or uncongenial statements as human opinion, rather than the Word of God. When Paul says for example

I (Greek: emphatic εγω) do not permit women to have authority over men: she must be silent
1 Timothy 2.12

It is all too easy for those so minded, to dismiss it as Paul's personal opinion, or even prejudice. As we stated in the case of the Old Testament, the Church risks becoming poorer and narrower in outlook if the passages from the Epistles are neglected or downplayed.

Preaching from the Gospel passage

As mentioned earlier the Gospel passage tends to be the most popular choice for the sermon at the Eucharist. There are several factors that contribute to this popularity.

In the Eucharistic Liturgy the sermon follows the Gospel immediately, so that a maximum degree of continuity is offered. It will not be a bad idea therefore for a preacher who has opted instead for the Old Testament or Epistle to make some reference in his sermon to the Gospel, to take advantage of this continuity.

In many churches the reading of the Gospel is heightened dramatically by placing it in the context of a procession, possibly with acolytes, incense and a congregational response. The congregation are positively urged to "Hear the Gospel of our Lord Jesus Christ" as the "Gospel of the Lord". Such a dramatic focus makes it *seem* natural for the Gospel Reading to be the subject of the sermon.

The Gospel Reading, unlike the other two readings, provides the congregation with direct quotations from Jesus, the centre of the Christian Faith. The Gospel therefore offers more direct access to Jesus than do the other readings, and therefore is likely to have a more immediate impact on the lives of the listeners. The Great Commission of Matt.28.18-20 is a command to go and "make disciples", where disciples are those who obey their Master's teaching, as well as seeking to emulate His lifestyle. For the disciple therefore the words of the Master are key. They need constantly to hear and absorb them. This is not an argument by any means for preaching on the Gospel Reading every Sunday; it is simply a possible explanation of why so many preachers do.

Amongst the less controversial conclusions of the Form Critics is the helpful observation that many of the units of the Gospel Tradition, the *pericopae*, were shaped by the preaching of the Early Church. They reach the modern-day preacher in preachable form already. Some of these units were labelled "pronouncement stories", because they invariably ended in a punch line or tag. The parable of the Sower (Mark 4.1-8) is followed by "he who has ears to hear, let him hear". This is often seen as simply a slogan of Jesus, repeated on several occasions. But it in fact a summary of the Sower Parable itself. Only those with ears to hear will have any understanding of what Jesus is saying.

A close study of the way Matthew and Luke use stories taken from Mark shows that very often the circumstantial details of the story are minimised in order to emphasise the exchange of words between the participants. The effect of this is to draw out the meaning of the story and in consequence make it more useful as a preaching vehicle.

The exegesis of Gospel material to render it suitable for preaching purposes will involve taking three important steps. To miss any of these steps out is to risk seriously distorting the message.

Firstly, the preacher must **understand the setting of the material in the ministry of Jesus.** It seems a balanced conclusion from studies of the Historical Jesus to assume that, whatever the precise details of transmission may be, that all the Gospel material has its origin at least in the ministry of Jesus. If we take once again the Parable of the Sower as our example, in its original setting it would be an explanation to the crowd of why not everyone responds positively to the message of the Kingdom of God. The different eschatological expectations that undoubtedly existed at that time meant that people had different understandings of what the signs of the coming Kingdom would be and what the appropriate response would be. So some will respond with great enthusiasm, Jesus says, but as the demands of entering the Kingdom begin to dawn on them, and the expectations of an easy ride, based on military conquest are disappointed, they will fall away. The message of the Kingdom is, however, not proved to be false because of this negative response, and will indeed provide its fruit.

The preacher will then go on to recognise the setting of the material in the life of the Early Church, asking why the Church preserved the material and why they found it useful. In the case of the Sower, the developing Early Church would find this message especially encouraging as they pushed out the boundaries in response to their Lord's command. They in turn would find that not everyone would receive the message of the Gospel eagerly. The eager, explosive response of the Day of Pentecost would not provide the pattern for the future. Some would greet the message with deaf ears. Others would greet it with fierce opposition. The pattern for Paul as he journeyed from city to city was to find an initial positive response followed by opposition. Indeed there seems to have been those who followed him round with the specific intent of stirring up such opposition. He says that while "a great door for effective work has opened for me" at Ephesus, "there are many who oppose me" (1 Cor.16.9). Acts 19.23-41 tells us of a great riot in that city as Paul's ministry was perceived as threatening the cult of the local deity Artemis.

To all the preachers of the Gospel in the Early Church the message of Jesus in the parable of the Sower would ring with meaning. They are not to be taken aback by the lack of response of by opposition to their preaching. It was only what their Lord Himself experienced. It will happen whenever the message of the Kingdom is proclaimed. But it will nevertheless bear fruit. The vital point for them to grasp is that *a varied or negative response does not mean that the message is invalid*. It is the soil, not the seed that determines the outcome of sowing.

Once those first two steps have been taken, the preacher will attempt to see the relevance of the material for his congregation's present day situation. It is vital he does not attempt this third step until the first two have been taken. But, if steps 1 and 2 have been executed properly, then the distance to step 3 will be a relatively short one. The discipline of applying the Gospel material first to the circumstances of Jesus, then to the circumstances of the Early Church will almost certainly provided pointers that will help us apply the material to the circumstances of the congregation. To go back to our example of the Sower: every modern day evangelist will see all the full range of responses to his message described above. Many will pose as a criticism of evangelism that many who respond initially do not seem to go on into discipleship. Now whilst it is incumbent on anyone involved in evangelism to ensure that follow up and pastoral care of those who respond to the evangelist is as organised and effective as possible, it remains a fact that in the ministry of Jesus many (perhaps in the end the majority) who responded initially to His message did not continue with Him. His plaintive cry to his disciples, "will you too go away ?" (John 6.67) is perhaps evidence of this.

Many a preacher, worried to distraction by the apparent lack of fruit from his weekly preaching labours can similarly find encouragement from the Sower. He must not automatically assume that it is his fault if no one *appears* to be responding in the way he hopes. Of course he must hone his preaching skills as carefully as he can. But, at the end of the day, what determines the response is not just the quality of the message or messenger, but the way that particular congregation is being touched by the constant battle between Light and Darkness in which the modern day Church is embroiled.

So the Gospel preacher will want to ask three vital questions of his material. What did it mean for Jesus and the people He is addressing in the passage under review ? That is the vital starting point. Secondly, what did it mean for the Early Church, the generation who caused the material to be written down ? Why did the Gospel writer include this particular saying or story in his Gospel ? What perceived question for the Early Church did it answer ? When all these questions have been addressed then, and only then, should the preacher move on to apply the material to the circumstances of his hearers.

The Gospels are a great treasure store of preaching material, for the reasons outlined above. But each gem has to be handled properly and polished carefully to be seen in its full splendour.

Following the Church's Year

Another aid for the preacher in the choice of his sermon material is the Church calendar, providing a wider setting for the Lectionary. Just as life has its physical rhythms, day/night, spring/summer/autumn/winter, so the Church's year is given rhythm by the Calendar.

The Calendar has a more specific and practical function however in ensuring that the congregation are continually reminded of the mighty acts of God in salvation. Thus Advent and Christmas remind us of the dramatic intervention of God into the world in the Person of Jesus, in fulfilment of long-made promises and as a foretaste of the consummation of all things at the end of time. Lent prepares us for Easter, just as Jesus' time in the desert prepared Him for His ministry and its culmination in Jerusalem. Holy Week and Easter remind us of the central acts of deliverance in the Cross and Resurrection of Jesus, whilst Pentecost calls to mind the endowment of the Holy Spirit to realize Christ's presence in

261

His Church. A preacher who faithfully observes these key points in the Calendar will therefore produce a congregation who will be securely grounded in the historical basis of their relationship with God.

Interspersed with these major celebrations are a number of "Saints Days" or "Holy Days" tied to specific days in the secular Calendar. The degree to which these days are observed will vary, often with the variation of churchmanship of the churches and preachers. Some churches observe only the main characters, Peter, John, Paul, James and so on, mentioned in the New Testament, whilst others will bring in famous Christians from subsequent Church History. Having said that, it is probably fair to say that churches of every shade see the value of remembering the great Christians of former generations. The writer to the Hebrews points us to the "great cloud of witnesses", those who exhibited faith in their lives, and who serve as an example for us (Hebrews 12.1,2). It is in the light of their example that we in our turn are to "run the race set before us". In context the writer is referring to the famous characters of the Old Testament, listed in Hebrews 11, but the principle holds true for Christian Saints of old. We have their examples to inspire us, and to remind us that we are what we are today as the result of a chain of witness stretching back through the ages. One of the practical difficulties in the observance of Saints' Days is that they will fall on a Sunday only every 6 years. To observe them annually means relating them to the nearest Sunday, employing a bit of imaginative flexibility at times !

Following the Church Calendar in our preaching has hidden snares and unexpected challenges. These challenges come in the very repetitiveness of the Calendar. Preaching every year at Christmas to the same congregation can sometimes stretch the resourcefulness of a preacher almost to breaking point. When tackling Christmas for the 15th time, how *do* you find a new approach ? Even though the Incarnation is a many-faceted phenomenon, it can at times be difficult to find a new way in.

Two things can help the preacher here. The first is the realisation (sadly) that few members of the congregation are likely to remember a sermon given five years previously. Therefore repetition *is* possible. If I had been approached at the end of a Christmas Service by someone who said "you said that five years ago" I would probably have fainted on the spot ! So it isn't an absolute requirement to produce a new sermon every year.

The other consideration is that there are excellent resources available when it comes to preaching the major Festivals. I would never use someone else's sermon in its entirety, and would never advise anyone to do so. A sermon delivered by someone else on an unknown occasion, with an unknown audience is not likely to properly fit another situation. But written sermons by others *are* valuable in providing a way in, a new angle or approach that will set another preacher's mind running. Now I certainly have done that, and gained a new insight from someone else that has set me on the course to prepare a sermon for myself. There is nothing wrong at all a preacher in drawing on the wisdom and imagination of others, as long as what is finally produced is truly his own and is suited to his own preaching situation.

Preparing the Sermon

One of the absolute prerequisites for effective preaching is good preparation. It is impossible to emphasise this too strongly. There is no substitute for it, and no excuse for neglecting it. Natural talent or even claims to inspiration from God will not justify being sloppy or negligent in sermon preparation. We have argued already that the writings of the Old Testament Prophets combined a closeness to God and an openness to the Spirit with careful, methodical literary construction. If it was good enough for them, it is good enough for modern preachers. Mounting the pulpit steps will be a joy if we combine our sense of the closeness of God with the realization that we have done our homework properly. I humbly confess that I find delivering the sermon infinitely more enjoyable than preparing it. Preparation can sometimes be a hard slog. But there is no alternative for the preacher who wants to be as effective as possible in speaking for God.

Taking on board what was said earlier about learning in community, a resourceful preacher may well wish to import these principles into his preparation. As well as having post-sermon feedback, the preaching will find great benefit from sharing insights with his congregation prior to the sermon. This could happen in a whole variety of ways, depending on the ingenuity and resourcefulness of the preacher. He may discuss the topic of the sermon with individual members of the congregation, or with his ministry team, or with some kind of focus group and so on. Where this is possible it greatly deepens and enriches the process of preparation, as well as creating greater confidence that the eventual sermon will reach its intended target. Nevertheless, even when all this is done, the moment still comes when the preacher has to sit down with open Bible and put it all together.

Engaging with the Text

Having arrived at the chosen text by whatever means the individual preacher has deemed appropriate, the process of what I call *engagement* begins. The drama of the sermon, referred to in the opening chapter, begins right there in the preacher's study. Just as the battle of the Cross was won in principle in the Garden of Gethsemane, so the struggle to discern the Word of God for the Sunday is played out on the Friday morning or whenever.

My personal practice is to begin preparation by sitting at my desk in front of the open Bible, with all the commentaries and resource books still firmly on the shelves. I read through the text several times, until I am thoroughly conversant with its contents, and indeed have allowed those contents to become part of me. I ask questions of the text, only to discover that the text is asking questions of me. After asking my questions I listen carefully for the answers, remembering that I am listening not simply for myself, but for the congregation. I do not rush into writing things down, because the effect of writing something can almost work like the closing of a valve, shutting off the flow of inspiration. I am content to allow this process of silent engagement to go on for some time before committing anything to paper.

A skilful interrogator will know the right questions to ask of the text. This will involve approaching the text from all the different angles described in an earlier chapter. In doing so he will constantly remember what many scholars forget, that is that the process of interrogation is not a one way street. The Bible is a unique book in that when we think we are the ones asking the questions, we discover that the Bible is in fact interrogating us, calling us to self-examination and new resolve.

This process of mutual interrogation, or engagement, is so much more than simply reading or even reading with understanding. The preacher must begin to find God in the text for himself before he can open it up to others. He must react to the dark places in his own life that the text illuminates before seeking to shine that same light from the pulpit.

The phrase "begin to find God" is used deliberately, because for all that preaching is monologue, it has a dimension of dialogue. The fullness of God's message will not be discovered by the preacher in isolation, but by the preacher in community. The hearing will be as important as the speaking. The charismatic renewal folk are onto something important when they remind us that the whole Church is a prophetic community, not just individuals within it. All Christians possess the Holy Spirit (Acts 2.37-39) and as such are equally heirs to Jesus' promise that the Spirit would guide them into all truth (John 14.26; 16.13).

The ultimate aim of the preacher is to involve the congregation in the same engagement with the text that has been happening in the study. The words of the sermon are aimed at building a bridge between the hearer and the Scriptures. And from this springs the most important dialogue of all - that between the hearer and God.

When to prepare ?

Being practical means recognising the difference between what is ideal and what is possible in the context of a busy parish ministry. I have for example heard some preachers say that preparation for their Sunday sermon begins the previous Monday morning. They have spoken of having a piece of paper on their desks on which they write thoughts and ideas that come up in the course of their daily ministry. Thus the Sunday sermon is the distillation of all their work of ministry in the parish.

I would be the last person to speak against this as an ideal. It is obviously right that the experience of the week before should feed into the Sunday address. The problem is that the Sunday sermon is not the only form of the ministry of the Word for the parish priest during the course of a week. In an average week he may well have to lead a Bible Study, do a school assembly, perform a funeral, lead a P.C.C. (yes, that needs good preparation) and so on. All will crowd in on the timetable and create pressure on the preacher's sermon preparation time.

In spite of all this it is absolutely crucial and beyond compromise is that sermon preparation is an absolute priority and should be given priority time, with nothing allowed to interfere. For most preachers I suspect this will be on a Friday, although preliminary sketch work could well begin earlier in the week. Friday for sermon preparation may well be dictated by the sort of pressures referred to above. In my personal view Friday should be the *latest* day for preparation, and preparing the sermon should not be left to Saturday. Friday preparation allows for second thoughts, further reflections and alterations that reveal themselves upon reviewing the written sermon. Then again, Saturday is often a family day in many clergy households, especially if the spouse works and children are at school. That day can be enjoyed all the more positively if the sermon is, so to speak, "in the can" and not hanging over the preacher's head.

What is equally important is that preparation time should be managed properly. This of course applies to the whole of a priest's ministry, but it is of crucial importance for sermon preparation. If a portion of time is allotted to sermon preparation, the preparation should be completed in that time. All of us can recall from College or University days the pressure of completing written assignments within a specified time. We fondly imagined that graduation meant escaping this kind of pressure. We have all learned by experience how mistaken a view this was. Now we value those earlier pressures as training disciplines that have served us well and stood us in good stead in the parish ministry.

Of course there will be from time to time things that disrupt us, a parish mini crisis, or someone with personal problems, and of course such things cannot be avoided. Only things of such magnitude should, in my view, be allowed to disrupt preparing the sermon. Happily they are rare. My personal preference is whenever humanly possible to start and finish the sermon in one sitting. This means making a conscious effort to minimise possible distractions. My own practice, developed over a number of years, was to actually move out of the study into another room, taking of course the commentaries and other aids with me. Staying in the study risked my eye falling on letters, forms and other things needing my attention. Physically getting away from these things offered a better opportunity for concentration. The other arch-destroyer of concentration and disrupter of preparation is of course the telephone. Thankfully the advance of technology has given us the answer machine, and avoided the necessity of jumping up to answer the phone every single time it rings. Yes, an emergency call *might* come in; but, unless we are in a difficult situation to begin with, with ten crises every day, such calls will be relatively infrequent. In my experience, the vast majority of crises survive being neglected by the parish priest for two or three hours ! It is certainly worth taking risk in order to enhance his ministry of the Word. My point is simply that effective preparation requires discipline, the sticking to the task until it is properly completed.

How long should we spend preparing the sermon ?

This last statement raises the associated question: "how much time should be spent in preparing the sermon ?". Here again we have to make a distinction between what is ideal and what is possible.

Two equal and opposite errors can be made here. There is the obvious danger of spending so long on sermon preparation that other things in the parish are skimped or neglected. One my curates invariably asked for 2 or 3 weeks notice of what she would be preaching on so as to have what she considered adequate time to prepare. Whilst we have argued that preaching is a top priority, there is not unlimited time to spend on it. On the other hand, the Priest who says "I am so busy doing things in the parish that I have no time to prepare sermons" may well be guilty of wrong priorities or (more likely) not yet succeeded in obtaining the discipline of good time management.

The question of how long should be spent in preparing an individual sermon is in fact an impossible one to answer, as there are so many variables. The facile answer would be "as long as it takes". The preacher must spend sufficient time to prepare thoroughly, so that he doesn't go up the pulpit steps with his address half-baked. Precisely how long this will turn out to be will vary from preacher to preacher. John Stott considers all the variables and then comes up tentatively with the formula of one hours preparation for every five minutes of the sermon.[7] This is a helpful guide, but is no more than a general rule of thumb, as Stott himself acknowledges. The point is that it is not the *amount* of physical time spent at the desk that counts, but the *quality* of that time. Going back once again to College and University days we can all remember hours spent over our text books and notes when we were tired or otherwise out of sorts when we were not really taking anything in. We fared much better after a good night's sleep or when we were otherwise relatively fresh. We need to ensure therefore that when we are engaged in the vital task of sermon preparation, we arrange things physically, using some of the ideas outlined above, so that the time we do spend on the task is of optimum quality. There will of course be other factors influencing us, including our spiritual and emotional state. These are less easily controlled and channelled, but with time and experience will come mechanisms that will help prevent them deflecting us from the task in hand. We will talk later about the preacher's relationship with God. For now we simply acknowledge that it is a vital influence on the way we ensure the quality of our time in preparation for preaching.

At different stages of a preacher's ministry differing amounts of time will need to be spent on preparation. By and large new and inexperienced preachers will need to spend longer in preparation than those further on in their ministry. As preachers gain experience not only in preaching but in ministry in general, so the fund of stories and illustrations grows larger, and the ability to put together a sermon becomes sharper. It becomes that much easier to make preparation time productive. The experienced preacher is still vulnerable to temptation, and still needs the iron discipline of dedication and time management, but generally speaking the going gets a little easier as time goes by.

The Aim of the Sermon

At theological college we were encouraged to write at the beginning of our sermon notes what the aim of our sermon was. We are not just mounting the pulpit steps to pass the time, or put ourselves on display in front of the congregation - we actually want to achieve something. We want to make a difference to our congregation and through them to the world by what we are saying week by week. The aim, written at the head of the sermon, is a salutary reminder than we have an object, an end in view.

The constituent elements of our aim can be summed up by the use of three Latin words, placere (to please), docere (to teach) and movere (to move or motivate).[8]

Placere reminds us that there should be something in the sermon that is pleasing to the ear, something that the congregation will enjoy hearing. It may take the form of a joke, a funny story, a human interest story or any number of other things. It will help if it is relevant to the main substance of the sermon, though this is not strictly always essential.

If it is included in the introduction to the sermon then it will grab the congregation's attention and make them want to hear more. It will make them feel "this is good" or "this is interesting". If however it is confined to the introduction, then the temptation will be for the congregation to develop a sense of anti-climax and switch off. Anecdotes or humorous stories should ideally be spread evenly throughout the sermon, so that the congregation's concentration can be sustained to the very end. The whole presentation should in a sense be interesting and pleasing, both in the way the preacher speaks and in what he says. God deliver us from boring and dull preachers ! Goodness knows, there are enough of them about. What we tend to forget is that people who come to church for the first time come with the expectation that it will be boring. We must do everything we can not to confirm them in their expectations.

Although I am aware there are many who would disagree with me, I personally am not afraid of using the word "entertainment" in connection with worship. There is from time to time much in common between the preacher and the entertainer. After all, not so long ago in our pre-radio, television and cinema age, if anyone can think that far back, people flocked to hear public orators in rather the same way people went to watch entertainers. What they said was often less important than the way they said it. I myself am often extremely impressed by the way entertainers grab their audience's attention and succeed in retaining it. I am convinced that there is much for preachers to learn here, if we have the courage and imagination to learn it.

Some might point out that many people who come to our churches for the first time come with felt needs, with heavy hearts, and with a burning desire to reach out for God. They will not feel their needs being met by a preacher who is prancing about in front of them, attempting to be funny and/ or entertaining when he really does not have the requisite gifts or abilities. Such a preacher is too terrible a phenomenon to contemplate. It is absolutely essential that whatever the preacher does or says at any point in the service that it should be natural to him, and flow from a transparently straightforward and honest personality. It is vital that people who do come with felt needs should have those needs met.

Nevertheless I am not persuaded that this is the most serious danger presented by preachers. I think a far greater danger is people dying of boredom in our pews who seem to project, like the writer of Ecclesiastes, that the whole of life is a wearisome burden.

The difference between the preacher and the entertainer is of course that the preacher goes way beyond entertainment. He seeks to tell a good story, maybe even to tell a joke to make his hearers laugh, just as the stage comedian does. But the preacher does always have a higher goal, that of edification. Even then there are links with ancient story tellers. They told stories to entertain, but often attached a moral or lesson to them. The story attributed to Aesop of the *Boy who cried Wolf* is a wonderful example. Gain a reputation as a liar and no one will believe you, even when you are telling the truth. The story entertains us, but it also teaches us. Preaching is much *more* than entertainment, of course; but I would contend that it is *not less.*

Docere, our second latin word, tells us that the sermon should convey information or teaching. The congregation should go away having actually learned something they did not know when they came to church.

This teaching may take the form of historical information, such as would illustrate the background of an Old Testament incident on which the sermon is based, or information relating to an incident in the Gospels or Acts. A passage from the Epistle may need to be set in the context of the writer's historical situation as he writes, or in the light of the general theological themes of his letter. This would be true for example of virtually any passage taken from the Letter to the Romans ! The preacher may want to give insight into some aspect of

Christian Doctrine, or relate his sermon to some contemporary event in the wider Christian world. There is endless scope.

Two notes of caution should be added here. If the preacher is seeking to impart factual information about something in his presentation, it is vital of course that he gets his facts right. A preacher never knows when someone in the congregation will catch him out, someone with expertise in an area of which the preacher is not aware. A weak grasp of factual knowledge will scarcely enhance his reputation in the eyes of the congregation and encourage them to listen to him.

The other thing to be aware of is that the sermon is not a lecture. The people have not come to be lectured and talked down to. In fact, as an educational medium, the sermon has great weaknesses. It presupposes a passive audience of mixed ability and mixed ages, and for an educationalist presents a nightmare scenario. However, we have to make the best of this, because for many, perhaps most, of the congregation it will be the only access to Christian education that they will have. This has been and remains a big challenge for the Church.

The word **Movere**, as we might guess from the sound of the word, has to do with motivation. The congregation are not to be left in the same place they were before the sermon. At the beginning of every sermon the preacher should ask himself the vital question "what do I want my congregation to *do* as a result of my sermon ?". Every sermon should have a clear aim, and seek to bring about a change in his audience. He will remember that "all Scripture is ..... profitable " and is meant to equip the reader for service (2 Tim.3.l6). So he will look for practical outcomes and identify them as far as he can discern them.

Well may we remember the response to Peter's sermon in Jerusalem on the Day of Pentecost, 'brothers, what shall we *do* ?' (Acts 2.37). There was an implied imperative in what Peter had been saying. Instead of simply contemplating their folly in crucifying the One who was "Lord and Christ", they should "repent and be baptised". As a result of John the Baptist's preaching, different groups of people, including tax collectors and soldiers, come to him for practical advice as to how their day to day lives should change as part of their response to his message (Luke 3.10-14).

This call to action is what distinguishes the sermon from the lecture or lesson. The primary purpose of the lecture is to inform; the purpose of the sermon, as well as the conveying of information, is motivation to action. If the sermon has disadvantages in educational terms, as mentioned in the opening chapter, that is because education is not it's sole or even primary purpose. All the elements of the sermon that comprise "education" and "entertainment" are geared to this motivation.

Motivation should be the aim of the sermon as a whole. Some preachers attach their practical application to the body of their sermon in rather the same way that a camper might attach a trailer to his car. The application should instead be part of the main fabric of the sermon. A good example of this is the Magnificat (Luke 1.46-55). The main application comes early on in the passage - "for he has been mindful of the humble state of his servant" (v.48). In other words, don't shrink from offering yourself in the service of God because you think you are too insignificant, for God sees strength and weakness differently. The rest of the passage is an illustration of this main principle. Viewed in this way, the whole sermon becomes application and motivation. What follows from the early statement of the theme is all application.

It may be useful sometimes to distinguish between a main aim and subsidiary aims. A relatively minor detail in a passage may have a practical application that is not part of the main

274

aim. There is no harm in picking this up as the sermon goes along, as long as it doesn't detract from the aim of the sermon as a whole. The well constructed sermon will achieve more than one purpose, and will ring bells with the congregation at all sorts of levels.

Having said all that, it is important to recognise that the preacher can suggest, but cannot control, the ways in which the congregation respond to the message, nor should he attempt to do so. Here Craddock and Lowry have important lessons to teach us. The actual response his hearers make will be determined by a whole host of factors outside the preacher's control, factors that work together to make up the life setting of each individual hearer. The response may be multi-layered, involving silence, submission, obedience, affirmation, repentance and of course the eucharistic celebration of receiving the Body of Christ.

The wise preacher therefore will not be too prescriptive in setting out his aims, presuming to know how the Holy Spirit, who "blows where He wills" will take and use our message. What the preacher wants his congregation to do, or thinks they should do may not be the same as what God wants them to do ! It is not an uncommon experience to find the sermon achieving surprising results, different from those the preacher anticipated. Contrary to what critics of the sermon sometimes say, this phenomenon does not imply a failure on the part of the strategy of the preacher. It is a reminder that God remains sovereign in this process of communication by preaching. Nevertheless each sermon should have a practical application, a call to action for the congregation. A sermon aimed at nothing is sure to hit the target.

The response may in addition be gradual, and not immediate. Most of us would testify that the moulding and shaping of ourselves that has been brought about by the preached Word is something we have come to understand and appreciate only over time. Over time our character changes, our view of the world changes, the way we see the poor, our money, our families - everything changes.

So, whilst not yielding an inch on the conviction that our sermons should aim to have practical outcomes in the lives of our hearers, we need to be flexible and humble about what those outcomes may be. Sometimes the benefits of a particular sermon may be gained in spite of us and not because of us as preachers !

Having, through our *placere* and *docere* walked people into the text, we now begin to accompany the text as it walks into their daily lives. We do this not by being prescriptive and by telling them what to do - that is a caricature of expository preaching - but, as one writer puts it, by borrowing pages from the playbooks of their own lives. As we preach they will see before their eyes their homes, their schools, their workplaces, their leisure activities, and into those situations the text is allowed to speak. We borrow these pages so that God can rewrite them.

Structuring the Sermon

Human beings are people of order and organization. We have a natural ability, when confronted with chaos, to impose order upon it. Thus, as those made in the image of God, we reflect His nature as creator. Our sermon therefore will have order and structure. It will begin life as random, disconnected thoughts, and will end in an ordered sequence.

The Structure of the Sermon and the New Homiletic

Those who have embraced Craddock's ideas see the inductive sermon as an event or experience. It is not the content of the sermon that is of crucial importance, it is the sermon itself. Preaching is not the conveying of a proposition or concept across the homiletically bridge between the horizons of the text and the hearer; it is an experience that is brought across.

These ideas have important implications for the structure of the sermon. If the sermon is regarded as the statement of theological and biblical propositions, leading to a summative conclusion, then the structure or form of the sermon will of necessity be predominantly that of a discursive lecture. If however, the sermon is seen as a journey of discovery, then the form and structure will be very different. Indeed, there will be no set structure. There will be as many structures as there are texts.

Craddock says

> Why should the gospel always be impaled upon the frame of Aristotelian logic, when the preacher's muscles twitch and his nerves tingle to mount the pulpit steps not with three points, but with the gospel as narrative, or parable, or poem, or myth, or song ? [9]

Genre and rhetorical criticism have emphasised the importance of the preacher respecting the literary form and rhetorical situation of the text under review when structuring his sermon. Form and meaning are undoubtedly connected, and it is all to easy to do violence to the meaning of the text by casting it in an inappropriate form. Whilst this has constantly be born in mind, we need to recall what we referred to earlier, that the New Testament writers themselves were not afraid to use their Old Testament texts in novel and imaginative ways. It is as always a matter of balance. The form of the original text must be allowed to influence the form of the sermon, but not be the sole, or even the dominant, factor in shaping that form.

Putting things together

It is clear in the light of the foregoing discussion that we cannot talk about a single paradigmatic or ideal structure for the sermon. Clearly there will be a number of factors that will govern the shape or form of the sermon:

i. The aim or purpose of that particular sermon

A sermon that is designed primarily to teach will clearly need a different structure than a sermon that is designed primarily to motivate, or call to action. The **teaching** or **didactic sermon** will have a significant propositional element within it, and may well be packed with scriptural references or allusions. In the **call to action sermon** the propositional element will be less prominent, and the application element brought to the fore. In an **evangelistic sermon** there may well be a preponderance of illustrations and human interest stories, relating the Gospel message to the individual lives of the hearers. Different purposes require different approaches and therefore different sermonic forms.

ii. The Form of the Text

This matter has come under discussion at various points in the development of the New Homiletic, and there are different understandings of it. And we have seen that New Testament writers often take surprising approaches to their Old Testament texts.

What we should say is that if our preaching is to be truly *biblical* preaching, then great respect has to be shown for the literary, historical, cultural and theological setting of the text in use. What we proclaim may not be without value altogether, but it will not be derived from what the Bible says, and therefore have proper theological justification. Honesty should compel the preacher in these circumstances to indicate the places where he is moving out of the Bible's hermeneutical tramlines, so that they can make the appropriate assessment of what he is saying.

Having said all that, the matrix of contextual factors listed above should not serve as a straightjacket for the preacher. Nor does it need to, for within the pages of the Bible there is a wonderful variety of sermonic forms to be used by the imaginative preacher, and no way he can justify imposing a single, uniform structure, however venerable that might be, upon his biblical material.

iii. What 'works' for the congregation

Some preachers might come back and retort that over the years some approaches work better than others for his particular hearers. Again, such a contention needs to be treated with respect. Over time the sensitive preacher will learn how his congregation listens to things, and what sort of elements of the sermon structure will aid their memories. Some would defend the traditional three-point sermon on this basis. One preacher I recall in Bristol resorted to elaborate (and often quite contrived) alliteration in presenting his preaching points. Contrived or not, his congregations remembered those points! Just as congregations vary, so the approaches to them need to vary also.

There is certainly no point in adopting approaches to particular congregations that do not ring bells with them, or aid their absorption of the sermon's message, a point that Craddock and Lowry might do well to remember. Doing what "works" for a particular congregation is fine as long as our previous point about resonance with the proper context of the sermon's text is observed, and inappropriate frameworks imposed upon it.

Elements of the Sermon's Structure

Whatever the form of the sermon may turn out to be, whether traditional, or inductive or narrative or whatever, there are elements of the approach that will remain the same.

i. The Introduction

The most important thing about the introduction to any sermon is that it should be attention-grabbing. There is nothing more disheartening for any preacher to see the congregation settling in their seats at the beginning of the sermon, ready for a nice snooze. The introduction stops them doing that. It tells the congregation that what is to follow will be important, interesting and well worth listening to. The introduction can do this in a number of ways. It may take the form of a humorous story, or a human interest story, or a reference to some contemporary event, or a mini-discourse on an important topic. Whether it is an explanatory statement, or one of Lowry's conflicts, it should be relevant in some way to the body of the sermon and display a connection that the hearer's can identify. Otherwise the story or whatever descends into entertainment.

ii. The Body of the Sermon

This will contain the main idea or thrust of the sermon. Haddon Robinson, from the expository sermon camp, encourages preachers to identify a single, unifying principle from the text under review, what he calls the "Big Idea".

> to ignore the principle that a central, unifying idea must be at the heart of every sermon is to push aside what experts in both communication theory and preaching have to tell us.[10]

He cites the writings of the prophets in support of this assertion, with each prophetic oracle conveying a single idea. He goes on to examine the sermons in Acts in the same way. Peter's sermon on the Day of Pentecost for example can be summed up as expressing the central idea, "let all the House of Israel know for certain that God has made Him both Lord and Christ, this Jesus whom you crucified" (Acts 2.36). Less certain is his analysis of Paul's address to the Ephesian elders at Miletus under the banner, "be on guard for yourselves and for all the flock" (Acts 20.28). There are other elements of a personal nature in this particular address not directly related to the duties of the church leaders Paul is leaving behind in Ephesus.

What Robinson fails to acknowledge is that some passages in the Bible are simply not capable of being expressed in one single idea, communicating in different ways and on different levels. Nevertheless his comments are helpful in encouraging the preacher to weave his material as far as possible into an integrated whole, rather than a collection of separate sayings. Some sermons I have heard do seem to resemble a string of beads, with stories, illustrations and saying strung together in a way that reveals only a superficial connection.

iii. 'Preaching Points'

But where a single, unifying idea has been identified, it may well still prove useful wherever possible to break it down into a series of preaching points, to ensure that all facets of the idea are displayed. Such a process not only helps to convey the full meaning of the Big Idea, but also acts as an aid to the congregation's memory. It is of course important that the individual points should be closely related, and complementary to each other. It is essential also, to repeat what was said in the previous paragraph, that they should arise naturally from the passage and not be part of a structure imposed upon it. If a passage or text simply cannot be broken down into individual preaching points, then the wise preacher does not attempt to do so. It may well be an indication that a different approach needs to be used for that particular text.

For many preachers down the years the classical three-point sermon has been of great value to both themselves and to their congregations. Often the three-pointer is parodied and denigrated by those in more contemporary preaching movements, especially those within the New Homiletic.

Looked at from one angle, it could be argued that the three-point sermon is old fashioned, hackneyed, and needs pensioning off in favour of more flexible and sophisticated approaches. Certainly it should not be regarded as the only approach to structuring a sermon, any more than any approach should.

From another perspective it could be argued that something that has proved its value over the years should not be easily discarded in favour of approaches as yet unproven.

I am certainly not disposed to argue that the three-point structure should be set aside. Although a text may throw up more or less of these points, three seems to be about right for some reason. It reminds me of the old joke, current in jazz circles, about trumpet players:

> *Question*: Why does a trumpet have three valves ?
> *Answer*: Because trumpet players can't count to four.

Whilst this is almost certainly not true of every congregation, for the average congregation, if there is such a thing, three points often seems to be right.

A text such as "Jesus Christ who has become for us wisdom from God - that is, our righteousness, holiness and redemption" (1 Cor.1.30), lends itself naturally to the structure:

> i. Introduction - Jesus, Wisdom from God
> ii. Preaching points -
> 1. Righteousness
> 2. Holiness
> 3. Redemption

In my view the three point sermon still has mileage in it. Three points seems to allow for a sufficiently comprehensive exploration of the Big Idea as may be possible in the time available, whilst at the same time provided a ceiling on the congregation's ability to retain the structure in memory.

What is of vital importance in biblical preaching is that the whole sermon, and not just part, should be permeated with that text. We still unfortunately hear preachers who begin with the statement of their text, only to wave it goodbye at the end of the introduction, never to encounter it again. It is worth remembering always that preaching is the setting forth of the Word of God, not a display of human ideas. Preaching gains the power it has through that Word of God, and whilst the display of human oratory and skill is important in setting forth that Word, it is no substitute for it. The Word therefore must be kept in view throughout the sermon, not merely at the beginning and at the end.

One major variation on basic sermon structure is the so-called **topical sermon**, which explores a subject using not a single text, but using multiple biblical texts. In general I am not a great enthusiast for this approach, since the risk of using texts in inappropriate ways at variance with their individual contexts, is virtually impossible to avoid. The justification for such an approach is often that the taking of a single Biblical text might not give the full picture. Preaching on money would therefore include such passages as

- Jesus and the Rich Young Ruler, Luke 18.18-30

- The Sermon on the Mount, esp. Matt. 6.19-24

- The Parable of the Talents, Matt.25.14-30

- The Unjust Steward, Luke 16.1-9

- Paul's words to the Corinthians, 1 Cor.9.1-18; 1 Cor.16.2; 2 Cor.8 & 9

- And so on !

What is immediately apparent from the foregoing sketch is the impossibility of covering a subject such as the Christian's attitude to money in a single sermon. The probable consequence of making such an attempt is to fail to do justice to any of the constituent passages, because of the constraints of time. In all likelihood also the congregation will be left confused or exhausted or both in the process. Far better is the construction of a mini-series of sermons on the topic, with one or at the most two individual Bible passages expounded in each sermon, with a final sermon to tie it all together.

Some might wish to defend the topical sermon on the grounds that it is important to display the fact that the different parts of the Bible fit together in an harmonious whole. The Bible is a library of sixty-six books, but at the same time a single book with a single message, inspired by the same Holy Spirit. Having moved through a phase when the diversity of the New Testament was being emphasised, as being an amalgam of distinctive theologies (Paul, John, etc) scholars are moving back to a position of emphasising the common ground between the individual writers. It is important for the preacher to be able to display this unity in diversity in his preaching.

There is the additional danger in any topical approach of subjectivity in the choice and combination of texts. I well remember listening to a sermon whilst visiting an Independent Evangelical Church in Manchester with my daughter whilst on holiday. The preacher preached a topical sermon on Christian Giving, beginning with 1 Corinthians 16.2:

> On the first day of the week, each of you should set aside a sum of money in keeping with his income, saving it up, so that when I come no collections will need to be made.

He then led us up hill and down dale through all the New Testament texts on giving, without as far as I can recall ever returning to his main text. It transpired in the course of the trip that he had a definite agenda, that of encouraging his hearers to give more generously so that they could build a new Church Centre. What he seemed not to recognise was that his main text from 1 Corinthians did not support this agenda. Paul is talking there about planned giving, not for themselves or for their church plant, but for the persecuted Christians back in Jerusalem, for whom Paul was enlisting support, and whose cause remained very close to Paul's heart as he journeyed around. Paul was calling them to disinterested giving, for people they had never met or would be likely to meet, and the fruit of which they would never see. This very far from the agenda of this particular preacher, who had a very close interest in what the money would be used for !

iv. The Summary/Conclusion/Resolution

This will gather together and integrate the thoughts contained in the main body of the sermon, especially the preaching point, or points, however many of them there may be. It will contain the resolution, complete or partial, of any conflicts introduced in the main body. It will spell out the practical application of the sermon in general terms, remembering what we said earlier about the sovereignty of the Holy Spirit in this process. If the congregation have dozed off in the middle of the sermon, the conclusion should give them some idea of what they have missed.

The conclusion should be short, pithy and to the point. It should contain only one 'finally'. It is amazing how refreshing the sound of the word "finally" can be to a congregation, as long as it truly is the end. Closed eyes miraculously open, flagging spirits are revived, and hearts leap for joy at the sound of that single word. If preachers at times have difficulty in beginning their sermon, they just as often have difficulty in bringing it to a conclusion. Knowing how to end the sermon is as important as knowing how to begin it. Many young preachers put me in mind of trainee aircraft pilots. They bounce on the tarmac several times before coming to a full stop. An indecisive ending tells the congregation that the preacher has not organized his thinking clearly enough.

Of course, no matter how long our sermon is, there is always more to say. It is neither possible nor desirable to exhaust the meaning of a particular text in a single sermon, no matter how hard I have heard young preachers try ! On several occasions Paul left his audiences wanting to hear more on another occasion. That is not a bad place to leave our congregation. The consumption of rich food leaves the diner with the desire to consume more of the same. Part of the purpose of preaching is to awaken and sustain just such a hunger for the Word of God.

CHAPTER SEVEN
ENDNOTES

[1] C.H.Spurgeon, *Lectures to my Students* (Revised Edition, London: Marshall, Morgan and Scott, 1954),89-91

[2] Christopher R.Seitz, *Prophecy and Hermeneutic: Towards a New Introduction to the Prophets*, (Grand Rapids: Eerdmans, 2007), 242.

[3] Exodus 19.6

[4] Isaiah 42.6

[5] see Jeremiah 31.31-34

[6] Among the more recent publication see the encyclopaedic work, ed. G.K.Beale and D.A.Carson, *Commentary on the New Testament Use of the Old Testament*, (Grand Rapids: Baker Academic, 2007).

[7] J.R.W.Stott, *I Believe in Preaching* (London: Hodder, 1982),258-9.

[8] I am greatly indebted to my tutor at Tyndale Hall, John Wenham, for these insights.

[9] Craddock, *As One without authority*, 45.

[10] Haddon W. Robinson, *Expository Preaching: Principles and Practice* (Leicester: I.V.P., 2001), 37.

8

THE PREACHER'S PERFORMANCE

DELIVERING THE SERMON

The preparation time is over, the work has been done thoroughly, and now the time for delivering the sermon has come. For all preachers there should be a great sense of excitement and anticipation, for in many ways this is the climax of the week, the high point of the ministry, an activity that sums up everything the preacher is about as a servant of God. If as a preacher he doesn't get excited about preaching, even when it is a weekly "routine", then something is wrong, and he needs urgently to re-evaluate his ministry.

In Anglican circles some would counter by arguing that it is the celebration of the Eucharist that epitomises the Priesthood, not preaching. But it is a false dichotomy, for at the heart of the Eucharist is the proclamation of the Word. The expression "Word and Sacrament" is an unfortunate one, since it suggests that the Ministry of the Word is something separate from what goes on in the rest of the service. On the contrary, it is precisely the uplifting of Jesus the Word that makes the actions with bread and wine sacramental. The sermon is in no sense therefore a mere preliminary to the "real business" of the Eucharist, but is that which gives meaning to the whole celebration. Eucharist without preached words is, in the words of the old Frank Sinatra song, like love without marriage. For those who are not old enough to remember that song, love and marriage go together like a horse and carriage.

Much time is wasted in the sterile debate about whether the ministry of the Word is more important than the ministry of the sacrament, or whether the ministry of the sacrament is more important than the ministry of the Word. The two ministries are complementary, or, better still, are two expressions of the one ministry. Whenever the minister of the Word prepares to preach he must remember that he is also the priest at the altar, and when the minister prepares to celebrate the Eucharist he must remember that he is also the minister of the Word.

A sermon is meant to be delivered. Sermons written on paper for people to read are not without their value, but are not achieving the real purpose of preaching. The oft-used definition of preaching as "truth through personality" implies that the essence of the sermon is that it is the dynamic, active delivery of a message by a living person to a living audience. The key to preaching is that it is "live". Even DVDs and videos of preachers, while by no means valueless, are placing this live encounter at a relative distance, as a secondary phenomenon.

If all this is so, we need to look at those practical issues that can enhance the delivery of the sermon and therefore determine whether this live encounter will be effective or otherwise.

From the Pulpit, Lectern or Where ?

The Pulpit

The traditional location for the preacher when delivering the sermon is of course the pulpit. The design of most Anglican churches identifies a special place just for the act of preaching. In the majority of churches the pulpit is elevated above the eye level of the congregation, reached by a flight of stairs. The present writer has over the course of time needed to navigate some quite circuitous routes to reach the pulpits of some churches, and indeed would on occasions have found a GPS navigation system quite handy ! The elevated position of the pulpit reflects the practice of the synagogue, which in turn recalls the incident of Ezra reading the Law to the people

> On a high, wooden platform built for the occasion
> *Nehemiah 8.4 (NIV)*

Pulpits very enormously in size and design, from the relatively simple structure referred to in the Ezra episode to the grand, elaborate structures found in many of our cathedrals. In churches that contain galleries, as of course the synagogue did, the pulpits are built high so as to put the preacher's head virtually on a level with the gallery. When preaching at a church named St. Michael and All Angels, Ashton under Lyne, a church within my deanery just outside Manchester, one is almost advised to take climbing gear and oxygen when venturing up into what is a distinctive, highly elevated pulpit.

In line with Anglican liturgical developments in the 19th Century, the period within which the vast majority of our churches were built the pulpit is set to one side, with the altar taking central place. In contrast, the design of most non-conformist churches still locate the pulpit in the centre, a construction usually of large dimensions, dominating the vision of the worshippers, with a small Communion Table set in front of it. Modern, newly-built Anglican churches still maintain a central altar, but often replace the pulpit with a movable lectern, which combines the function of a place from which to read the lesson, as well as the locale of the preacher. This lectern can be placed centrally or off-centre, to suit the requirements of the particular church. A multi-purpose lectern has the advantage of reducing clutter at the front of Church, opening up the congregation's view of the liturgical action, and reducing the number of *foci* for their attention. It helps to integrate a number of liturgical actions, such as reading, preaching, praying and the giving of notices. Others would argue however for the value of movement and the highlighting separately of reading and preaching. There is legitimate room for a difference of opinion here.

The pulpit does offer the preacher certain practical advantages. It maximises his visibility and audibility for example. With or without a microphone, it offers the congregation the maximum opportunity of hearing the preacher. Discreet spotlights enhance the visual impact, without risking turning the Church into a theatre. The pulpit dramatically emphasises the idea that what the preacher is doing is something very special, distinct from other things that are happening in the service.

It offers also the very useful practical possibility of hiding the preacher's notes and other visual aids with which the preacher is working until such time as he wishes to display them. The pulpit hides unlimited secrets. I remember very vividly being half-way through a sermon in a church in Droylsden, also in Manchester, when I felt a certain warmth around my ankles. I looked down briefly to discover the blind organist's guide dog tucked away, comfortably asleep, in the pulpit. It was his apparently his customary place of refuge during the service. You can be sure I was very careful what I said, especially about organists, in the rest of the sermon ! Although occasionally a place of danger, the pulpit more often offers the preacher a sense of physical security, a secure base from which to launch his proclamation.

This physical separation from the congregation can be viewed both positively and negatively of course. The sense of authority conveyed can be a false one, rendering the preacher as it is said "six feet above contradiction" and well beyond the range of any rejoinders from his listeners. It also places certain physical restrictions on the preacher, restricting him to one spot, and thus reducing his scope for hand and other physical gestures to back up his words.

Certainly the Revivalist preachers described earlier would find many Anglican pulpits extremely restrictive indeed. Whilst physical gestures can all too easily be overdone, they do undoubtedly add weight to sermon presentation.

Platform/Lectern

As previously mentioned, modern church buildings often replace the traditional pulpit with a movable, multi-purpose lectern situated on a platform/stage at the front of the Church. The platform would be raised above congregational level, but not to anything like the same extent as the traditional pulpit. The fact that it is portable allows the preacher to locate it in the place where it expresses most clearly his relationship to the congregation.

For most preachers this location will be at the front centre of the stage, where he has a real sense of being in amongst his listeners as he speaks. It gives the sermon much more immediate impact, the preacher being "in the face" of the congregation, making a proclamation to them, whilst in a very real sense one of them. It offers the preacher a degree of freedom of movement and gesture denied to the preacher by the fixed pulpit, whilst at the same time giving the congregation a single visual focus.

These advantages might be countered by the impression given that preaching is simply one liturgical activity amongst many, and not the special, climactic activity suggested by the pulpit. Be that as it may, the location of the pulpit in a newly-built church will be decided by the principles governing the design of the church as a whole, and not those governing preaching alone.

The Roaming Preacher

Some preachers enjoy casting off all restraint completely and wandering round amongst the congregation whilst preaching. This is of course taking the principles of nearness and immediacy to their fullest extreme. Strange as it may seem to many, there are occasions where this is most appropriate. I myself have used this technique many times at baptismal services, where I have known that the majority of people attending have been those very unfamiliar with worship in Church and therefore unaware of normal liturgical practices. I found they responded very readily to someone standing there in a friendly, informal and undemanding way speaking directly, from the heart about Jesus. The liturgical mystique is thus stripped away and the congregation find themselves at the centre of things. It is also a medium they will find themselves familiar with from the pubs and clubs that make up their everyday lives.

There are two basic requirements for preachers if they are aspiring to use this approach. The first is that they should feel at home doing it. Not everyone is able to get close up and personal with the congregation in this way. It requires a personality that is relatively extrovert and personable, who is able to relate to people at close quarters and speak to people in a natural manner. If the preacher does not have that kind of personality, and if getting close up is not the natural thing to do, then he should not attempt it. But if a preacher is able to do it, then it offers a marvellous opportunity, on those occasions where it is appropriate, to present the Word very directly and personally. It ensures all the congregation is involved in the sermon all the time. Very few will dare to fall asleep if they think the preacher may come and stand next to them at any moment !

The second requirement is that the preacher should be able to preach without notes. It is simply not possible for the preacher to the leave the pulpit or lectern and take his script along with him. Having to glance down repeatedly at notes takes the preacher's eye off the congregation, risks irritating them in the process, and destroys much of the immediacy of the impact. This is often compounded by the fact that, if the notes are not written properly, the preacher takes a second or two to find his place in the notes, creating a stop-start effect, which spoils the flow of the address and lessens its force. The use of autocues in television broadcasting, especially for newsreaders, emphasises the point, allowing the newsreader to look at the audience through the camera throughout the broadcast.

The very important point should be made here that preaching without notes is not at all the same thing as preaching *extempore*. The latter implies that no previous thought has been given to the matter of the address. Circumstances have forced the speaker into make it up as he goes along. There are a few talented preachers who can get away with this, but in my experience vary rarely does off-the-cuff speaking result in an effective sermon. Nearly always the preacher ends by recognising important things he has omitted, as well as being aware of saying things he was "led" to say but which he later regrets. As I have said, where circumstances allow, there is simply no substitute for thorough preparation.

It is perfectly possible however for preparation to have been so thorough that the main substance of the sermon is so burned into the mind of the preacher that he is able to stand and deliver without recourse to notes, rather in the same way that an actor delivers lines on a stage. Thus speaking without notes is not a sign of too little preparation, but rather the opposite. It takes *more* preparation to speak without notes, rather than less. It is not of course a technique for beginners, unless that beginner is so bursting with natural talent that all the rules may be broken. For the majority of us it takes time and experience to be able to reproduce thoughts, arguments and stories from mere headings.

For those who are able to preach without written notes the advantages are obvious and considerable. It means the preacher can focus all his attention on his audience and upon his delivery to them. He can hold constant eye contact with them, without having to look up, down or sideways at a script. But, as with all forms of preaching, good preparation is the key.

The Preacher's Script

With the exception of those who opt for the technique outlined immediately above, the vast majority of preachers work from a script which they take to the preaching locus with them. The form of this script will be tailored to the individual preacher's requirements, and will vary widely from preacher to preacher. There is no general rule governing the form a preacher's script should take.

Less experienced preachers will tend to use full scripts, with everything set out in long hand. This has the obvious advantage to the preacher, since all the thoughts and ideas in the sermon will of necessity have needed to be thought through and worked out in the course of the preparation. It cuts out the need for the preacher to think on his feet, and therefore minimises the risk of the careless, ill thought out phrase that the preacher later regrets using. It can have the disadvantage of making the delivery mechanical and impersonal, the preacher reading to the congregation rather than preaching to them. It is also quite restrictive on the preacher, making him the slave to his script, rather than freeing him to speaking directly to the situation in which he is preaching. I recall vividly being in a service where the preacher, admittedly young and inexperienced, never lifted his eyes once from his script to look at his congregation or acknowledge their existence. The mischievous thought passed through my mind that they could have all slipped quietly out of the church or died in the course of the sermon without him even noticing. The sermon delivered from a full script is in effect the one given birth in the study on the Friday morning or whenever, rather than the one bursting into life in the pulpit itself.

Those who have been preaching for a longer period will be able to preach from headings, or from otherwise more abbreviated forms of notes. As was mentioned previously, the more abbreviated form of script does not betoken lack of preparation - rather the opposite. It simply means that ideas and arguments can be called to mind and delivered from something considerably less than a full script. An illustration or personal story for example may be recalled and subsequently recounted from a single word or phrase. Judicious use of underlining, or a highlighter pen will also enhance the process of emphasising headings and key words.

This more sophisticated approach frees the preacher from many of the problems of the full script as outlined above. Most importantly, in my view, it maximises eye contact with the congregation, something I regard as extremely important. Eye contact strengthens greatly the immediacy and dramatic impact of the delivery. The congregation are made aware that the sermon is for them personally. In the same way that the eyes of the portrait on the wall seem to follow the viewer all round the room, so the preacher's eyes follow each member of the congregation. "He was looking at *me* personally when he said it" is the feeling that can be engendered in each member of the congregation individually. The sense of the sermon as an encounter between God and the listener, is in the last analysis something enabled by the Holy Spirit, but is enhanced and made all the more real by the preacher's eyes, as well as by his voice.

Abbreviated notes, customized for the individual preacher, also allow space for flexibility and spontaneity. Every preacher will tell you that unexpected things happen in the pulpit. Many a preacher comes down the pulpit steps saying to himself "where did that come from ?". Full-scripted sermons can have the effect of restricting or eliminating this "surprise" factor. We must go back again, however, to emphasise that flexibility and spontaneity are skills acquired with time and experience, and therefore the developing preacher is better sticking with relatively full scripts until he has mastered these skills. What he thus delivers will at least have the merit of being rounded and well thought out, something that is of vital importance for the congregation.

The Preacher's Voice

Just like the tennis player's racquet, or the golfer's clubs, the preacher's voice is his stock in trade. He will nurture it very carefully, and laryngitis or tonsilitis will for him represent great crises. Gestures, visual aids and other things will be employed, but at the heart of the delivery of the sermon will be the preacher and his voice. One of the common denominators in an otherwise diverse group of revivalist preachers, such as Wesley and Whitfield was their ability to command the attention of great crowds by the force of their oratory alone. In the history of preaching therefore the sermon has become synonymous with powerful, distinctive oratory. This method of delivery is one of the major things that distinguishes the sermon from the lecture.

Not all preachers, especially in Anglican circles, can afford to be Wesleys or Whitfields. Yet there are certain basic minimum requirements for any preacher's voice:

It should be interesting to listen to

The sermon is more of a wake up call than a lullaby. The preacher has to grab the congregation's attention right from the start and hold onto it. His voice will convey passion and commitment, and tell the congregation that the preacher really cares about them and wants them desperately to hear what he has to say to them. Because he is passionate about his message, he wants them to become passionate also.

Note that being passionate is not the same thing as being intimidating or threatening. Sometimes the line between the two becomes blurred. The congregation are not there to be bullied into submission, and their right to listen or not as they choose must be rejected. If they choose not to accept the message it is not as far as the preacher is concerned because they are thick or obdurate; maybe - just maybe - it is the preacher who is not expressing the point clearly enough. A little humility on the part of the preacher goes a long way.

The preacher's voice will have light and shade. It will make full use of rise and fall, of changes of pace, of changes of volume and so on to emphasise particularly points and to prevent the delivery becoming predictable. What it will not be is a flat monotone. It is not at all necessary to adopt a special, "ecclesiastical" tone for the sermon that the preacher does not employ elsewhere. The delivery should be "natural" in the sense that it expresses the preacher's normal personality, which the congregation recognise is not alien to him, but which nevertheless acknowledges the special nature of the preaching task.

Just as we don't see ourselves as others see us, so we cannot hear ourselves as others hear us. Playing back a tape recording of yourself preaching can be traumatic and extremely revealing. Allowing for the fact that all but the best quality recorders will have an element of distortion in them, hearing yourself on tape will be quite instructive if not downright embarassing, and every preacher should do it from time to time. My own voice for example is relatively high pitched, and when I wish to increase the volume to emphasise a point, the tendency is to go higher still in pitch. I have to make a conscious effort therefore at key points in the delivery to keep my voice low and prevent it going off the scale altogether. Listening to myself on tape has been a key factor in recognising and dealing with this particular problem.

Other problems recordings can help us to deal with include the tendency of some preachers to end each sentence on the same note. No matter how much rise and fall they employ in the early part of the sentence, they invariably come back to the same note at the end of the line. As preachers we need to focus not just on the sermon as it leaves us, but on the sermon as it arrives at the congregation's ear.

The Diction should be clear

It goes without saying that the congregation should be able to tell what the preacher is saying. They generally don't have the opportunity to interrupt the preacher and say "I'm sorry, I didn't catch that, can you say it again, please ?". They must hear it and absorb it first time. This means the preacher must and trouble to enunciate his words clearly, making proper use of his mouth and vocal cords. This doesn't necessitate elocution lessons, though they will undoubtedly help, but does require discipline and the making of every effort to speak clearly.

Regional accents can complicate communication between preacher and congregation. In general terms, a preacher with an accent wholly alien to his congregation will have difficulties, and it is worth honestly recognising this when patrons consider appointments. However, accents are not inevitably a barrier to good communication as long as both sides make the appropriate effort. This involves the preacher aiming to speak clearly and articulate his words properly, and the congregation making a genuine effort to tune in. Undoubtedly the Church should accept the modern understanding, in the media and elsewhere, that accents are "in" and not attempt to flatten them into a consensus English. Indeed, accents can help the delivery to sound more interesting, as discussed above.

The Preacher should be audible

This ties in closely of course with the point made about diction. There is no point in the preacher's voice being crystal clear if it still cannot be heard, although clarity will always assist audibility. This means the preacher will need to learn the art of projection, aiming to be heard on the back row rather than on the front rows, which are usually empty anyway.

In my own case I was very fortunate in this respect. In the first place I was married to a teacher, well-used to making her voice heard amid the pandemonium of the average classroom, a level of ambient noise not usually found in the average Church. She taught me particularly that a voice projects further when kept at a lower pitch. It is not volume alone, but the combination of volume and low pitch that ensures maximum projection. The natural acoustics of the building will play a part, but nevertheless the principle, volume plus low pitch, holds good.

The other thing that proved an invaluable aid was membership of a local amateur operatic and dramatic society. Again I learned the basic principles of projection, of timing the delivery of lines and phrases, as well as the use of rise and fall in the voice for dramatic effect. The preacher who wishes to be effective in his delivery will never be afraid of learning from others engaged in one way or another in the art of oratory, including those involved in the entertainment business.

Some preachers, because of their physical stature, will have a natural advantage when it comes to volume. Because of the larger volume of their lungs they will have less difficulty in making themselves heard than others. Those lacking these natural advantages will need therefore to compensate. By maintaining the basic principles of projection (volume plus low pitch, etc) and by aiming for the back rows not the front, the relatively weak-voiced preacher will succeed in maximising his delivery.

Fortunately science and technology has come to the aid of the preacher here. In common with most other forms of electronics, public address systems as they have advanced have become cheaper and come within the economic range of most churches. Such systems can be as simple or complex as the needs of a particular church requires. Worship leaders and preachers can use stand microphones, fixed to a particular point, or can use radio microphones which tend to me more temperamental, but which offer the speaker freedom of movement. Movements of the head whilst speaking will not cause loss of volume with a radio mike, whilst fixed mikes require the speaker always to face in one direction.

What is worth remembering is that a sound reinforcement system is not there simply to aid the preacher with the quieter voice. It offers all preachers considerable benefits. It means that the speaker can employ variations in loudness and softness for special effect, knowing that even when he is speaking softly he will still be heard. By always having power in reserve, the preacher has a whole range of vocal effects available to him that he would not possess if he were having to concentrate on volume. The more loudly a speaker has to speak unaided by electronics the smaller the range of vocal effects he has available to him.

In purchasing a sound reinforcement system, there are one or two important things to bear in mind.

A Church should **buy the best system it can afford**. When it comes to the realm of electronics, buying cheaply is definitely false economy. I have suffered, like many others, listening to preachers through cheap and nasty systems that distort the voice and which are often quite literally a pain to listen to. A bad system will disturb the congregation and distract them from the task of listening to the preacher. Rather than being a help, a bad system will be a hindrance. Of course, if that is all a particular Church can afford, then so be it. But it is well worth aiming as high as possible in this particular area.

A Church should also **buy an integrated system, rather than putting one together piecemeal**. In other words, buy microphones, speakers and amplifiers that are compatible with one another, rather than buying components that come from different systems and different sources. Seek good professional advice when installing a system. There are around the country a number of sound system companies that are very familiar with and sympathetic towards the needs and requirements of churches. Seek their advice not only on buying the system, but on setting it up. Microphone feedback howls may provoke laughter in the congregation, but are a relatively easily avoidable distraction. The occasional bursting in of a police broadcast or a Rugby League commentary (as happened to me once) into the middle of divine worship may also be highly amusing, but is also avoidable.

Where possible, a Church should have a system that is controlled. Many churches now, even traditionally-built ones, manage to accommodate a mixing desk, where a controller sits adjusting and balancing all the microphones being used, as well as DVD-players, lap top computers and anything else the Church may be employing. Again, it is well worth paying the extra money if possible to add a mixing desk to the system, as it makes the whole presentation smooth and effective. Controllers will of course need to be trained, but in our modern world there are enough people computer and electronically literate to provide such training. In passing it is worth noting that a controlled system obviates the need for preachers and worship leaders to fish under their robes to find the tiny button that switches the transmitter on and off, something that preachers greatly appreciate !

The Preacher should speak at an appropriate speed

The speed at which a preacher speaks is often overlooked when considering the practicalities of preaching, but is actually of great importance. Too rapid a delivery will mean that important words are lost and phrases will be garbled. The congregation will at the end be left with a feeling of exhaustion, not to mention the preacher himself. On the other hand, too slow and deliberate a delivery risks the congregation nodding off, or having their minds drift off onto the thousand and one other things they could have been doing instead of coming to Church. The pace has to be sufficiently quick to persuade the congregation that what the preacher is saying is important, urgent and actually exciting, without losing anything in clarity. Given a choice, I would prefer to err on the side of being too quick rather than too slow, but a good balance is of course the best option of all.

Creative use of changes of pace will, just as in a piece of music, enhance the congregation's interest in the sermon. This is the technique of the storyteller. Exciting elements of the story are delivered at greater pace, whilst parts that need more careful thought are delivered more slowly. From time to time interest grabbing suspense can be created by careful use of pauses. Some less discerning members of the congregation may be misled into thinking the preacher has lost his place in the sermon and forgotten what comes next, whilst others will have their attention riveted all the more closely by having been temporarily been left hanging in mid-air. When changes in pace become cleverly combined with changes in volume, the delivery becomes virtually irresistible. At times a creative imagination is one of the best gifts a preacher can possess. The number of variations in presentation is therefore virtually without limit.

The length of the Sermon

How long is a piece of string ? This is only a slightly harder question to answer than "how long should a sermon be?". There are so many variables that it is impossible to give a simple answer.

It depends for example on **the ability of the preacher as a communicator**. I have listened to sermons that have lasted for an hour when that hour has seemed like only five minutes, so good and effective was the preacher. And I have seen a congregation almost lose the will to live when an address lasting only a few minutes has seemed endless.

A visiting preacher went to help out at a neighbouring Church. On arrival he was greeted by the churchwardens, who explained that it was their custom to have a cup of tea with the preacher at the end of the service. They explained that one of them put the kettle on at the commencement of the sermon, so that when the preacher heard the lid of the kettle rattling, he knew the tea was ready and it was time to stop. Thinking this seemed a very civilised custom, the preacher politely enquired as to how long that gave him for the sermon.

"Twenty minutes" came the reply. "Mind you" the warden said, "for some preachers we only half-fill the kettle!". I guess for some preachers even that would be over-generous. One factor in determining the length of a sermon will therefore be the ability of the preacher to present an interesting, lively and effective sermon that will sustain the concentration of the congregation. Alongside that will on the other hand be **the ability of the congregation to listen to a sermon.** For the vast majority of the congregation, the sermon will be the only occasion when they have to sit passively for any length of time and listen to somebody else speaking. In a multi-media, interactive age, that is not how they acquire the vast bulk of their information. We are told for example that at least 70% of the information we absorb comes in through our eyes, and only 20% through our ears. And yet in receiving the sermon, it is almost exclusively the ears that are employed. This will impose severe restrictions therefore on a congregation's ability simply to listen passively for any length of time.

The preacher will need to work hard therefore to sustain his congregation's concentration. He cannot take it for granted. We have already made reference to one or two ways in which the congregation's attention can be refreshed as the sermon goes along (variations in loudness, pitch and pace), and will deal with the use of humour in a separate note. Without being unduly pessimistic however, it is fair to say that with most congregations the sustenance of concentration levels for a significant length of time will be an uphill struggle. As a preacher gets to know his congregation he will gradually get to know how full the kettle should be.

What ultimately will hold the congregation as they listen to the sermon? It will not be the excellence of the speaker, his sunny personality or rapier wit, but it will be the feeling that what they are listening to is important to them and their lives. They will be held by the feeling of being transformed and shaped by what they are hearing. When this is happening time will stand still. The Sunday roast, the impending visit of Auntie Flo that afternoon, and the thousand things that press on them will all be forgotten. People in fact have all the time in the world for things that are important to them.

Having said the foregoing, it nevertheless remains true that for all congregations there will be a **minimum length** of time for a sermon. If the sermon is to be based on good, solid Biblical exposition, as I believe it should, and if the fruits of that exposition are to be passed on to the congregation, then this cannot be done within a certain length of time. Although other commentators might say something different, my view is that this minimum time is ten minutes. Anything less than that cannot possibly do justice to the biblical text at all. As preacher and congregation work together and grow together in the disciplines of preaching and listening, so the minimum level can be pushed on, and the levels of concentration extended beyond this basic ten minutes. I personally would feel myself failing if I were to drop short of twenty minutes, but I do recognise that preachers and their congregations differ widely. If the ten minute minimum were observed everywhere, then that would be an advance on what I strongly suspect is the situation in many Anglican churches today.

Theoretically there is no **maximum length** of a sermon. Some congregations will be able to absorb longer expositions than others, and with some preachers, admittedly few, the congregation would feel short changed if the delivery lasted less than an hour. Local factors will determine the optimum length. Then again, the sermon's liturgical context will impose a maximum length on the sermon, unless the whole service, especially if it is the Eucharist, becomes inordinately long.

In one sense you could argue that artificially determining the sermon's length is unnecessary and irrelevant. If God gives the preacher a message, his responsibility is to stand and preach until the delivery of that message is complete. Time will not come into it. What needs to be said must be said. In practice of course the length of delivery will work out approximately the same week by week, as the preacher's skills develop. Yet in a very real sense preaching is timeless, and the preacher must not allow his delivery to be dominated by his watch or the Church clock.

It should be said in passing that preaching to postmoderns does not inevitably mean that a sermon needs to be short. The same dynamics prevail as they did with preaching in any age. If a sermon has caught fire, why should it end after 20 minutes ? Once a sermon has begun burning on its own, let it. Don't quench the Spirit at this point. Let people have what they need.

One of the things that cause the length of the sermon to vary is the ability of some preachers to finish. If starting is important, then finishing is every bit as important. "Stand up, speak up and then shut up" is a maxim well worth remembering. Some preachers are like trainee fighter pilots, bouncing on the tarmac three or four times before the plane comes to a complete stop. I can recall one young preacher using the word "finally" twice and the phrase "so then" five times in the last five minutes of the sermon. It goes without saying that "finally" should be used only once, to indicate genuine finality, and "so then" used only sparingly, lest the congregation have their hopes raised, only to have them dashed as the sermon continues. To go back to aviation parlance, take-offs are optional, whereas landings are compulsory. It is important that the conclusion of the sermon is concise, direct and brings things to a natural, clean halt. Just as the congregation may well hold the introductory words of the sermon in their memories, so the final words of the sermon, if pithy and striking, will remain with the congregation all the following week.

A Note on the Use of Humour

The Bible is a serious book, there's no doubt about that. Its theme, from Genesis to Revelation, is the most important message in the history of humankind. But, contrary to many people's ideas, the Hebrew and Christian Scriptures are not the dry, humourless writings many imagine them to be.

The idea that God laughs is mentioned several times in Psalms. In Psalms (2:4), the Psalmist says: "He who sits in heaven will laugh, the Lord will mock them." Psalm 37:13: "My Lord laughs at him for He sees that his day is coming." Psalms 59:): "But as for You, God, You laugh at them; You mock all nations." These verses all indicate that one day the Lord will laugh at evildoers. Of course, the type of laughter described here is not a happy, fun-loving laugh, but a sarcastic, derisive one. The Psalmist is describing a contemptuous, sardonic laugh aimed at the wicked who do not realize the futility of their plots if God does not approve.

Jesus displayed a likeness to his Father in every way, of course, not the least of which was his sense of humour. Matthew records Jesus' encounter with a paralytic. When the Lord assured the cripple that his sins were forgiven, some in the crowd secretly accused Jesus of blasphemy. Knowing their thoughts, Jesus responded, "Which is easier: to say, `Your sins are forgiven,' or to say, `Get up and walk'?" Turning to the man (and, I like to imagine, with a knowing smile on his face), Jesus said, "Get up." In twenty-first century vernacular, he might have shrugged his shoulders and said to his sanctimonious critics, "have it your way--but I will heal him no matter what you say."

Jesus' love of humour s repeatedly betrayed in his parables. We see He is capable of telling a story that would have half his audience fuming with anger and the other half doubled with laughter.

307

One such story is the oft-misunderstood story of the friend at midnight (Luke 11.5-8). The story tells the tale of a man whose friend comes knocking on his door to borrow some bread for an unexpected late-night visitor. Jesus has the man respond from inside the house, "Don't bother me. The door is already locked, and my children are with me in bed. I can't get up and give you anything." Jesus' first-century listeners would have imagined that, as was common, the man's dog, goats, chickens, and sheep would be locked inside with the family. The picture is one of a household aroused, if not by the persistent knocking of the friend, then certainly by the two men talking back and forth through the closed door. Jesus must have smiled himself at the image of the man's stubborn refusals waking his wife and children--as well as his dog, goats, chickens, and sheep!

There are many different types of humour in the pages of the Bible. These include puns, wordplays, riddles, jokes, satires, lampoons, sarcasm, irony, wit, black humour, comedy, slapstick, farce, burlesques, caricatures, parody, and travesty. The differences among these different humour types is not always great. In particular, burlesque, caricature, parody, and travesty are very much alike and refer to literary or dramatic works that mimic serious works in order to achieve a humorous or satiric effect. Likewise, the difference between satire and lampoon is not that great. The bottom line is that humour has the ability to make people laugh, smile, or chuckle, at least inwardly. Perhaps it does the same for a divine being.

The Hebrew Bible therefore employs many sorts of humour, but its purpose is not to entertain. The major goal of the Hebrew Bible is rather to teach humanity how to live the ideal life. Much of the humour found in the Hebrew Bible has a purpose, namely, to demonstrate that evil is wrong and even ludicrous, at times. The punishments meted out to wrongdoers are often designed to mock them and to hoist them by their own petards.

Many celebrated preachers down the years have employed humour as an effective means of communication. Anyone reading Luther's writing, especially on the subject of the Pope, could not fail to be impressed by his use of the sharpest, biting caricature, describing the Bishop of Rome on one occasion as being like "an ass playing a harp". Charles Hadden Spurgeon would have his congregations rolling in the aisles, though not so much as to cause them to miss the point of what he was saying. Dr. Martyn Lloyd Jones, whilst not exactly famous for his one liners, would nevertheless emphasise the error of positions he was criticizing by gently poking fun at them. Humour is then a firmly established part of Christian preaching tradition, reflecting quite properly the fact that "seeing the funny side" is very much part of the human personality.

What does humour in the sermon achieve ?

The first thing it does is to create a mood. By creating in them a "feel good" factor, it places the hearers in the mood to hear more. It tells them the preacher is a human being, like them, with some understanding of all aspects of life, the lighter parts as well as the darker parts. He is not deadly serious about everything in life, but can take a step back from time to time and acknowledge those aspects of life that are genuinely funny.

Preaching is of course not simply entertainment. It is a serious business where the serious truths of life, death and eternity are being set before the congregation. But being serious is no justification for boring the pants of the preacher's congregation. On the contrary, what is not often understood is that the use of humour can actually make people *more* receptive to serious truth rather than less. By sensitive, skilful use of humour opposition can be disarmed, hostility dissipated, and many otherwise difficult debates can be conducted in a way that is palatable to both sides. By use of sympathetic (that which does not put down or denigrate its object) humour many explosive situations can be defused, and constructive discussion enabled.

Humour in theological debate often works by pointing out the ridiculousness of those attitudes and positions that are causing people to resist the truth. Such use of caricature can be seen on the lips of Jesus on a number of occasions. When for example He is being accused of casting out evil spirits by Baalzebub, the Prince of demons, he caricatures the position of His Pharisaic accusers by pointing out that this is tantamount to Baalzebub declaring civil war on himself (Matt.12.24-29) ! Caricature, whilst a useful tool, must of course not be used to the point where it distorts the position under review to the point where it becomes unrecognisable. Some might argue that distortion is of the essence of caricature, and therefore it should not be used at all. But true caricature, as in the example used by Jesus here, is a drawing out of what is already there, the leading through of an argument to its logical conclusion.

As part of the dynamics of a sermon, humour can play an important role in refreshing the congregation's concentration, especially in the middle of the address. When a preacher has been "serious" for a while, and the congregation is beginning to flag or feel beaten down, it can be good to throw in a funny story or joke, to perk them up and prepare them for the final assault. Mind you, this can be risky, for if a preacher says something he knows is funny, because he's used it before, and nobody laughs, it is a sure sign he has lost his hearers. Ever noticed why so many preachers put most of their funny stories into their introduction ? That's the reason !

Pulpit Comedians Beware !

As many comedians will tell you, getting people to laugh is just about the hardest task an entertainer can attempt. Anyone attempting to use humour in the pulpit ought therefore to be aware of the many pitfalls.

As all preachers know only too well, **humour can be risky, and its success is not guaranteed.** If someone sings a song in public, providing they sing reasonably in tune and articulate the words well, they will get applause at the end of the song, even if much of that applause is merely polite. Someone telling a joke on the other hand cannot be certain at the end that *anyone* will laugh ! Humour is in fact a very adventurous thing to attempt, because it is highly contextual. It works only if the humorist is aware of the beliefs and assumptions of the audience, and to some extent shares them. A comedian encouraging his elderly audience to reminisce about the good old days of rationing, bread and dripping, and rickets will always get a sympathetic reception. A preacher telling the one about the Bishop who turned up to a half-empty church who remarked "there are not many here, did you not tell them I was coming ?", only to be told "No, but word seems to have got round !" will on the other hand get a laugh only from those who recognise that bishops and other ecclesiastical dignitaries are on occasions inclined, ever so slightly, to be pompous. The bottom line is that simply because a comedian can get one audience to laugh, it doesn't follow he will be able get another different audience to laugh in the same way. The preacher who is able to get his audience rolling in the aisles will not necessarily enjoy the same success at the local working men's club or at the legendary Glasgow Empire. The humorist must always get to know his audience and what will tickle their funny bones.

Humour can be misplaced. This is usually because the preacher has not done the required homework to get to know his congregation. I can remember coming back from Canada one year, and in my first sermon after returning making some comment about Canadians having no sense of humour, only to subsequently discover there was a party of visiting Canadians in Church that morning. All my skills were required in retreating from that one. There are other occasions where I have spectacularly "bombed" is similar circumstances. It underlines that humour is indeed a high risk business.

It scarcely needs saying that preacher must be very careful at whom he targets his humour. Jokes about people's natural "challenges" such as height, weight, shape are not likely to go down well with sections of the congregation, as are comments about accents, or colour, or race. Jokes about sex are not totally taboo, but that area bristles with so many minefields that the subject is probably best avoided altogether. As always the golden rule is "know your congregation", and have some idea how they are likely to respond to your material.

Sometimes the preacher gets it wrong, usually because he has forgotten the basic principle mentioned above of knowing his audience, and has not put in the necessary homework in order to gain that knowledge. By and large however, humour has for me been far more of an asset than a liability, and the relatively few occasions when it has gone wrong have been appropriate occasions for learning.

Another important thing to recognise is that **humour requires a sense of humour on the part of the preacher.** This seems almost too obvious to state. And yet not every preacher has the natural talent of a Peter Kay or Ken Dodd. Making people laugh simply does not come easy to some preachers, if it comes to them at all. Someone with a totally humourless disposition attempting to be funny is probably just about the worst thing that can be inflicted on a congregation, as Trollope would readily have agreed. Having said that, I would want to ask what anyone with no sense of humour at all is doing in the ministry in the first place. The ability to laugh, especially at yourself from time to time, is absolutely essential for anyone in modern ministry. Lacking this ability, and the tendency to take yourself seriously all the time, is in my experience a recipe for total disaster and a rather short career. All of us who have survived in the ministry for any length of time have relied to a greater or lesser extent on a sense of humour and the ability to see the funny side of many situations we have found ourselves in.

Note however that laughing at yourself is not the same thing as public self-deprecation. All of us have weaknesses of which hopefully we are well aware. These are things to laugh at privately with friends rather than to advertise from the pulpit. The preacher who is constantly saying things like "I know I'm not a very good preacher" or "I'm not putting this very well" is wasting his breath. The congregation will already well aware of these things, and therefore it is not necessary to advertise them. Presenting yourself either as Supervicar or Rubbishvicar are not the only options. A self confidence that is based on the authority of the Word the preacher is proclaiming, delivered with a sense that it is the Spirit who makes the preaching effective rather than natural talent, will strike the right balance.

Then again, **humour can be overdone**. The preacher must always remember that he is delivering a sermon, not a stand-up comedy routine. Hearing your congregation laugh, an all too rare experience in many churches, is wonderful and can also be intoxicating. It can constitute a kind of power trip, as the preacher realises he is able to manipulate his congregation's emotions in at least one respect. If, at the end of the sermon, the only thing the congregation can say to the preacher is that he was very funny, the sermon will have missed the mark.

Learning from Professionals

I personally enjoy good stand-up comedians, and greatly admire many of them, not simply for their comedy, but for the way they interact with their audiences. I have tried to make a modest study of their techniques, because I believe there are many things preachers can learn from them. I am a particular admirer of the old "greats" such as Frankie Howerd, Ken Dodd, Stan Boardman, Frank Carson, Max Miller, George Burns, Bob Hope and Jackie Mason, as well as successful modern comedians such as Peter Kay. Don't tell them, but I have used material from all of them from time to time !

Of the mainstream comedians I admire most I would pick out just two for special comment.

A true colossus of comedy, **Ken Dodd**, know in his eighties, still commands full houses for his live shows up and down the country. Amongst the many things he is renowned for is his stamina. I was privileged to be at one of his live shows recently in my local theatre. He came on stage just after 7 p.m., and was still going strong at midnight, when I reluctantly tore myself away so as to be properly awake for Church the next morning. How many preachers could hold their audience for anything approaching that length of time ? We may recall that on one famous occasion "Paul kept on talking until midnight", with disastrous results for at least one of his listeners, but few preachers today would attempt to emulate him (Acts 20.7).

There are two things in my view that contribute to Ken Dodd's holding power. The first is that, like many successful comedians, he develops a common, sympathetic bond with his audiences, using as comedy vehicles situations that are familiar to their everyday lives. He is very much one of them. In this sense he reflects the approach of the parable teller. The second factor is something unique to him, and that is the pace of his delivery. Once the audience have begun to laugh (and he would probably recognise that this is the hardest part) he never lets them rest. The jokes carry on coming relentlessly like machine gun bullets, so that the audience are never allowed to stop laughing. Indeed a later joke can be missed by the audience because they haven't stopped laughing at an earlier

314

one.   None of the jokes are hilariously funny in themselves. It is the sheer pace at which they are delivered that causes the audience to keep on laughing.

Peter Kay is a modern counterpart of Ken Dodd. Using his Bolton origins as a springboard in much the same way Dodd uses his Knotty Ash heritage, Kay bases his humour on enabling his audience to see the funny side of things in ordinary life that we take for granted. Unlike the so-called "alternative comedians" his satire is pleasant and sympathetic. Again his humour is based on the establishment of total sympathy with his audience and a sharing of values with them. He is laughing *with* them, not *at* them.

Let me in passing say a quick word about "alternative" comedy, for which I confess to have no enthusiasm at all.   I have no problem with the proposition that alternative comedy is needed to question cosy, conventional assumptions about society, to prick pomposity and to present alternative ways forward. Alternative comedy seeks to invade areas of life where conventional comedy fears to go. Humour is as good a way as any of doing all those things. My personal feeling is however that comedy should not stray beyond the bounds of good taste and, to labour the obvious, that it should actually be *funny*. In my personal view alternative comedy fails on both counts, although my children think that in saying that I am showing my age !

Sympathy for the object of humour is of great importance. Just as it is essential the congregation do not feel they are spoken down to, so they must not feel they are being laughed at or made to feel ridiculous by the preacher. Above all, the preacher as well as the comedian must never fall into the temptation of scolding his congregation/audience for lack of response. I think it was Dame Edith Evans who once said that there was no such thing as a bad audience, only audiences to which the key had not yet been found. If an audience is not laughing at the comedian's jokes, it is as much likely to be his fault than theirs. Perhaps he needs to get new material. Scolding a congregation will only alienate them from the preacher and make them less likely, not more, to respond to the message.

In summary, we can say that humour is a very useful tool, a touches everyone at important points in their lives. Used skilfully and sensitively, noting the cautions listed above, it will make congregations more responsive to the preacher's message. Yes, as I said at the beginning, it carries risk, but then little if anything is achieved in ministry by playing safe all the time. The preacher who is timid, and stays within safe, smooth channels all the time, never venturing into uncertain yet potentially fruitful areas, will produce a congregation in the same mould.

9

THE PREACHER'S PRIVILEGE

PREACHING AT BAPTISM, WEDDING AND FUNERAL SERVICES

A good deal of a parish priest's time is taken up with going out in order to recruit and maintain a congregation to which to preach. There are regular occasions however when people come to us and ask us to preach to them. They don't put it that way of course - they are coming for the baptism of their child, or for marriage, or for the funeral of a loved one. But they accept that a "talk" from the Vicar is part of the package they are asking for. They accept that at some point in proceedings they will be on the receiving end of an address. In my experience they accept this with equanimity. It is no big deal. It is worth therefore addressing a few remarks in our survey of preaching towards preaching at what the Church is pleased to call "The Occasional Offices".

The first thing to note is that in many parishes they are often far from "occasional"! In parishes with large populations they can come thick and fast. My experience was that there has been over recent years a significant fall off in the numbers of Church weddings, a situation that reflects a national trend. But there does not seem to have been any comparable reduction in the numbers of requests for "christenings" or "funerals". The ministry of the Church in these areas appears to be just as sought after as ever. These services are of course called "occasional" because they are not part of the week-by-week schedule of services, but come as and when they are requested. The parish priest needs a policy for approaching them therefore. They are too frequent for any off the cuff approach which takes each occasion as it comes. The way of dealing with them needs a well thought out and considered plan.

Is "preaching" an appropriate term to use for these services? I actually think not. "Preaching" seems to me far too grandiose and pretentious a term to use for speaking to congregations made up almost entirely of people who do not attend Church with any regularity, and who therefore have no experiencing of, and therefore any conditioning for, listening to conventional sermons. Different rules and principles will apply from the ones I have been previously setting out. I prefer therefore to use the much more flexible term "address" for the time when the Parish Priest speaks directly to the congregation in these services, and that is the term I shall use from now on.

Adopt a Positive Approach

The common denominator for baptisms, weddings and funerals is that in applying for these services people are coming to us, asking something from the Church and from God Himself. So many people in our land treat the Church as irrelevant to their lives that it is to be appreciated and valued when people do come to us. It is vital that when people approach us for our help we should adopt a positive approach to them. They should receive a "yes" and not a "no" from us. What they are being offered will not necessarily be everything they are seeking - for I fully realise that people sometimes come with bizarre and unrealistic requests - but it should be the offering of *something* positive. They should not be turned away empty-handed at the vicarage door. Such an experience can create a scar that may never heal. It makes no difference that we feel we have good, sound reasons for turning people away. They will not remember our reasoned arguments. They will instead respond to the feeling of rejection.

What is an absolute necessity of any form of parish ministry is that it should not give way to cynicism in dealing with the people of the parish. Cynicism towards the public is an abomination in a parish priest. I have many times come across in my colleagues what seems to be the attitude that people are out to exploit the Church, seeking its services without intending any form of commitment. There may be times when we strongly suspect this is the case. However there are other times when it becomes a self-fulfilling prophecy. So what if people do try to exploit us ? Rather than cynically assuming they are attempting to draw us into playing their game, we should rather recall that we are there to do God's will and demonstrate that all-embracing love can and does win out over cynicism and exploitation. To put it another way, we can say that we are there to open ourselves up to the possibility of being exploited, to show unchanging, unwavering love even when that love is thrown back in our faces. In doing this we are of course following in the steps of Jesus, who loved and forgave even those who were nailing Him to the Cross. Interestingly, although people like the Rich Young Ruler, the crowds of John 6.66, and even Judas walked away from Jesus of their own accord, Jesus Himself remained inclusive and turned no one away, whatever their attitude. We must be as inclusive as Jesus was.

Occasional Offices are important because they place us on the frontier between what we may term "folk religion" and authentic Christianity. In what we might term the "rites of passage" the material world and the world beyond intersect in the thinking of men and women, and provide a window of opportunity. In the happiness and wonder of a new human life, in the joy of mutual commitment to a shared life, and supremely in the reminder of human mortality people glimpse a reality beyond the daily round of life in a material world and are, if only temporarily, open to receiving a new understanding. It is for us in the Church to grasp the opportunity that these occasions give us. This is another reason for approaching them positively. We can waste the opportunity if we dwell on the fact that the enquirers do not come to Church most of the time. The important thing is that they have come *now*, and we must respond positively to the window of opportunity as part of our mission.

One of the complicating factors in doing so is that on this folk/authentic frontier is that we will confront some rather strange ideas about what is going on in the service that is in view. People do not come to us in a vacuum. They come already with their own thoughts and beliefs. They may apply for baptism because someone has told them that "the baby comes on better after being christened", or that an unbaptised baby will automatically go to hell. The ideas of what has happened to their loved one after death may in some cases be far removed from any biblical teaching. On the principle outlined above we seek to respond positively, and not show disdain or contempt for any of these understandings, no matter how bizarre. Criticising people's beliefs and rejecting them will be perceived as rejecting the people holding them, no matter how hard we try to maintain a distinction. The point is that in coming for these services people are reaching out to us, prompted by these beliefs. No matter how inadequate or mistaken we feel these beliefs are, we need to take them seriously. The golden rule in any kind of ministry, and in any kind of preaching, is to begin where people are. We cannot be like the Irishman who answered a request for directions by saying, "well, if I were going there I wouldn't start from here".

We can't choose our starting points. They are presented to us. We take heart from the fact that they are only starting points. It is our privilege to begin there and take people on.

Preaching at Infant Baptism

Although happily adult baptisms do occur not infrequently, by far the most common form of baptism performed in the Church of England in modern times is that of infant baptism, and it is to this form of the service we will look at.

One of the things I could not fail to notice is that people turn up for baptism services, whether or not part of the main service, in increasingly large numbers. By far the largest congregations I have ever addressed have been baptismal congregations. Such large numbers present dynamics not encountered (sadly) in regular Sunday worship, and present consequent challenges and opportunities. I personally used to love those occasions. I would walk out of the vestry, see the vast numbers of excited and curious faces, and get a real buzz. The adrenaline would flow, and I could not wait to start speaking. Other clergy and laity may well react differently. For me the experience was very much a positive one.

What was even more curious for me was that the largest numbers would come from what we might term "alternative" families (single parents, unmarried parents, etc). After pondering awhile as to why this was, I came to the conclusion that it was probably because in such families there were fewer opportunities for gathering together than in others. Some families gather together at almost every conceivable opportunity, whilst other families seldom gather. With no prior wedding ceremony, the baptism of the child was probably the first opportunity for some while for that family to gather together with their friends. On the principle again of being positive, we accept that the service is performing an important social function, if perhaps little else.

There would of course have been the opportunity to meet beforehand with the parents and godparents, and take them through some form of preparation process. If the job has been done well, then the parents and godparents will at least approach the service with some degree of understanding. Most however will not, and we must accept that we will be speaking to a congregation with little or no understanding of the Christian Faith or Gospel. Some evangelists will tell you that no understanding is better than a false understanding of the kind described above. It gives us as preachers a blank canvas on which to paint a picture of the Christ who loves them and died for them.

If it is essential for the priest to approach the sermon or address positively then, curiously enough, he will find that the congregation does also. For people who have not been in Church for a long time, if ever, there will be a real curiosity factor. What *do* vicars believe ? What *is* the Church all about ? Why should *I* bother about God ? As the priest stands up to speak we will momentarily feel like Jesus in the synagogue at Nazareth, when "all eyes were fastened on Him" (Luke 4.20). There will be a real invitation for the Vicar to give it his best shot. How long this moment lasts will depend entirely on us and our ability to grip the congregation with our presentation.

At this point parish priests may wish to employ visual aids, power point and so on, to give the congregation something on which to fix their eyes. That is fine, as long as the strictures on the use of technology mentioned in Chapter One are observed. My person preference was not to do that but to adopt an informal style, wandering around with a hand held microphone, to speak to people directly and at close quarters. I recognise that not everyone can do that, and people will gain nothing by adopting a style that is not suited to them. For me this seemed to work. It gave me close contact with my audience, even those hiding on the back row, so that I could interact with them and check the "temperature" of things as the address developed.

Symbolism is of course important, and an address that is just words will struggle to hold people. But then of course the Baptism Service is replete with symbolism, much of which can readily be absorbed into the address and the presentation of the Gospel. There is the candle, lit in the early part of the service, reminding us that Jesus is the Light of the World and that becoming a Christian can be compared to coming out of the world's darkness into the Light of Christ (Acts 26.18). The signing with the Cross reminds us that the Cross is at the heart of the Christian Gospel and that it is at the Cross that Christian discipleship begins. Water has of course a multi-faceted universal symbolism. In relation to baptism it represents life, eternal life, union with Christ and washing from sin. Putting on the new garment is a reminder that becoming a Christian means shedding the old, discredited values of the world, and putting on the new values of the Kingdom of God (Eph.4.22-24). There is a rich vein of symbolism already present in the Baptism Service for the preacher to use without importing things from outside.

The service takes part hopefully as part of the Church's missionary outreach. The large numbers at baptisms are reminders of the mission field in which God has placed us. It is to be hoped that the regular congregation will see it in this way, and not resent the large numbers that come and appear to swamp them once a month or whenever. I have to admit from personal experience that it is not always easy to get congregations to see baptism this way, and it can be a real test of the parish priest's powers of persuasion. Unless they do then baptism will not normally be the way into the Church that it ought to be for many of the people who come to us on the occasion of their baby's birth.

If baptism is part of our missionary outreach, it follows that the thrust of the address will be evangelistic. The difficulty is that people of the calibre of Billy Graham would have an hour or so to set out their message, the parish priest will have only 10 minutes or so at his disposal. He cannot hope to set out the full Gospel in that time. His only realistic target in the time available is to make some sort of impact that will penetrate the defence mechanisms of his congregation, start them thinking and create a desire to want more. His aim will not be to "spell it out", for he hasn't the time to do that. He will of course have had the liturgy of the service itself to introduce people to the subject matter of the Gospel and therefore he does not need to explain everything from scratch in the address. His approach in the address will be very like the teller of parables, who appeals to imagination, curiosity and conscience to start things moving in people's hearts and minds.

This last point is particularly important. Most people's understanding of "sin" is not that of the Bible. Sin in biblical terms is the condition into which we are born, the natural tendency within us that alienates us from God and causes us by our thoughts and actions to live lives that fall below His standards. The outsider, unschooled in Pauline Theology sees sin as wrong actions, usually of a sexual kind, that are of a different order to our normal human failings. If the preacher were to label them as sinners therefore, they are likely to see the preacher accusing them of great moral lapses, and take appropriate umbrage. Yet we cannot and should not avoid the subject completely. People who come to Church for the first time, or for the first time in a while, come with expectations that it will be boring, but also with the expectation that they will be chided and scolded for not having been before. I well remember my dentist telling me that all his new patients, when they come for the first time, immediately offer an apology for not having been sooner. I responded by commenting that new people in Church often use that as an opening gambit, and that dentists and vicars therefore have something important in common ! The consciences of people at baptism service does indeed offer us a point of contact and a way in, but it must be treated sensitively.

Above all they must be assured by the sermon and by all the service that they are welcomed by us just as they are by Jesus. Non-verbal communication will be as important, if not more important, than verbal. More than ever in the baptism services *how* we say something will be more important than *what* we say. Jesus was incredibly positive in His attitude to children.

> Let the children come to me, for to such belongs the Kingdom of God. I tell you the truth, whoever does not receive the Kingdom of God like a little child will never enter it.
> *Mark 10.14,15*

What Jesus is saying here is not simply that those who would enter the Kingdom of God must be child*like*. He is saying that in some way the Kingdom belongs to children. We recall the Pied Piper of Hamlin taking the children off to his new kingdom, away from all the complications of life among adults. Peter Pan is of the very firm conviction that to become an adult will mean the end of all that is good and worthwhile in life. There is a grain of truth in that, so that children represent the paradigm for those receiving the Kingdom of God.

> I tell you the truth, unless you change and become like little children, you will never enter the Kingdom of Heaven. Therefore, whoever humbles themselves like this little child will be the greatest in the Kingdom of Heaven.
> *Matthew 18.3,4*

In the same passage Jesus speaks of the reality of a child's faith

> Whoever welcomes a little child like this welcomes me. But whoever causes one of these little ones *who believe in me* to

sin, it would be better for him to have a large millstone hung around his neck and to be drowned in the depths of the sea.

Matthew 18.5,6

Working with children and their families is always a great privilege. Preaching the Gospel to them is not only a privilege, it is a great opportunity also.

Preaching at Weddings

In the case of both baptism and funerals, the service in Church celebrates an event that has happened some time previously, a birth and a death. In the case of marriage, the parish priest is actually at the heart of a major event of life as it actually happens. To me this is always a great privilege. Even though I am involved, as the one conducting the service, I feel that I am in one sense an invited guest, an onlooker as two people make the greatest act of voluntary commitment human beings can make to other human beings.

However, the conduct of marriage services presents the parish priest with a number of important challenges. There is of course the consciousness than weddings take place within a legal context, with the pressure to get all the legal procedures right, not always easy when the priest has had not legal training.

But more than that, the priest has to cope with changing social patterns. He has to recognises that he faces a much changed situation from that of two decades ago. People now have a bewildering variety of options when it comes to deciding where and how to hold their marriage ceremony. In the last two or three decades there has been a sharp rise in the number of couples living together prior to marriage. From a situation where cohabiting prior to marriage was the exception, it is now the norm, even amongst many churchgoers. The proportion of those cohabiting prior to second marriages is even higher. The majority of those living together eventually marry their partner, but even this proportion is declining, in spite of the contradictory nature of this position. Where people live together long term without contracting marriage, it brings marriage itself into question. It is arguable of course that people in such relationship are *de facto* married, so that marriage is questioned only in the formal sense. This is not the place to discuss the various factors that have led to this situation, and to guess how it will work out. There are a number of big questions, not least as to whether it would be a great tragedy if the Church ceased to have a legal role in marrying people altogether. That is a discussion for another day.

What we are addressing here is the situation where people have come to us, by whatever path, to be married. We need to work with the situation as it is, and not as we would like it to be. As with baptism, our approach should be positive. The couple may not have come to us at what we would consider the right moment, but at least they have come to us. Better late than never. They have come asking for our ministry, and it is important that we welcome them and offer that ministry. We have the consolation at least that, although a Church wedding is no longer the norm, those who have come to be married in Church are more likely to have come for the right reasons, and therefore are likely to be more receptive to our ministry. There is the further prospect that, if we provide a good, quality ministry to couples who come to us for marriage, then word will get round, and marriage in Church will continue to be an attractive option compared to what is in my experience rather sub-standard services provided by hotels and other registered marriage venues. It is sadly the case that there is a correlation between the degree of casualness and informality of the setting of the marriage ceremony and the degree of seriousness with which couples approach their marriage vows. Certainly I believe the Church has no reason to be defensive or apologetic about what it offers to couples seeking marriage by way of an option for their planning. In the case of marriage there will at times be legal and ecclesiastical reasons why we ourselves have to qualify the help we give, but we must do everything we can to support and encourage them.

There are of course other implications for the contemporary ministry of marriage in Church. The prevalence of cohabiting requires a distinct change of emphasis in preaching. The preacher can no longer speak so much of "new adventures" and "new beginnings" in the way he could when bride and groom has both been living independently. In one sense marriage will bring about very little that is genuinely new for the couple. This is a real loss, and I detect a change in the general atmosphere of weddings today because of this. The very precious atmosphere of excitement and anticipation, and the sense of moving into new, uncharted territory has largely gone.

Nevertheless in the marriage service we are doing something extremely valuable. What we are doing is marking a transition, not the setting up of something new, but a transition to a new level for the relationship the couple already possess. The keyword for the service and the address may well turn out to be "commitment". What is happening in the marriage service is that the bride and groom are standing up in Church, in front of the priest, in front of their family and friends, but most of all in front of God, to say that the relationship they possess is the real thing, "till death us do part". Whilst not ideal, this still gives the parish priest great scope for ministry and teaching about the nature of marriage as part of God's creation plan for men and women. We should therefore approach it as a real opportunity, just as we saw was the case with baptism.

The reference to creation brings us on to an important point. Marriage is God's norm for everyone, not just those who belong to the covenant community. There may well be a qualitative difference between the marriage of Christians than others, although the fact that bride and groom are Christians is no guarantee of success for the marriage, but the marriage of non-Christians is in God's sight still a valid marriage and the fulfilment of His creation ordinance:

> For this reason a man shall leave his father and mother and be joined to his wife, and the two shall become one
> *Genesis 2.24*

The validity of marriage, is based on both husband and wife having common origins in the flesh of Adam, and is not dependent on the couple being part of the Christian community, no matter how desirable that might be.

This brings us on to the second major change in the approach to marriage in Church, and that is the change in the Church's rules on divorce, and the consequent rise in the number of people applying for a second marriage in Church whilst their first partner is still living. This presents the parish priest with many difficult challenges and will often cause him to use all his qualities of tact and diplomacy.

Once again we repeat what is fast becoming our slogan, "be positive". Hesitancy should not give way to cynicism. Cynicism should not lead us to assume that people who come for second marriage are dishonourable, seeking to exploit the parish priest and the Church for their own ends, prepared to lie and mislead in order to get what they want. As mentioned in the case of baptism, I have with great sadness heard many of my colleagues in discussion utter views pretty close to this. Our calling as priests involves, I believe, taking people at face value and treating them as honest until evidence proves irrefutably to the contrary. That will happen fewer times than might be imagined. If an individual parish priest for reasons of conscience feels he cannot go ahead with remarriage for a particular couple, he should also in conscience be honest with them and point them in the direction of another parish priest who will help them.

My experience tells me that we are not, as is often alleged, in an open floodgates situation. As we have already said, the prospect of being married in Church has become less attractive for everybody, so it is most unlikely that we will ever have a queue at the vicarage door of people applying for marriage, whether for the first or the second time.

Nevertheless, I do recognise that an application for remarriage does place the parish priest in a difficult situation. Whatever the legislation may say (and here *I* give way to cynicism) in practice it will be the parish priest whose attitude will decide whether the remarriage goes ahead or not. This responsibility is not materially affected by the option of Blessing after Civil Marriage, which still requires the parish priest to accept in principle the appropriateness of a particular couple marrying. My aim was always to discuss the matter fully with the couple concerned, *to decide between the three of us* the appropriateness of going ahead or not. Rarely if ever did I find myself in the position of saying "no". Where the second marriage did not go ahead, it was always the couple themselves who withdrew.

Following through on the principle of being positive, my experience was that the process of sitting down and speaking to a couple about their previous experience and previous marriages was in itself extremely valuable pastorally, irrespective of whether the second marriage took place at the end of the process or not. Old wounds were opened, past mistakes faced up to, tears often flowed, and there was the opportunity for healing. I could never escape the conviction that this was what I was called to do as a parish priest, and I would have denied myself the opportunity of doing it if I had turned the couple away at an earlier point.

The Gospel of Jesus tells us that the past can be forgiven, and new beginnings are always possible. We must as a Church

330

beware of proclaiming that this is true everywhere except in the area of marriage. I cannot believe that the words of Jesus in Mark 10.1-12 can be pressed to mean this. Jesus is recalling the Pharisees to first principles, and God's ideal for marriage, at the same time acknowledging, in His reference to the Levitical certificate of divorce, that God recognises that men and women often fail to achieve those standards.

We must also beware of imposing standards onto divorced people that we do not apply to others, especially cohabitees. They may walk out of a long-term relationship, a break up caused by their unreasonable behaviour, make no proper provision for children, commit all sorts of other improprieties, and yet still be married in Church. A divorcee may have done none of those things and yet still be subject to stringent discipline.

What is also of vital importance is that once a decision to remarry has been taken, it should be applied ungrudgingly and without restraint. The parish priest should not treat it in any way as a second-class marriage, but do whatever he can to see that it is founded as securely as he can.

In connection with this Rod Symmons raises the interesting point as to whether the previous relationship and its breakdown should be mentioned in the marriage service or not.

> In preparing the address, the preacher will need to consider whether reference should be made to the previous relationship.[1]

The principle that causes this to come under consideration is the principle that the address should have a sense of honesty and integrity

That reflects the reality of the circumstances of the marriage[2]

No one would disagree with the principle of honesty and integrity, and the need to reflect this in the wedding service. For example, everyone (except perhaps the bride's father) welcomes the dropping of the pretence of the father giving away his daughter, especially when that daughter may have been living with the groom for a number of years. No one even mentions this change in practice now.

The question it devolves into is how far the principle of honesty should be pressed. It is one thing for everybody present in the Church to be aware of past mistakes and failings, but quite another to air them publicly. Why is it necessary to do so, and what does it actually add to proceedings ? Are people not entitled to put the past behind them and make a new start ? Why do they need to be reminded *in the service* of that past ? There are plenty of opportunities for the parish priest quite properly and quite profitably to talk to the couple about the past and how much the couple have learned from it, indeed it is essential to do so, but not necessarily in the wedding service itself. And how fair is it to the marriage partner who has not been involved previously in divorce ? Should it be applied to all marriages or just second marriages ? Should previous cohabiting be mentioned, even when no divorce has been involved ? There are so many questions that spring to mind that the parish priest may feel he is walking through a minefield. One false step, no matter how small, may cause a disastrous explosion. I remain unconvinced, and feel that the dangers far outweigh the advantages. I feel that the principle of honesty and integrity can be better maintained, perhaps by what the priest does not say, rather than by deliberately introducing what may be perceived as a discordant note into the service.

The aim of the parish priest therefore is to give everyone than comes to him, whether for the first or second time, the best possible marriage experience, so that their marriage may be set on the best possible foundation. We may well feel that marriage preparation classes and the marriage sermon provides all too little opportunity to do that - but we must do what we can.

The challenge involved for preachers at a celebration of a marriage consists in trying to preach in a way that is inclusive of those in the congregation who are not practising Christians—and sometimes this will include one or both of the two people getting married. The aim is to communicate a vision of Christian marriage without appearing to reproach those whose life-style or relationships may fall short of Christian ideals and who might feel alienated by the message. The opportunity that presents itself in the marriage service is to preach a sermon that helps the couple to see the relevance of Christ to their marriage, whilst at the same time attracting members of the congregation to the Christian faith and to a Christian understanding of marriage. The same spirit of inclusion prevails as that we saw in the baptism service.

However, the congregational audience at a wedding will be even more diverse than that at a baptism service. It will be made up of the families of the bride and groom of course, plus a collection of friends and acquaintances. Many will treat it as a purely secular occasion, with very little regard for the spiritual nature of the service. This will present a particular challenge to the preacher, as he will often need to battle to grasp and retain the attention of the congregation, whose attention may be solely directed towards the appearance of the bride and bridesmaids, as well as the exotic variety of hats usually represented on these occasions ! The parish priest may well feel he is being marginalized, treated as a side show, when really the happy couple are the centre of everyone's attention. A good dose of humility is therefore a useful attribute for the vicar at a wedding. To counterbalance this, however, the congregation at a wedding will usually be a happy congregation, in good spirits and anxious to contribute what they can to the positive atmosphere of the service. They will not wish to do anything that might spoil the service for the couple getting married. This cannot be said of the majority of services the parish priest will preach at, so he should make the most of it.

Who is the address for ? Who is the preacher targeting in his talk ? He will have already had plenty of opportunity to speak to the couple, either personally on in a group of wedding couples (my preference), so that there is no need to repeat what has been previously said, apart from giving certain things emphasis. It will not be a discourse on the Christian view of marriage, although it will be grounded in it. In the address therefore the preacher will regard the congregation of the day as his targets. It will of course be natural to use the couple as the focus of the talk, and the wedding service as its framework. Some remarks will rightly be addressed to the couple, but to direct the address wholly at them risks isolating the congregation and reducing them to eavesdroppers or voyeurs. In any case, it is most unlikely that the bride and groom will be in any condition on the wedding day to take in anything significant that is said to them. The state of near nervous collapse (sometimes exaggerated by alcohol) that most couples are in sometimes means that for them simply remembering their names will turn out to be a major achievement !

Rod Symmons makes the important observation that the Common Worship Liturgy changes the place of the wedding address from after the marriage ceremony to a place in between the legal declarations and the vows.[3] This will change the focus of the address from being a reflection on something that has happened to an explanation of something that is about to happen. It gives the opportunity of speaking about the nature of marriage by reference to the vows the couple "are about to make". When therefore the congregation hear those vows, they will understand them that much better because of the priest's prior explanation of them.

The nature of the wedding congregation, present at a wedding but probably never seen again means that it is possible to use basically the same address at every wedding. Sometimes we will find ourselves marrying brothers and sisters of people we have previously married, but in my experience that situation is rare. In most cases one or two basic address structures on which we can weave variations will suffice. This is not in fact a counsel of defeat, or an attempt to justify laziness or a lack of adventure. There are, after all, only so many things that can be said about marriage ! My own personal approach was the vary the lead in according to the circumstances of the particular couple, so that no two marriage addresses began the same way. I might lead in with references to the occupations of the bride and groom, or their hobbies and interests, or some personal knowledge of them. But then, like trains going through Crewe Junction, the addresses would all converge onto the same basic point.

That same basic point would be "love", presented as the cement that holds the marriage relationship together and makes a success of the marriage itself. Given the opportunity to choose, most couples will choose 1 Corinthians 13, where Paul discusses the importance of love (1-3), the essential characteristics of love (4-7) and the persistence of love (8-13). Marriage is of course not the original context of the passage. That context was Paul's discussion of the use of spiritual gifts in the Church at Corinth. He warns them that spiritual gifts without love are worth nothing. Love is the quality to be desired most of all, because love will outlast spiritual gifts. Nevertheless, the decontextualisation of this particular chapter is no great crime, since love has the same basic characteristics in both contexts.

For me the key phrase in the passage as it relates to marriage is in v.5 - "love is not self-seeking" (ου ζητει τα εαυτης), variously translated in different versions. This verse gives the perspective and focus for everything else Paul says here about love, and gives very solid meaning to the nature of love.

The concept of self-giving love gives of course a solid link to the Gospel. God's love is expressed supremely in the self-giving of Christ on the Cross. Paul uses this as the link between marriage and the Church in Ephesians 5. Husbands are to love their wives in the same way that Christ loved His Church, giving Himself on the cross so that the Church, as His bride, could be presented without spot or wrinkle.

In an all too short time it is simply not possible to discourse on marriage, even if the congregation were disposed to listen. There would simply be too much that would need to be said to fit it into a relatively small compass. The danger of missing out something vital is all too real.

Then again, humility might cause us to pause and ask how far we are qualified to discourse and lecture on marriage. As is the case with all our ministries, our lives have to back up what we preach, and, if we are married, the quality of our own marriages will either strengthen or weaken what we preach about marriage. It is sadly all too common to find clergy husbands and wives struggling, often because of the pressures of ministry, in their marriages, some even to the point of break up. Marriage is a complex and testing relationship, needing to be worked on day by day, and only a fool would pretend to have all the answers. Moreover, we may indeed sometimes discover that some of the people we marry are accountants, or solicitors, or teachers, or social workers, and therefore often know a lot more than we do about many of the practical aspects of marriage. We may avoid dropping spectacular clangers if we have the humility to recognise that.

What we need to do is to concentrate on what we do know, and what as parish priests we are specialists at, that is, presenting God's ideal for marriage in the light of the Gospel as read in the pages of the New Testament.   Once a couple have caught a glimpse of how their marriage relationship mirrors and reflects God's love in Christ, then their marriage will be truly set on the best possible foundation.

Preaching at Funerals

When we discussed baptism services earlier, the point was made that non-verbal communication is as important as verbal communication.   The same point is just as true, if not more so, at funerals.   The problem at funerals is not merely discerning what people are thinking about, but determining the extent to which people are thinking at all.   People approach funerals at the level of feelings rather than of thought.   In trying to determine what he might say to engage mourners' minds, the parish priest much first work out what is happening at the level of their feelings.

Mourners will come to a funeral with a complex mixture of feelings, often unresolved and at war with each other.

There will be **grief and an overwhelming sense of loss.** This will be true of all funerals, but the feelings will be particularly strong if the death has been sudden, tragic, untimely or all three. In those circumstances people will frequently go to one of two extremes.   They will either weeping uncontrollably (and noisily), or they will be in a state of silent shock.   One lady at the funeral of her 40 year old son in law was literally rigid with shock, and could scarcely move physically at all.

Some mourners will appear **emotionless** and scarcely aware of their surroundings. In some cases this state will have been induced by well meaning doctors prescribing something to "help you along".   This almost catatonic state can be strengthened further by a sense of denial. They are going through the motions with no sense of the grim reality that the service represents.   These funerals I find the hardest to take.

Nothing the priest says appears to register or produce any kind of reaction whatsoever. Outward appearances can be deceptive I suppose, and so I have often ploughed on more in hope than expectation. Frequently I have felt like suggesting abandoning the service and going straight to the graveside to get the essential business done.

Many at funerals will be **disturbed** by the reminder of mortality, and the knowledge that one day it will be them in the coffin at the front. If the death has been sudden and unexpected, they will be reflecting on how slender the thread separating life from death can be. Some will of course will react to the *momento mori* by seeking to repress it and to drive it from their minds.

Some mourners will be possessed with **guilt,** aware of things left unsaid or undone, especially of unresolved disputes with the deceased which now have no opportunity for resolution. Funerals of people who have committed suicide often produce great amounts of guilt, as everyone is consumed with thoughts of what they could have done to prevent the tragedy. I well recall conducting the funeral of a 14-year old boy who had died from taking ecstasy tablets. The congregation was packed with young people, and I think it would not have been an uncharitable guess on my part to imagine that a number of them were also taking drugs. Their feelings of guilt and concern were almost tangible.

Perhaps there will be **anger** as well. This anger may be directed at other mourners, who they feel did not treat the deceased properly. There may be a pending dispute over the will, and other practical matters. The anger may even be directed at God, who has taken someone away too soon. In such circumstances the wise parish priest will hesitate before using the words "The Lord gave and the Lord has taken away" in the introduction. This does not mean he should not use them, but only that he should think twice before doing so.

At some funerals there will be, mixed in with all of the above, a genuine **sense of thanksgiving** at the thought of a long life, lived well, and which has touched the lives of many people. Thanksgiving and sorrow are not mutually exclusive. Although sad to have lost them, people will gather in order to give someone a good "send off".

At a funeral service therefore people do not listen to the address in a vacuum, but in a continuum created by the interaction of many if not all of the above factors. In the pre-funeral visit to the chief mourners, the parish priest will hopefully have learned enough to allow him to discern the best approach to the service as a whole, and to recognise which of the above factors is likely to be uppermost on the day. At the Church door or the chapel gate he will speak personally to the mourners, to discover how they are feeling. He will use the first part of the service to measure the emotional temperature of the congregation as a whole. He will hopefully have gathered enough information by the time he begins the address to have a clear idea of where to pitch it.

In his general approach he will try to find a balance between warm informality and dignity. It is important that the seriousness of the occasion is recognised. It is not a time to be chatty, or for knockabout comedy routines, although humour need not be entirely absent altogether, as we shall see. Nor is it an occasion for overdone solemnity and gravity. I recall being in the congregation at one funeral where the Vicar's voice literally changed as he passed through the Church porch. Suddenly he became the perfect imitation of John Lawrie from Dad's Army, with his famous catchphrase "we're all doomed". The family are already upset enough, without the Vicar rubbing it in. Whatever else he does, the parish priest should exude a warm and caring attitude, positive towards both the deceased and those who mourn the deceased. Although he more often than not will not have known the deceased, *they* did, and they value that knowledge. The priest's daunting task is in a relatively few words to speak on behalf of the family and sum up the value of that person's life. It is a great challenge as well as a great privilege.

One of the great pressures of speaking at funerals is the fact that every word is weighed, more so than at any other service. People will remember what the Vicar said at so-and-so's funeral for years to come. The preacher cannot therefore afford to get it wrong. He cannot make throw away remarks or make statements for which he might later need to apologise. He must prepare extra carefully for every part of the service, not just the sermon, but the introductions he plans to give to each part of the liturgy. Nothing must be left to chance or left to be made up on the day.

Curiously enough, as was implied above, this does not necessarily rule out the use of humour at a funeral. Indeed, if the deceased were known to be an amateur comedian or joker, humour may be actually appropriate. I recall taking the funeral recently of a man who was indeed known as a practical joker. On the coffin the family reflected this by placing a photograph of him pulling a funny face and sticking his tongue out. By one of those wonderful "co-incidences" that occur from time to time, his funeral took place on Red Nose Day ! There was simply no way of delivering the address without commenting on this fact in the service. It is however scarcely necessary to list all the warnings and caveats involved in injecting humour into a funeral service. The consequences of misdirected humour on those occasions is of course incalculable. Unless the humour has in some way been introduced by the family themselves, as in the case above, it is best avoided altogether.

The eulogy given by a member of the congregation is becoming so popular now as to be almost standard. I personally welcome this development, for a number of reasons. In the first place, it greatly lightens the preacher's load in that he doesn't have the responsibility of having to say everything about the deceased. That responsibility is shared by someone else, someone moreover who knew the deceased well and is less likely therefore to say something inaccurate or misleading. In the second place therefore the eulogy introduces an element of realism, and makes the whole service much more personal. People expect vicars to say certain things at a funeral - that's their job. When a lay person says the same thing it somehow has more force and impact.

Some clergy display a degree of nervousness about the idea of a "loose cannon" lay person speaking in the service. Nick Watson, in his Grove Booklet, *Sorrow and Hope: Speaking at Funerals,* tells us that he asks to have a typescript of the eulogy beforehand.[4] Where this is possible, it would undoubtedly be a help. But there could be many reasons why it is not practicable or advisable. The person concerned may live a distance away, or may not compose the speech until the last minute. The eulogist may actually consider it to be impertinent, especially if he is a professional person or someone used to speaking in public. They may consider themselves better at public speaking than the Vicar - and they may actually be right ! I think it is one of those things that should be labelled highly desirable, but in the last analysis not something the parish priest can insist on.

It could actually be argued that such insistence stems from a sense of insecurity on the part of the parish priest, and is part of a desire to keep in full control of the funeral process. In my experience such fears are by and large groundless, and over the years I have heard some quite wonderful things in eulogies, some of the best coming from some very unpromising looking people. Just before the funeral of a teenager I was approached by another teenager, who asked if he could stand up and say something about the deceased. I admit it was something of a risk, but something told me to give him the green light. This lad subsequently stood up and spoke quite simply, from the heart, about his mate, something that was more powerful than anything I could have said.

My task in preaching after a eulogy is to pick up on what is said by the speaker, and try to find keywords or themes that will link into my own presentation. Obvious examples would be words like "love", "friend", "family" or "helpful", that can be used as bridges to the Gospel. This requires very careful listening on my part, as well as a degree of flexibility and ingenuity in building those bridges. Where this is done it does in my view link up the ministry of the parish priest and that of the congregation beautifully, and make the whole presentation infinitely more powerful. My only regret is that I caught on to these opportunities late in my ministry.

Another fear is that eulogies may introduce alien ideas about the future hope into the service. Again, that is not really borne out in my experience, though I acknowledge it as a genuine fear. People who give eulogies more often than not will stick to their brief about speaking about the deceased, and recognise that the whole area of life after death is the province of the parish priest. It does highlight however that just as mourners do not come to a funeral in an emotional vacuum, they do not live in a vacuum of belief either. Each mourner will be seeking to cope with the situation in his or her own way, and will have mechanisms for doing so. These mechanisms may well include strong beliefs about the significance of death and what happens afterwards. This is true of people who would, in any other circumstances, not own up to any kind of religious beliefs at all. As one person said to me the day before a funeral, "there will be no atheists at the crematorium tomorrow". Investigation and conversation will very quickly tell us that many of these beliefs are not founded on the biblical truth that we are committed to proclaim. They will often involve such notions as immortality of the soul, universalism and reincarnation, as well as a whole variety of ideas drawn from New Age culture.

The dilemma for the parish priest is that many such beliefs, no matter how bizarre or unbiblical, will bring real comfort to the bereaved. The notion for example that Grandad is watching over the family as they live their everyday lives, or that Grandad is now a star in the sky to which the family can point, is very powerful. Where Christian theology comes in at all, it will involve the assumption that, wherever or whatever heaven is, Grandad is there. The notion of judgement and separation is missing. Because these beliefs are so strong, the parish priest who seeks to engage with them and destroy them is going quite literally where angels fear to tread.

One example of how folk beliefs and Christian beliefs intersect is presented by the regular use of Henry Scott Holland's work "Death is Nothing at all"[5]. In the above-mentioned Grove Booklet Nick Watson offers a detailed critique of Scott Holland's poem, arguing that it represents society's attempts to minimise the impact of death, when in actuality is "something" significant and not nothing at all.[6] In that respect it is true neither to human experience, which recognises the reality of death and bereavement, nor authentic Christian hope, which is based on the fact of resurrection rather than the survival of the soul. The idea of continuity which the poem embodies is in his view based on some New Age philosophy rather than the teaching of the Bible.

Watson is certainly right to point us to hope based on biblical truth rather than other ideas as the basis for our approach to funerals. But in attacking Scott Holland the way he does Watson underestimates two important things. The first is that the very popularity itself of Scott Holland, and the regularity with which his poem is chosen points to the fact that it *does* genuinely resonate with human feelings linked with bereavement. Many bereaved people testify that alongside the sense of loss is often a strong sense of the deceased's "real presence" continuing with them in their homes and wherever they may be. There is the understanding that while death has

343

indeed brought about a significant change, there is a sense of continuity, at least in the sense that the deceased lives on in the memory of the bereaved. This sense can be particularly strong if the death has been sudden and unforeseen. The poem also tells them that the life of the bereaved has not ended with the death of the deceased. They must carry on with the example and inspiration of the loved one. In the aftermath of a death people don't operate always on a rational level. They operate on the level of feelings, and it is *on this level* that Scott Holland's poem is a help to them. We recall that Jesus Himself wept at the grave of Lazarus, even though He knew what He was about to do. He wept for the disruption to the created order that sin had brought, a disruption that had involved His friend Lazarus.

Again, Watson is correct in underlining the fact that Christian hope is based on the doctrine of the resurrection of the body, rather than the Greek notion of the immortality of the soul. Jesus takes up the Jewish notion of general resurrection, based on Daniel 12.1,2, and applies it to His own ministry in John 5.24-29. He is the key, not to participation in the general resurrection, for all participate in that, good and bad. He is the key to the destiny of people in that resurrection. What is startlingly new in Jesus' presentation is that He speaks of this resurrection not simply as something that will happen on the Last Day (John 6.39,40), but as something that is brought into the present. In His conversation with Martha He draws from her an affirmation of the traditional view of future resurrection

> I know that he (my brother, Lazarus) will rise again on the Last Day
>
> *John 11.24*

Jesus astounds her by going on to say that the resurrection is not simply a matter of the remote future.

I (emphatic εγω) am the resurrection and the life. He who believes in me, although he dies (aorist tense: at some point in the future) will (continue to) live. He who (thus) lives and believes in me will never die.

John 11.25

There is therefore real continuity, even within the Christian doctrine of resurrection. To the dying thief on the Cross Jesus gave the promise that "today you will see me in Paradise" (Luke 23.43). Because of this we can have reasonable hope of being able to give some sort of answer to the question every parish priest dreads being asked after a death, "where is my loved one *now* ?". Watson belatedly recognises this when he states that "the only hope we have warrant to proclaim is that of resurrection to a life *continuous with this earthly life*, yet transformed by grace."[7] In seeking to attack Scott Holland therefore Watson overlooks things that are important in his concept of continuity.

Watson's desire to be critical of contemporary attitudes to death sees him also taking a dim view of euphemisms such as "fallen asleep", or "departed", in order once again to minimise the impact of death. Now I myself am not in favour of using unnecessary euphemisms. When asked I tend to say that someone has "died", so that there is no misunderstanding. The unfortunate thing about the two euphemisms Watson selects for criticism is that they are both biblical euphemisms ! Paul urges the Thessalonians not to be concerned about those who have "fallen asleep" (των κοιμωμενων, Thess.4.13), whilst to the Philippians he announces his desire to "depart" (αναλυσιαι, Phil.1.23). He tells Timothy that the time of his "departure" (death) is near (ο καιρος της αναλυσεως μου εφεστηκεν, 2 Tim.4.6). No one is helped ultimately by pretending death is something other than what it is. But neither is there any justification for being insensitive and brutal at the time of the funeral. There will be a time for precise explanations, but that will usually be later, when people are getting over the initial shock.

What are we aiming to do in the funeral address itself ?   I suggest that we are aiming to do three things (although these do not constitute the three points of the address !)   Nor are these in order of importance. All form part of the funeral ministry.   In the first place, we are **celebrating the life of the deceased.** It is appropriate for us to make some reference to the deceased, using whatever information we have been able to glean from family and friends. I usually make a framework of that life, comprising references to early life, school, work, family and pastimes.   We speak good things about the deceased without making them out to be a saint (unless of course they were a saint). It will generally not be wise to refer to shortcomings or faults, unless there is strong warrant from the family to do so. Even then I would hesitate. It is best to follow the old adage that "if you can't say anything good, say nowt", and leave the congregation to fill in the gaps.

At the same time we are **seeking to bring comfort to the bereaved.**   Watson is of course perfectly correct to remind us that what we say must be based on Bible truth.   We must not reinforce incorrect notions, either intentionally or unintentionally. But there are always things we can say that are positive and bring support to the bereaved. At the end of the day, God is a God who loves His creations, and will always do what is right, just and loving. If I didn't believe this about God I would not be in the ministry in the first place. And as always, that love of God is something that communicates by what we are and how we behave as much if not more than by what we say.   As Archbishop Robin Eames once said, "long after people have forgotten what we have said, they will remember that we were there".

While in the mood for quoting Archbishops, I was present at a service in Manchester Cathedral when Robert Runcie was discussing why it is that mourners at funerals always compliment the Vicar and say how wonderful the service was, irrespective of the quality of ministry. I have had people say that to me at the end of a service when I have known in myself that I didn't get it right and was not on the ball, perhaps because the service was first thing on a Monday, or last thing on a Friday. Archbishop Runcie's conclusion was that what people were responding to was not necessarily anything specific that was said, but an individual standing at the front who was apparently firm and unmoved amongst the emotional wreckage of death and bereavement. It is once again our non-verbal communication that is speaking louder than words.

Finally, we are **proclaiming the Gospel.** As was the case with baptism, we are not able through pressures of time, especially at the crematorium, to preach a full evangelistic address, always assuming that a funeral was a suitable occasion for doing so. Nevertheless, the Pastoral Services book issued with Common Worship describes our task as "proclaiming the Gospel in the context of the death of a particular person". The statement, while it sounds clear, needs in fact a little unpacking. What I interpret it to mean is that our task is to show that the Good News of Jesus Christ has implications for mankind's last and greatest enemy, death. The victory of Jesus over sin and death through the Cross and resurrection means that death can be faced with equanimity, knowing that it is not the ultimate disaster that people suppose. The eternal consequences of the Cross will be the focus of our Gospel presentation. In the time allowed it will not be easy to get this across, but if it is done in a positive, loving way, through our non-verbal as well as verbal communication, then our task is a far from impossible one.

CHAPTER NINE
ENDNOTES

1   R.Symmons, *Preaching at Weddings* (Cambridge: Grove, 1995),10-11.

2   Symmons, 11.

3   Symmons, 8.

4   Watson, N., *Sorrow and Hope: Preaching at Funerals* (Cambridge: Grove Booklets, 2001), 15.

5   Canon Henry Scott-Holland, 1847-1918, Canon of St Paul's Cathedral. From 'The King of Terrors', a sermon on death delivered in St Paul's Cathedral on Whitsunday 1910, while the body of King Edward VII was lying in state at Westminster: published in Facts of the Faith, 1919.

6   Watson, N., *Sorrow,* 9,10.

7   Watson, *Sorrow,* 10.

10

THE PREACHER'S PERSEVERANCE

SUSTAINING THE PREACHING MINISTRY

At the beginning of this book I had occasion to mention the plethora of books on the subject of preaching. I attempted a justification for the writing of this book on the grounds that relatively few dealt with preaching from within an Anglican context. It is noticeable also that many of these books are essentially manuals for beginners. They give valuable guidance on how to master the basic techniques of preaching and establish a personal preaching pattern and style. What is rarely recognised and acknowledged is the fact that such a style, once established, has to sustain a preaching ministry that will last for the whole of the parish priest's active ministry. As that ministry develops and changes with time, so the preaching will change and develop with time - or ought to. A priest ought not to be preaching in the last few years of his ministry in the same way he was preaching at the beginning. The myriad of experiences, good and bad, that come the way of a priest during his ministry, as well as new knowledge gained from comprehensive and disciplined study, should constantly be feeding into his preaching work, shaping and moulding it as he goes along.

In this closing chapter I want to answer the question "how does a Priest sustain and develop his preaching ministry over a number of decades ?". I want to examine the important influences on the shaping of a preaching ministry as well as development opportunities for the preacher, so that this ministry keeps up to date with changing times and gains in ineffectiveness by adapting to those changes.

The Fact of Change

It scarcely bears reflection on the part of the preacher to recognize that preaching changes with time. Hopefully such change is for the better. Any preacher reviewing the text of sermons he preached ten or twenty years earlier will generally be grasped by a sense of their inadequacy, and will at times wonder how he ever had the nerve to stand up and preach them in the first place. Time has given a new perspective. He is simply not the same person he was when he preached those sermons. He has moved on, and his hearers have moved on with him. Because of that it is rarely possible to repeat old sermons. The changed circumstances of the preacher's own life as well as that of his congregation will generally preclude such repetition. So much editing and adaptation will be needed that it is rarely worth the effort. The preacher will find it better and easier to produce something new.

It could be however that the statements of this paragraph are somewhat optimistic. Change often is imperceptible. Just as we can't see ourselves growing, we can't see ourselves changing. But just as surely as we can see that we have grown (maybe older and fatter) so, on looking back, we will be able to see that we have changed in all aspects of our lives, not least in our approach to preaching.

The other problem is that as human beings we are often resistant to change. When we do recognise it happening, we often fight against it. As preachers we may get to the stage when we feel we have "arrived". We have cut our homiletical teeth, in our curacy or just after, and have arrived at what we regard as *our* style of preaching. We begin to say, "well, that is the way I do it; that is what works for me", without questioning whether it is still the right way. Undoubtedly it was the right way at one time, but cultural currents around us may need us to go in for a reappraisal. Sadly, many priests close their eyes and ears and plough on regardless, in well-worn grooves, using tried and trusted methods. They may in fact not need to go in for large-scale revisions and changes; but at least the questions should be asked in a spirit of openness.

Age on the other hand will hopefully have brought with it maturity, and a genuine humility. Models of Ordination that see it as in some sense "graduation" should be avoided. It is not a end, but a beginning. The newly-ordained minister, because he possesses several degrees, and has mastered a host of complicated, unpronounceable subjects, may be tempted to think he knows all the answers. That feeling normally survives ordination a week, if that, before being shattered by the realities of parish ministry. The priest of even a few years experience has long recognised that he alone is not the answer to the Church of England's prayers, and that it is entirely of the grace of God that he has been of any use at all. Indeed, in that time there will have been moments of self-doubt, though hopefully they will have passed. But there will also be the confidence of knowing that he has learned important truths both by theory and practice, that need to be passed on to his present hearers. He knows this because of the way such truths have proved themselves in the past.

So Killinger comments:

> The older ministers become, the humbler they feel. Gone is the bumptious confidence of youth, when they knew too little

to know how truly finite and limited they were. In its place is the sobriety of age and, if they are lucky, the confidence of another kind, born of experience and technique, the confidence of having practised a craft so thoughtfully over the years that they can rely on what they have learned to get them out of the tightest places. [1]

The Minister's Spiritual Life

It goes almost without saying that the quality of a priest's preaching will go hand in hand with the quality of his spiritual life. If his walk with God is fresh and real, and developing every day, then this will shine through his preaching. His preaching will have the ring of reality about it, because he will be passing on truths that are well-grounded in his life and experience. On the other hand, if his spiritual life has become a matter of dry routine, of going through the motions only, then his preaching will become the arid repetition of standard forms and phrases that will have nothing of the Holy Spirit in them.

The preacher's walk with God should not only be fresh and real, it should be constantly developing and maturity. Paul spoke figuratively of growing spiritually from childhood to maturity, a process that enabled him to "put away childish things" (1 Cor.13.11). Paul had a great sense of moving on in his life and in his ministry "pressing on to the goal" (Phil.3.12-14). He could not conceive of standing still, much less of going backwards.

This is of course not the place to discuss fully the area of ministerial spirituality. We can however set out a basic principle. The spiritual life of the preacher must be developing and not stagnating. To ensure this, the preacher will want to keep all his spiritual disciplines under constant review. He will want to ensure that his prayer life, his Bible study, his participation in the Eucharist, his consultations will spiritual directors, and so on, are developing and maturing with time.

He should not, by and large, be using the same personal Bible Study scheme was using ten or twenty years ago. His prayer discipline should reveal a deepening experience of the richness of prayer, and be increasingly open to different streams of tradition and practice current in today's Church.

Desert experiences inevitably come, times when the preacher will feel far away from God, an experience brought about by a whole combination of factors and circumstances. For the preacher this can have particularly disturbing consequences, as the ideas dry up and the period sitting in front of a blank piece of paper get steadily longer. The experienced preacher is encouraged in such times to hold on and maintain discipline, because these dry periods do not last for ever. To go back to the comment of Killinger, set out above, we can be encouraged to know that good habits of disciplined preparation and good technique can see the preacher through in such times.

Another encouragement comes from the knowledge that whilst the effectiveness of a sermon is strongly influenced by the condition of the spiritual life of the preacher, it does not entirely depend on it. After all, we must not forget that as well as preacher and congregation there is a third party involved in the preaching event, that is, God the Holy Spirit. He is able to take the worst sermon in the world from the worst preacher in the world and make the words effective. All of we preachers will testify to occasions when we have felt in ourselves that a particular sermon was neither prepared nor delivered well, that it fell far below the standard we feel is our best, only to discover that the sermon is welcomed and appreciated by our hearers. We are not the measure of spiritual maturity - that measure is the Living Christ. He chooses to use preachers to bring people to that level of maturity through our preaching, which He wants to be of the best standard it can be. But He is quite capable of doing it without us ! It is sometimes thoughtlessly said that a preacher cannot take his hearers higher than he is himself. If that were true, then many of us would have real cause to be worried. But happily it is not true. The statement falls into the same trap mentioned previously. When it comes to spiritual maturity, Jesus Christ is the measure, not us. He is both the measure of growth to maturity and the true agent of that growth. Hopefully many of the preacher's hearers will be stirred to develop their God-given gifts to the point where some of them outstrip him eventually in spiritual maturity and spiritual gifts. Some preachers might be tempted to consider that failure, when it is in fact success. It is a sign that God the Holy Spirit is at work within the congregation through our preaching. We must not therefore as preachers place a lid on the possibility of growth in our congregations, especially a lid set at the level at which we find ourselves.

Keeping the Mind Alive

Just as the physical body needs regular sustenance to enable it to grow strong and vigorous, so does the intellect. A healthy mind is needed in order to apply what has already been learned as well as to analyse new situations as they arise and devise appropriate solutions for them. Because a particular approach has worked in the past, it does not follow it will always work. People change: situations change. The parish Priest who is intellectually alive will be able to detect when a particular set of ideas and practices have had their day and need to be replaced by novel approaches.

Then again, however thorough a particular priest's training may have been, there will be situations arising in the modern parish that could never have been anticipated in that training. The priest will need to have the intellectual and spiritual agility to build on the past in order to tackle these new situations from first principles and devise appropriate responses without the luxury of established practice to fall back on.

How does the preacher resist the slide into intellectual stagnation and keep himself mentally fit for the work of preaching in a world that constantly changes with time ?

By the Books he reads

Even the briefest of glances at a preacher's bookshelves will give a good clue as to where that particular preacher is located in his thinking and how fresh that thinking is. Amazingly, in an age where books on Theology and Bible Study are readily available, it is still possible to meet preachers who have not read a serious book on theology for 20 or even 30 years. For them their college training was the end of serious theological study. For them sermon preparation involves recycling the same tired series of commentaries (tried and tested, admittedly) written in another era.

It is not of course the case that something is automatically good simply because it is modern, or worthless because it is dated. We might cynically paraphrase Ecclesiastes by saying that "of the making of fresh approaches there is no end" and that closer examination of these fresh approaches reveals there really is nothing new under the sun. The preacher will need to keep his critical faculty finely honed in order to discern what is good in the newer writings and what is of lasting value in the older ones. Having said that, it remains regrettably true that very often something as simple as inertia prevents much modern theological writing from being properly appreciated.

The modern preacher will not of course confine his reading to theology only. He will read well beyond the boundaries of what is termed "theology" in order that the knowledge and understanding of the world that underpins his preaching will be as broad as possible. We may well ask which is better, a detailed knowledge of a few subjects, or a shallower knowledge of many ? In my view, for the preacher the latter is preferable, and will allow him to speak with a degree of authority and understanding on a broad range of topics. Broad and shallow, rather than narrow and deep will be of greater value by and large to the preacher. The preacher must always be honest and humble enough to confess the limits of his knowledge and not pretend to be an expert on everything. Should he fail to do that, people will soon see through him, as sooner or later he makes some glaring factual gaffe and loses respect. I remember an enthusiastic curate once preaching passionately about repentance and repeatedly asking "can the tiger change his spots ?", to be told gently later that tigers of course have stripes, not spots ! Honesty and openness with the congregation remain the best policies.

This links with the delicate question of how far the preacher's background reading should be precisely that, *background* reading, and how far it should intrude into the sermon itself. What is the place of direct quotations from other writers in sermons ? Now of course the preacher will want to show that what he is saying is in line with contemporary understandings, and may well wish to illustrate this by quotations. My feeling is that this is OK provided the source of the quotations is accessible to the congregation, so that, should they wish to, they can check it out. It could well be that no one in the congregation will ever avail themselves of this opportunity, but the opportunity should be there nevertheless. The whole point of giving accurate details of academic references is to enable the reader to check them out. Quoting from some recondite ancient source may sound very impressive, but may not always be totally honest. It is not of course the purpose of a quotation to impress the congregation. Quotations should be used at all only if they significantly add to or illuminate the point being made.

Obvious reading for any preacher keeping up with developments in the contemporary world are the **newspapers**, although news programmes on television have in many ways supplanted them. Newspapers offer a more immediate way of getting in depth coverage of news items, however. The preacher will read the papers therefore, though the choice of newspaper will vary. Time available to read them will be a factor in the choice. I simply could not find the time to read lengthy articles the so-called broadsheets, though some of my ministerial colleagues apparently could. For me news had to be available in more condensed time-efficient format. So I don't argue that preachers should read only the so-called quality papers. Preachers may wish to vary their choice of newspaper from time to time, to minimise the effect of the political bias evident in all of them. He will be aware that there is virtually no such thing as objective news reporting.

Bible commentaries will be important components of a preacher's reading material. Generally the preacher will have two types of commentary on his bookshelf. He will have an exegetical/critical commentary on each book of the Bible, if possible based on the Hebrew or Greek text. This will enable him to engage with the text at its deepest level. For New Testament books the International Critical Commentary series is excellent, many of the volumes having been reprinted or revised. The Word Series Commentaries are also excellent, though rather wordy. One volume commentaries on the Bible or New Testament are better than no commentary at all, but inevitably can only skim the surface of any particular passage. In addition (not instead of) this type of commentary he will have an expositional/devotional commentary, to assist in bringing out the practical implications of the text. In this regard the outstanding series is "The Bible Speaks Today", produced by IVP. Some commentaries will of course bridge the gap by combining both textual exegesis and devotional exposition, the Zondervan NIV Application Commentary series being a commentary series that springs to mind here.

Commentaries will always need to be handled carefully, as a means to an end and not an end in themselves. But they are invaluable, essential tools for the preacher.

Preaching is an exercise in communication, and good communication skills will require a reasonably high level of literacy. Good literary skills in turn can be developed only by immersion in good quality literature. The effective preacher will therefore be a regular reader of **novels and other books** that explore ideas at some depth, as well as handling language effectively and creatively. As teachers aiming to teach young children literacy skills quickly learn, children will develop the ability to write and speak well if in the first instance they are reading good literature and hearing good spoken language in their daily environment. If the preacher has been fortunate enough to have received a good education, he may well already be familiar with the English classics, and therefore have a good literary grounding. His reading will not of course be confined to the classics, but will hopefully take in the full range of contemporary literature. This will ensure the preacher's horizons stay as broad as possible and in turn provide endless resources for his oratory.

One or two words of caution are appropriate here. What the preacher reads should in some way engage with the literary world of his readers. If he is constantly quoting the classics, when they spend their time reading Stephen King or Ian Fleming, then he will present himself as a snob and alienate them. Associated with this is the indirect snobbery that sees reading only as intellectual enlightenment. When I am on holiday I ensure that I do not take any "serious" books with me on theology and the like, preferring instead the enjoyment and relaxation of a thriller. There is absolutely nothing to be said against reading for enjoyment as well as enlightenment.

The other important issue is the one referred to above, the issue of time. Time for reading the newspaper has a degree of priority, whilst for the busy parish priest time for reading novels tends towards luxury. Most of my novels I would read late at night, when the day's work is over, or on holiday. Careful management of time will create space for longer reading sessions. But in the cut and thrust of parish ministry novels are to be regarded as highly desirable, but not essential.

By the Courses he attends

Talk to clergy about their days at theological college, preparing for ordination, and you will get a variety of opinions. Most will say they enjoyed it and found it of great benefit. An extremist few will write it off as largely a waste of time, leaving them unprepared for the tasks and challenges they currently face. Even amongst those who enjoyed their training will come the ready acknowledgement that it failed to prepare them for every contingency of parish ministry. I vividly recall spending just the second Monday after my ordination cleaning the Church Hall after someone had broken in and splattered harvest parcels everywhere. I remember thinking "when did we cover this at college ?".

The truth of course is that there is no way College training can prepare an ordinand for all the situations he is likely to meet in the course of a life in ministry. The best it can do is provide him with a solid grounding in theology that will provide a frame of reference by which he will be able to deal with the constantly changing world in which he is called to minister. My impression, gained from visiting a number of theological colleges in the last year, is a very positive one. Theological training is much more diverse and effective than I recall it being in the sixties, when I trained for ordination. Two things have contributed to this. The first is the abolition of the General Ordination Examination (G.O.E.). This was a centrally-administered examination, comprising 13 subjects, that all candidates were required to pass before ordination. This limited the ability of colleges to devise their own courses and made huge impositions on their time. Linked with this change was the **upgrading of Theological Colleges to enable them to award their own academic qualifications**. This came about through the development of links with local Universities and their Faculty of Theology. So Trinity, Bristol linked with Bristol University; Wycliffe with Oxford; St. John's with Nottingham and so on. These links enabled the qualifications awarded by the colleges to be recognised by the National Academic Awards bodies. The colleges were thus enabled to get the balance between academic and pastoral training they had wanted for so long.

In parallel with this post ordination training, generally reckoned to cover only the first three years of ministry, was abolished by the dioceses in favour of some form of Continuing Ministerial Education (C.M.E.). This was based on the insight, now widely accepted right across society, that education is for the whole of life, not just for the early part. All local authorities have Adult Learning Centres, most of which are extremely popular. All dioceses in turn have budgets for C.M.E., and all clergy are encouraged to regularly attend courses, both those organised by the diocese itself, as well as those organised externally. The extra-mural departments of most universities hold a whole variety of courses for the public, with little or no academic requirements for the courses. For the preacher who wishes to keep his intellect alive and active, there is plenty of scope to do so.

Some may wish to take the matter further by taking on courses leading to academic qualifications, such as University Higher Degrees. I myself held off from this for years thinking I could not possibly find the time to do a degree as well as run a busy parish. It was only when a then Director of C.M.E. of the Diocese of Manchester put it to me that a parish priest who was being stretched and challenged intellectually would be of much better value to a parish in all sorts of ways compared to one that was intellectually stagnant, that I overcame this hesitation. After years of hard work and rigid time management, I was able to gain both a Masters Degree and Doctor of Philosophy through part time study at the University of Manchester. It is hard work, and it is not for everyone, but it *is* possible. Rigorous, part-time study from within the parish has the added advantage of linking together the academic and pastoral worlds, preventing them becoming divorced from each other.

Looking after the Body

The parish priest's lifestyle will be an important back up to his preaching, as well as to the rest of his ministry. A healthy lifestyle will enable the preacher to place all the energy and resources into the sustaining of that ministry. This lifestyle will establish and maintain a proper balance between work, study and recreation.

What the congregation see of the minister in the pulpit can be the tip of the iceberg only. Behind that apparently calm exterior can lurk a stressed and pressured mind, and the consciousness of a hundred jobs not yet completed. Often clergy live under total dominance of the diary, having little or no time they can call their own. The importance of this for our present task lies in the fact that often one of the first things to get squeezed out is sermon preparation time. Instead of rightfully having an appropriate block of time suited to its priority, it gets relegated to the cracks, being fitted into the time between meetings and other activities. In the jazz musicians' world (to which I belong) the saying goes: one day without practice the musician knows; two days without practice and the bandleader knows; three days without practice, everybody knows ! When sermon preparation gets downgraded to the fag ends of time, it is not long before all the congregation recognises what is going on.

The answer to diary domination is of course good management of time, with the essential ability to distinguish between what is important and what is of lesser importance. Along with this goes the ability to graciously say no to certain requests. Being faithful servants of Christ does not inevitably mean acceding to every request made to us. Many clergy fail at this point, and spend their time rushing round trying to perform so many tasks that they pretty soon exhaust and frustrate themselves. The outcome tends also to be that the more tasks taken on by the preacher, the less likelihood of any individual task being done well, including the vital task of sermon preparation.

Good time management will include factoring in time for recreation, seen in its most literal sense of *re-creation*. The trick is to see recreation as being so much more than time off work and see it as time to recharge batteries and to renew ourselves so that we may in turn become more effective workers. A preacher who is physically shattered all the time is no use to anyone, least of all God.

Recreation may take many forms, including holidays and travel, hobbies, sport, theatre and cinema, reading, and so on. Recreational patterns will vary from individual to individual. An idea I used to find useful was to belong to some group or society in which I was not the leader, but was simply in the ranks. Clergy can so easily forget what it is to be accepted for themselves, rather than the rank they possess. This is not always completely possible, as people eventually get to know what you are in your job, and begin to confide in you and seek your help. Nevertheless, involvement in such groups puts the preacher in close contact with people *at their level*, an experience that enriches and develops the preaching ministry in its turn.

Although such matters are not always within his control, the preacher will look after his general health. Recognising that his body is indeed a temple of the Holy Spirit, he will not deliberately indulge habits that he knows will damage that temple (1 Cor.6.19). Diet and exercise will become important, not for what they are in themselves, but as a way of honouring God in the body, so that in turn he may serve

Him more effectively in the ministry of preaching to which he has been called.

'All life would become a sermon'

Parish priests come in all shapes and sizes. Their personalities differ widely, and accordingly their temperaments will vary. Some will be great activists, ready at all times to get on with the job. Others will be more contemplative, preferring to consider carefully and long, sometimes too long, before going into action. Some will be possibility thinkers, seeing the positive side and the potential of everything, whilst others will focus primarily on the drawbacks and snags inherent in any suggestions put to them. Some will be academics, with a Public School/University history behind them, whilst others will be practical men, ex-plumbers and engineers, natural doers rather than thinkers. All these different types have their place in ministry. Whatever their differences, the vital thing they have in common, perhaps all they have in common, is the call of God.

These wide differences in temperament and personality will lead in turn to widely differing lifestyles. Nevertheless, what these lifestyles have in common is that they will be on public view. Clergy live their lives in a giant goldfish bowl, open to everyone's gaze, something that many clergy find particularly testing. They try various techniques and tactics to ensure the same degree of privacy that others enjoy. One suspects that nearly always they are fighting a losing battle. At the end of the day it simply is the case that the sort of privacy that most of the public enjoy is something that is sacrificed the moment the Bishop lays his hands on the candidate's head at ordination. Like the Royal Family, the Vicar and his family are public institutions, and very little of what goes on in the vicarage will remain truly private. The vicarage, owned by the Diocese, is in the true sense a public house, as well as a private residence. Parishioners are reasonably entitled to have a degree of access to that house. The wise parish priest accepts this and recognises that ministry has a number of compensating privileges, not least of which is relatively free access to other people's homes in the parish.

What becomes vital therefore is that the preacher's home and family life, lived under public scrutiny, should be consistent with and back up his preaching ministry. "Do as I say, and not as I do" is simply not acceptable from a preacher. His personal conduct should always exemplify the ideals he sets forth from the pulpit. That this puts great pressure on the preacher is undeniable, and that this pressure is greater than that on those sitting in the pews has also to be acknowledged. But to anyone proposing to complain about this I would say: "that's just how it is; if you can't handle it, then stay out of the pulpit". Persistent problems in the preacher's private life will seriously affect the reception of his preaching, and may in time undermine it, something that the preacher has to take seriously.

Of course, preachers are only human. Congregations do not expect their preachers to be superheroes, removed from all human temptations. From time to time preachers do fall from grace, sometimes quite spectacularly. The wise congregation will not rush to judgement, but will seek to understand fully what has happened, and the circumstances surrounding the event. They will acknowledge that just as they are not perfect, then neither are their preachers perfect. Nevertheless, depending on the seriousness of the moral lapse on the part of the preacher, their confidence in him and their ability to listen to him cannot but be affected to a certain degree by what has happened. It is not so much a matter of judgement, as a matter of confidence and trust, and all preachers must accept this.

There is of course a positive side to public observation of the preacher's life. The birth of children to the preacher's family will be occasions of great rejoicing for the whole congregation.

Should the preacher actually get married during his time in a parish, all the more rejoicing ! Good things that happen to the preacher and his family will be celebrated publicly, just as times such as bereavement will be shared by everyone. There is a real sense in which the life of the congregation ebbs and flows with the life of the Parish Priest.

In one sense of course this puts extra pressure on the parish priest. He cannot cope with tragedy, illness or bereavement privately. They are for him public experiences, just as everything else is public. The congregation will watch, to see how he copes. "After all", they say, "if the Vicar can't cope, what hope is there for us ?". This point is very real for me. Sadly, my wife suffered a disabling stroke, and after three years of being pushed around in a wheel chair, died. Through that period I had to cope with continuing to run a busy parish, as well as being Area Dean. It was a particularly testing time. On reflection, two positive things came out of it, in terms of my preaching ministry. The first is that the compensating privilege for the preacher suffering personal loss is that he has support and encouragement from the congregation, more support than people in other walks of life can call upon. This is naturally extremely valuable, particularly in the early months. The other thing is that suffering and loss in the life of the preacher inevitably adds depth to the things he says. People come to realise that what he is doing in the pulpit is not some sort of game or role play, but is extremely serious. He is speaking of the great issues of life and death, of time and eternity. He is saying something even more staggering than this, that the response the congregation offer to what he preaches can actually *determine* the issues of time and eternity. The congregation are offered the opportunity of seeing these truths in a whole new light because of what has happened to the preacher and his family.

I well remember meeting Noel Proctor, Prison Chaplain at Strangeways in Manchester, some time after his wife's death.

Noel was always a very lively, energetic and humorous preacher. After his wife's passing he was still all that, and yet I saw in his eyes and sensed in his manner a new depth, a new understanding, that made his preaching all the more effective.

The preacher's personal life and personal experience can therefore shape his preaching ministry in all sorts of ways. Indeed it will do this, either positively or negatively, whether the preacher is conscious of it or not. Whether the effect will be a positive or negative one will depend on the preacher, and his ability to respond to the ups and downs of life by feeding those experiences into his preaching.

These lines, taken from "As You Like It" describe in caricature something of the preacher's outlook on life and on his response to the experiences of life.

> And this our life, exempt from public haunts, finds tongues in trees, books in running brooks, sermons in stones and good in everything.

As we noted earlier, the genius of the prophet lay in his ability to look beneath the surface of events to see what was really happening. The apocalyptic strain of prophecy took this to extremes, and saw behind the appearance of earthly things the eternal conflict in the heavens between God and satan, between the Kingdoms of light and darkness. Their message of encouragement came in the sure knowledge that in this conflict victory for the forces of light was assured, as God intervened dramatically to not only conquer His enemies but to bring history itself to its glorious consummation.

So preachers will read the news, will observe what happens in the world around them, and see behind these events and happenings ideas that speak of the Kingdom of God and its growth. He will learn to see everything from the point of view of the work God is doing in the world. If he is wise he will avoid apocalyptic excesses. Sometimes events that occur in the course of his ministry do not merit the status of examples of the light/darkness conflict, but constitute human relationships problems that are to be resolved much more quietly by means of quiet pastoral work. I have known colleagues who have all too easily given in to the temptation to attribute their problems to satanic interference, when a look in the mirror might well offer a solution much closer to hand.

With this caution in mind, the experienced preacher learns more and more to draw out principles from the happenings in the world around him, both close at hand and far away, that will constitute the basis of illustrations and stories for his ministry. In time it will become a natural and unconscious process. As he learns to look on the world with a preacher's eye, so illustrations will leap out at him. He will be able to call them to mind with scarcely a moment's thought. He will be able to reverently paraphrase Michel Quoist, whose poem was entitled "All life will become a prayer" into "all life will become a sermon"[2].

The process is made all the more effective if the preacher's world, from which he draws his life illustrations overlaps significantly with the world of his hearers. Occasionally one hears of square pegs being put in round holes. A young man with only public school and university experienced being placed in a parish populated by manual workers. Their spheres of life will scarcely overlap at all. That young man will have great difficulties in relating his preaching to the day to day lives of his hearers, as they will have very little in common at all. We he inevitably fail ? By no means. He will need to throw himself into the world of his hearers and identify with it as far as possible, as we earlier noted Bishop Westcott did at Durham. His preacher's eye will enable him to see his parish as a scenario in which the values and principles of the Kingdom of God are being played out. It is by no means an impossible task for the preacher, whatever set of circumstances in which he is appointed to preach.

367

The ability of a preacher to sustain a preaching ministry throughout the full course of his parish ministry will depend on two things, namely a relationship with God that matures and develops throughout that ministry, and an ability to look at the world in which he lives with God's eyes, responding to the work of the Kingdom of God as it continues to grow around him.

Over the years, as he sees lives changed and revolutionized by the Word of God he preaches, the sense of privilege will grow as he recognises more and more that in succession to the prophets, apostles and even Our Lord himself, he has been called to the greatest work to which God can call anyone on earth.

> We are ambassadors for Christ, God making His appeal through us.
>
> *2 Cor.5.20*

CHAPTER TEN
ENDNOTES

[1] J.Killinger, *Fundamentals of Preaching* (Minneapolis: Fortress Press, 1996), 199.
[2] M.Quoist, *Prayers of Life* (Logos Books, 1963))

SELECT BIBLIOGRAPHY

Aune, D.E. *Prophecy in Early Christianity and the Ancient Mediterranean World*. Grand Rapids: Eerdmans, 1983.

Barr, J., *The Semantics of Biblical Language* (Oxford:OUP, 1961)

Bauckham, R., *Jesus and the Eyewitnesses:The Gospels as Eyewitness Testimony* (Grand Rapids: Eerdmans, 2006).

Birch, T., *The Life of Dr.John Tillotson, Lord Archbishop of Canterbury* (1752)

Blench, J.W., *Preaching in England in the Late 15th and 16th Centuries* (Oxford: Blackwell, 1964)

Boucher, M., *The Parables* (Wilmington: M.Glazer, 1980).

Bowen, R. (ed) *A Guide to Preaching* (London: SPCK, 2005)

Brown, A., *Preaching at Baptisms* (Cambridge: Grove Booklets, 2008)

Brown, C., *Religion and Society in 20th Century Britain* (Pearson International: Longman, 2006

Bruce, F.F., *The Speeches in the Acts of the Apostles* (London, 1944)

Buttrick, D., *Homiletics: Moves and Structures* (London: SCM, 1987)

Carson, D.A.(ed), *Worship by the Book* (Grand Rapids: Zondervan, 2002)

Cazelles, H., "The Canonical Approach to Torah and Prophets," *JSOT* 16 (1980), 28-31.

Chapell, B., *Christ Centred Preaching* (Grand Rapids: Baker Academic, 1994)

Childs, B.S., "Retrospective Reading of the Old Testament Prophets," *ZAW* 108 (1996), 362-77.

Collins, R.F., *Preaching the Epistles* (New York: Paulist Press, 1996)

Coggan, D., 'Paul the Preacher' in ed. G.Hunter, G.Thomas and S.Wright, *A Preacher's Companion*, Oxford: BRF, 1990),

Craddock, F.B., *As One Without Authority* (Ohio: Phillips, 1957)

--------- *Preaching* (Nashville: Abingdon, 1990)

Davis, H.Grady, *Design for Preaching* (Philadelphia: Muhlenberg, 1958)

Day, D., *A Preaching Workbook* (London: SPCK, 1998)

--------Embodying the Word: A Preacher's Guide (London: SPCK, 2005)

Dodd, C.H., *The Apostolic Preaching and its Developments* (London: Hodder & Stoughton, 1944)

--------*The Parables of the Kingdom*. New York: Charles Scribner's Sons, 1961.

Drane, J., *Cultural Change and Biblical Faith,* (Carlisle: Paternoster, 2000)

Dowley, T. (ed), Eerdmans' *Handbook to the History of Christianity* (Grand Rapids: Eerdmans , 1987)

Earey, M., *Liturgical Worship* (London: Church House Publishing, 2002)

English, D., *An Evangelical Theology of Preaching* (Nashville: Abingdon ,1996)

Eslinger, R. (ed), *Intersections: Post Critical Studies in Preaching* (Grand Rapids: Eerdmans, 1994)

---------- *Narrative and Imagination: Preaching the Worlds that Shape Us* (Minneapolis: Fortress Press, 1995)

Gee, Henry, and William John Hardy (eds), *Documents Illustrative of English Church History,* (New York: MacMillan Press, 1896),

Gill, R., *Changing Worlds: Can the Church Respond ?* (London: Continuum, 2005)

Graves, M., *What's the Matter with Preaching Today ?* (Louiseville: Westminster John Knox, 2004)

Green, J. (ed) *Hearing the New Testament* (Eerdmans: Grand Rapids, 1995)

Greer, R., *Anglican Approaches to Scripture: From the Reformation to the Present,* (New York: Herder & Herder, 2006)

Greidanus, S., *The Modern Preacher and the Ancient Text* (Leicester: IVP, 1988)

---------- *Preaching Christ from the Old Testament* (Grand Rapides: Eerdmans, 1999)

Hengel, M., *The Hellenization of Judaea in the First Century after Christ* (London: SCM, 1989)

Herbert, A.G. (ed), *The Parish Communion* (London: SPCK, 1937)

Ilion Jones, *Principles and Practice of Preaching* (Abingdon: Nashville, 1956)

Johnston, G., *Preaching to a Postmodern World* (Leicester: IVP, 2004)

Jones, C.,(ed), *The Study of Liturgy* (London; SPCK, 1992)

Jones, K.B., *The Jazz of Preaching* (Nashville: Abingdon, 2004)

Keck,L.E. *The Bible in the Pulpit: The Renewal of Biblical Preaching* (Nashville: Abingdon Press, 1978)

Keir, T.H., *The Word in Worship* (London: OUP, 1962)

Killinger, J., *Fundamentals of Preaching* (Minneapolis: Fortress, 1996)

Leech, K., *The Sky is Red: Discerning the Signs of the Times* (London: Darton, Longman & Todd, 1997)

Lloyd Jones, D.M., *Preaching and Preachers* (London: Hodder, 1971)

Long, T.G., *Preaching and the Literary Forms of the Bible* (Philadelphia: Fortress, 1989)

Lowry, E.L., *Dancing on the Edge of Mystery,* (Nashville: Abingdon, 1997)

---------- *The Hermeneutical Plot: Preaching as Narrative Art* (Louiseville: Westminster John Knox, 2nd ed., 2001)

MacCulloch, D., *The Later Reformation in England , 1547-1603* (London: MacMillan, 1990)

Marsh, S., *Christianity in a Post-Atheistic Age* (London: SPCK, 2002)

McDill, W., *The Twelve Essentials to Great Preaching* (Nashville: Boardman, 1994)

Motyer, J.A. *The Prophecy of Isaiah* (Leicester: IVP, 1993)

Miller, C., *Market Place Preaching : Returning the Sermon to where it was* (Grand Rapids: Baker Academic, 2005)

Newport, K.G.C. (ed), *The Sermons of Charles Wesley: A Critical Edition with Introduction and Notes* (Oxford: O.U.P., 2001).

Noren, C.M., *The Woman in the Pulpit* (Nashville: Abingdon, 1992)

Peterson, D., *Engaging with God: A Biblical Theology of Worship* (Downer's Grove: IVP, 1992)

Piper, J., *The Supremacy of God in Preaching* (Leicester: IVP, 1990)

Quicke, M.J., *360 Degree Preaching: Hearing, Speaking and Living the Word* (Grand Rapids: Baker Academic, 2003)

Robinson, H.R., *Biblical Preaching* (Grand Rapids: Baker, 1980), 2nd ed. 2001)

Runia, K., *The Sermon under Attack* (Exeter: Paternoster Press, 1983)

Seitz, C.R., *Prophecy and Hermeneutics: Towards a New Introduction to the Prophets* (Grand Rapids: Baker Academic, 2007)

Silva, M., (ed), *The Foundations of Contemporary Interpretation* (Leicester: IVP, 1997)

Smyth, C., *The Art of Preaching: A Practical Survey of Preaching in the Church of England, 747-1939* (London: SPCK, 1953)

Spurgeon, C.H., *Lectures to my Students* (London: Marshall, Morgan, Scott, 1954)

Standing, R., *Finding the Plot: Preaching in Narrative Style* (London: Church House Publishing, 2004)

Stevenson, G., *Pulpit Journeys* (London: Darton, Longman and Todd, 2006)

Stevenson, G. & S.Wright, *Preaching with Humanity: A Practical Guide for Today's Church* (London: Church House Publishing, 2009)

Stott, J.R.W., *Between Two Worlds* (Grand Rapids: Eerdmans, 1982)

----------- *I Believe in Preaching* (London: Hodder, 1982)

Sweazey, G., *Preaching the Good News* (Englewood Cliffs: Prentice Hall, 1976)

Symmons, R., *Preaching at Weddings* (Cambridge: Grove, 1995)

Thompson, J.W., *Preaching like Paul: Homiletical Wisdom for Today* (Louisville: Westminster John Knox Press, 2001)

Townsend, M.J., *Thinking about Preaching* (Peterborough: Epworth Press, 2007)

Tyson, John R., *Charles Wesley on Sanctification* (Grand Rapids: Astbury Press, 1986)

Vanhoozer, K., *Is There a Meaning in the Text ?* (Leicester: IVP, 1998)

---------- "God's Mighty Speech-Acts: The Doctrine of Scripture Today", in P.E. Satterthwaite & D.F.Wright (eds) *A Pathway into the Holy Scripture* (Grand Rapids: Eerdmans, 1994), 143-182.

Veith, G.E.Jr., *Postmodern Times: A Christian Guide to Contemporary Thought and Culture,* (Wheaton: Crossway, 1994)

W.Ward Gasque and R.P.Martin (eds) *Apostolic History and the Gospel: Essays presented to F.F.Bruce* (Exeter: Paternoster, 1970)

Warren, M.A.C., *The Day of the Preacher,* (London: Mowbrays, 1966)

Watson, N., *Sorrow and Hope: Preaching at Funerals* (Cambridge: Grove Booklets, 2001)

Webb, J.M., *Preaching Without Notes* (Nashville: Abingdon, 2001)

Weber, M., *The Sociology of Religion* (ET Boston: Beacon, 1963)

Westermann, C., *The Parables of Jesus in the Light of the Old Testament*. Minneapolis: Fortress Press, 1990.

Wilson, P. Scott, *The Practice of Preaching* (Nashville: Abingdon, 1995)

---------- *The Four Pages of the Sermon: A Guide to Biblical Preaching* (Nashville: Abingdon, 1999)